PLURALISM

Cultural, moral and religious diversity is a pervasive feature of modern life. Yet, the resulting issue of pluralism has only recently become a focal point of intellectual debate, and our understanding of the philosophical questions relating to it is still in its infancy.

Pluralism: The philosophy and politics of diversity is the first volume to link pluralist themes in philosophy to politics and political theory. Bringing together philosophers and political theorists, it advances recent debates on pluralism in a range of essays which challenge or defend established ideas of pluralism. The volume is divided into three parts. The first part is an investigation of philosophical sources of pluralism, including the work of William James. The essays in the second part discuss the political dimensions of pluralism and its connections to liberalism. The last part investigates the practical implications of pluralism in conditions of cultural diversity.

Pluralism is a valuable source for all students of philosophy, politics and cultural studies, and all those interested in the problems of accommodating diversity.

Contributors: Maria Baghramian, Raphael Cohen-Almagor, John Gray, Iseult Honohan, Will Kymlicka, Susan Mendus, Martha Nussbaum, James R. O'Shea, Philip Pettit, Jonathan Riley and Jonathan Wolff.

Maria Baghramian is Lecturer in Philosophy and **Attracta Ingram** is Professor in Politics, both at University College Dublin.

PLURALISM

The philosophy and politics of diversity

Edited by
Maria Baghramian
and
Attracta Ingram

London and New York

First published 2000
by Routlege
11 New Fetter Lane, London EC4P 4EE

Simultaneously published in the USA and Canada
by Routledge
29 West 35th Street, New York, NY 10001

Routledge is an imprint of the Taylor & Francis Group

Typeset in Galliard by Saxon Graphics Ltd, Derby
Printed and bound in Great Britain by TJ International Ltd,
Padstow, Cornwall

British Library Cataloguing in Publication Data
A catalogue record for this book is available from the British Library

Library of Congress Cataloging in Publication Data
Pluralism: the philosophy and politics of diversity/edited by Maria
Baghramian and Attracta Ingram
p. cm.
Includes bibliographical referernces and index.
1. Pluralism. 2. Pluralism (Social sciences) I. Baghramian, Maria
II. Ingram, Attracta.
BD394 .P545 2000
147'.4–dc21   00-055334

ISBN 0–415–22714-3 (pbk)
ISBN 0–415–22713–5 (hbk)

This book is dedicated to
Robert Farhat
and
Alec Cornelius

CONTENTS

vii

CONTRIBUTORS

Maria Baghramian teaches in the Department of Philosophy, University College Dublin. Her research interests are in philosophy of language and contemporary American philosophy. She is the author of *The Problem of Relativism* (Routledge forthcoming,) and the editor of *Modern Philosophy of Language* (J.M., Dent 1998, Counterpoint 1999).

Raphael Cohen-Almagor is Senior Lecturer at the Department of Communication, University of Haifa. In 1992 he was Visiting Professor at UCLA School of Law. He is the author of *The Boundaries of Liberty and Tolerance* (1994), *Speech, Media and Ethics* (2000) and editor of several books, among them *Challenges to Democracy: Essays in Honour and Memory of Isaiah Berlin* (2000), and *Medical Ethics at the Dawn of the 21st Century* (2000).

John Gray was educated at Oxford. He was a Fellow of Jesus College, Oxford, from 1976–1998. In 1996 he was made Professor of Politics at Oxford. Since 1998 he has been Professor of European Thought at the LSE. His books include *Mill on Liberty: a Defence*, *Isaiah Berlin* and *Two Faces of Liberalism* (forthcoming).

Iseult Honohan teaches historical and normative political theory in the Department of Politics, University College Dublin. Her research interests include ethics and public life and feminist thought. She is the author of *Civic Republicanism* (Routledge Problems of Philosophy series, forthcoming).

Attracta Ingram is Professor of Politics at University College Dublin. Her research interests include human rights and national self-determination. She is author of *A Political Theory of Rights* (Oxford Clarendon Press 1994). She is co-editor (with Gerard Quinn and Stephen Livingstone) of *Justice and Legal Theory in Ireland* (Oaktree Press 1995).

Will Kymlicka is the author of four books. His publications with Oxford University Press include: *Liberalism, Community and Culture* (1989), *Contemporary Political Philosophy* (1990), *Multicultural Citizenship* (1998). He is currently a Queen's National Scholar at Queen's University, and a recurrent visiting professor in the Nationalism Studies programme at the Central European University in Budapest.

Susan Mendus is Professor of Politics and Director of the Morrell Studies in Toleration programme at the University of York. Her main interests are in liberal political philosophy, and feminist theory. Her book, *Feminism and Emotion*, will be published by Macmillan Press in 2000.

Martha Nussbaum is Ernst Freund Distinguished Service Professor of Law and Ethics at the University of Chicago. She holds appointments in the Philosophy Department, the Law School, the Divinity School, the Classics Department, and the Center for Gender Studies. Her most recent book, *Women and Human Development: Capabilities Approach,* was published in 2000 by Cambridge University Press.

James R. O'Shea is a lecturer in the Department of Philosophy at University College Dublin. He has published several articles on Hume and on Kant, and is currently working on intentionality in William James and a longer work on Kant's philosophy of nature.

Philip Pettit is Professor of Social and Political Theory, Research School of Social Sciences, Australian National University and a regular Visiting Professor of Philosophy at Columbia University, New York. Among his recent books are *The Common Mind: An Essay on Psychology, Society and Politics* (Oxford University Press 1993) and *Republicanism: A Theory of Freedom and Government* (Oxford University Press 1997).

Jonathan Riley is Professor in the Murphy Institute of Political Economy, Tulane University. In addition to numerous articles, his recent publications include *Mill's Radical Liberalism* (Routledge 2001), a co-edited volume on *Constitutional Culture and Democratic Rule* (Cambridge University Press 2001) and the *Routledge Philosophy Guidebook to Mill on Liberty* (Routledge 1998).

Jonathan Wolff is a Professor of Philosophy at University College London. He is the author of *Robert Nozick* (1991) and *An Introduction to Political Philosophy* (1996) and editor with Michael Rosen of *Political Thought* (1999) and with Martin Stone of *The Proper Ambition of Science* (2000). He is currently working on issues of equality and economic justice.

FOREWORD

In the present volume, the two editors have brought together a distinguished collection of essays on one of the most important and difficult topics of our time. Indeed, if the topic is difficult, it is so in more than one sense, just as 'pluralism' has more than one sense, as the reader of this collection will quickly perceive. Perhaps this is even appropriate: why shouldn't a volume about pluralism itself exhibit pluralism as well as discuss it?

In truth, the 'difficulty' of dealing with pluralism is as much human and political – learning how to live together in a world in which diversity can no longer be ignored and unity cannot be achieved by 'the method of authority' – as it is intellectual. However, the intellectual difficulty is also 'political' in a deeper sense, for overcoming stereotypes is always of human importance, as Ludwig Wittgenstein tried to teach us. Two stereotypes of pluralism keep us from seeing how complex a phenomenon the plurality of pluralisms actually is: on the one side, there is the stereotype that holds that there is no such thing as 'the truth', that even talking of some views being right and some being wrong is just a 'repressive gesture', and on the other side there is the stereotype that holds that there is always one right view and a plurality of errors, and 'reason' requires that we reject any other account as a capitulation to 'irrationalism'. But as these papers collectively testify, both stereotypes are falsifications. Not only is there such a thing as partial truth and partial falsity, but it is not even always the case that *apparently* contradictory accounts of the facts are really irreconcilable. This is something I discussed in detail in a little book titled *The Many Faces of Realism* some years ago. The greatest difficulty, intellectually speaking, in dealing with a case of 'pluralism' lies in determining the nature of the plurality that confronts us. That is why we need a number of different models of 'pluralism, and that is what the present book beautifully provides.

Hilary Putnam

ACKNOWLEDGEMENTS

This material was developed as part of the Faculty of Arts project on pluralism undertaken by members of the philosophy and politics departments in University College Dublin. Several of the contributions were delivered at a joint conference organised by the Royal Irish Academy Philosophy Committee in conjunction with the project. The editors received a great deal of help from the Faculty of Arts, and the departments of philosophy and of politics. Those who participated in the discussions of pluralism, who contributed papers and comments, included colleagues from Trinity College Dublin, and from the US, Australia, Israel, Canada, the UK, and Germany. Tony Bruce, the editor at Routledge, has been unfailing in his encouragement and sound advice. The comments by anonymous referees have made this a better book than it otherwise would have been. Gayle Kenny, Eleanor Smith and Gillian Wylie helped us with the preparation of the manuscript. We are very grateful to them all. A grant from University College Dublin Publications Fund covered the cost of indexing this collection.

Permission given by the following copyright holders and authors is gratefully acknowledged.

'Women and Cultural Universals', from *Sex and Social Justice* by Martha Nussbaum. Copyright © 1999 Martha Nussbaum. Used by permission of Oxford University Press, Inc.

'Ethnocultural Minorities in Liberal Democracies' by Will Kymlicka and Raphael Cohen-Almagor from *Challenges to Democracy: Essays in Honor and Memory of Isaiah Berlin* edited by Raphael Cohen-Almagor, Ashgate Publishing Limited, 2000.

INTRODUCTION

Maria Baghramian and Attracta Ingram

Pluralism pervades our lives. We find ourselves in a world in which there is a plurality of different ethical, philosophical, religious, and cultural beliefs. Pluralism is not a new phenomenon, nor indeed one that separates contemporary western societies from others, now or in the past. What is new is the development and spread of pluralism in the world of ideas. Discussions of pluralism, first opened up by philosophers, linguists, and anthropologists, have now found their way into the political and social sciences, psychology, literary and cultural studies, history, and education. Behind this explosion of interest in pluralism is the excitement of a transformative idea – the thought that there can be more than one 'correct' or 'true' account of a given subject matter. Pluralism, thus understood, challenges the old philosophical faith in a single right answer to questions of what there is, what knowledge consists in, and what morality is about. The pluralist picture of the world enjoins us to recognise that there can be many diverse and incompatible conceptual and moral frameworks, many belief systems and ultimate values, without there being an overarching criterion to decide between them as to 'truth'.

The collapse of old certainties in religious, ethical, and scientific arenas, has been instrumental in motivating the intellectual examination of pluralism. Science in particular has played a leading role in this development. The discovery of the possibility of non-Euclidean geometries followed by a sea change in theories of physics gave strong support to the idea that there can be many 'rationally acceptable' but incompatible descriptions of the universe and its laws. The significance of this shift in ideas was noted by William James, writing at the beginning of the twentieth century:

> Up to about 1850 almost everyone believed that sciences expressed truths that were exact copies of a definite code of non-human realities. But the enormously rapid multiplication of theories these latter days has well-nigh upset the notion of any one of them being a more literally objective kind of thing than another. There are so many geometries, so many logics, so many physical and chemical hypotheses, so many classifications, each one of them good for so much and

1

yet not good for everything, that the notion that even the truest
formula may be a human device and not a literal transcript has
dawned upon us.

(James 1975b: 40)

The developments in science to which James draws attention have gone hand
in hand with philosophical discussions of the relationship between human
thought and the world. Much of this discussion has centred on metaphysical
problems associated with conceptual pluralism and relativism. The roots of
conceptual pluralism may be traced back to Immanuel Kant's distinction
between the data of our sense experiences and the principles of organisation
or categories we use to organise them. Kant believed that all thinkers necessarily apply the same categories or conceptual schemes to the undifferentiated flow of their experiences. We cannot talk about a world independently
of our conceptualisation of it. The world as it is or *the thing in itself* apart
from our conceptions of it, is not open to us. While Kant defended a unique
universal classificatory framework, once his distinction between a conceptual
scheme and the content of that scheme was available, it was easy to accept
that there may be more than one system or scheme of organisation and the
idea of conceptual or metaphysical pluralism was born.

We see the fruits of this distinction in twentieth century discussions of
conceptual pluralism and ontological relativism. In order to make sense of
our experiences, it has been argued, we must impose upon them some conceptual or linguistic framework. However, there is no such thing as a single
unique and correct conceptual scheme, and no determinate facts to enable
us to choose between different frameworks: conceptual plurality and relativity are thus the inevitable consequences of our attempts to make sense of the
world.[1]

Debates on pluralism and relativism have been fed from another direction
also. Increasing awareness of the extent of diversity of beliefs, practices and
customs of different cultures and different historical epochs has cast doubt
on the universality and objectivity of our judgements, and in particular our
ethical judgements. Isaiah Berlin's analysis of value pluralism has provided
the touchstone for much of the discussion in this area. According to Berlin,
there may be irresolvable conflicts among the ultimate values espoused by a
single moral system, as well as the different moralities and values espoused
by different cultures. Pluralism, for Berlin, is the recognition that values are
incommensurable and constitutively uncombinable. However, Berlin argues
that this type of incommensurability does not preclude the possibility of

> members of one culture [being able], by the force of imaginative
> insight, [to] understand the values, the ideals, the forms of life of
> another culture or society, even those remote in time or space. They
> may find these values unacceptable, but if they open their minds

2

> sufficiently they can grasp how one can be a full human being, with
> whom one could communicate, and at the same time live in the light
> of values widely different from one's own, but which nevertheless
> one can see to be values, ends of life, by the realisation of which men
> could be fulfilled.
>
> (Berlin 1990: 10)

Thus for Berlin, value pluralism does not lead to relativism. But Berlin's
vision of an objective plurality of values is not shared by everyone.
Objectivity remains a critical concern in discussions of pluralism. The fear is
that if we allow the possibility of many incompatible and true pictures of the
world, and many incompatible goods and virtues, then we are undermining
the whole notion of the true and the good. The spectre of relativism haunts
pluralism and the boundaries between the two seem quite hazy.

The problems of pluralism are not merely abstract philosophical problems.
Pluralism as a social fact presents us with a variety of different and often conflicting beliefs, values, and ways of life. What attitude to adopt in the face of
the fact of pluralism is itself a matter of disagreement. Pragmatically, we may
take the view that we should accept the fact and design social arrangements
that can accommodate pluralism in a just social order. This seems to be a sensible social and political response designed to deal with the conflict and intolerance that can result from difference. It leaves aside contentious disputes
about the legitimacy of pluralism and its implications for truth, relativism, and
what there is. However, schemes for the practical accommodation of difference in society are themselves contested. Strategies of assimilation, integration, and politicisation of cultural difference all have adherents and opponents
in the practical arenas where disputes over the treatment of minorities, or
claims to self-determination, or identity rights, are fought out. And these
practical disputes often feed on assumptions that are matters of vigorous theoretical dispute. Some versions of the politics of identity, for example, refuse
to contemplate the possibility of defending a way of life on the grounds that
its propositions about how to do things cannot be intelligibly debated across
languages or cultures. But assumptions of non-translatability and different
rationalities are strongly contested in theoretical debates.

So while the political significance of the fact of pluralism is readily admitted, the legitimacy of our responses to the phenomenon is a more difficult
matter. The defence of political principles and policies for the accommodation of difference raises questions about the connection of these principles to
more deeply entrenched philosophical and moral beliefs. Our wished-for
responses to pluralism may conflict with these beliefs. They may also be facilitated and given direction by these beliefs. Or, we may find that pragmatically driven impulses to accommodate difference open up a fruitful
engagement between theory and practice that both revises background
beliefs and proposes a theoretically defensible practice.

This book attempts to address some of these issues of theory and practice by examining three main themes: the first is concerned with the philosophically core issue of conceptual pluralism and its implications for questions of truth and intelligibility; the second with the connections between pluralism and liberal ethical and political outlooks; and the third, with the implications of pluralism for both the more abstract, as well as concrete and practical issues, of political obligation in liberal democracies. The collection is organised so that the themes and chapters build on each other, but each chapter can also be read as an independent unit.

Philosophical sources of pluralism

One of the first figures to recognise fully the significance of pluralism in modern philosophy was William James, and his work has bequeathed to us some of the main lines of approach to the problems of pluralism. James provides a way into what is now called 'conceptual scheme pluralism', and this is the focus of the opening essay by James O'Shea. This piece shows, that, for James at least, pluralism is a consequence of an answer to a deeper philosophical question: how exactly do concepts enable us to grasp any truths at all? In elaborating James's answer to this question, O'Shea is able to show how certain doctrines about the function and limits of conceptualisation provide the grounds for James's radical pluralism. O'Shea focuses on James's account of the role of concepts within perceptual experience. This is an interpretation of concepts that concentrates on their functional use and value in triggering inferences that map regularities exhibited by the kind of thing the concept represents. James regards conceptual map-making as a means of adaptation to 'an immense environment'. O'Shea suggests that representation as adaptation lends plausibility to James's notorious identification of 'true' and 'useful'. We claim truth for our ideas when they are useful, in the way maps and other symbol systems are useful, in representing the properties and relationships of things, and thus guiding us successfully among the things themselves. A second crucial aspect of this theory is the relativity of conceptualisation to human interests and purposes. O'Shea stresses that this is a claim about the selectivity of our conceptions: that we are always attending to a particular *aspect* of reality, and that the aspects we select are always selected in light of some interest or end in view. O'Shea observes that these notions of the concept-dependence and interest relativity of our dealings with reality have now become an accepted part of the fabric of our philosophising – our philosophical toolbox. More controversial is James's idea that 'there is no really inherent order' apart from the various orders we impose on reality. This is the key rejection of the monistic belief in the world as a connected unity. It is supported in James by two main arguments, one a critique of abstractionist mishandling of concepts, the other a critique of a priori claims for the necessary unity of the world. Pluralism and monism can

4

then be understood as fallible hypotheses about the way in which the world is connected, and James believes that pluralism – the hypothesis that the 'unfinished' universe may always remain 'incompletely' unified – is the better hypothesis.

If pluralism is to be treated as a fallible hypothesis about the world, it must be coherent. The fundamental issue is how the apparently conflicting truths of a plurality of conceptual schemes can be understood. James has a number of strategies for dealing with this issue: instrumentalism, scheme-relativity, truth-convergence, and the plenitude of the given, all of which have been influential throughout the twentieth century, but each of which, O'Shea suggests, presents serious difficulties to be overcome.

James thought that the conflicting truths of different conceptual schemes call for an overhaul in the very idea of truth. But in recent years, it has been the very idea of conceptual scheme pluralism that has attracted the overhaul. As the piece by Maria Baghramian notes, conceptual pluralism has fallen out of favour with those hostile to cognitive relativism and to empiricism. Conceptual scheme pluralism is rejected by Donald Davidson on the grounds that we can admit the possibility of an alternative conceptual scheme only if such a scheme is untranslatable into our language, that is, into our conceptual scheme. In that case we cannot intelligibly compare or contrast schemes. If translation fails, we cannot speak of a plurality of schemes. But neither can we speak of one scheme, as if we could make sense of what it would be like to be more. So it seems that conceptual pluralism is, at the very least, a philosophical error, and perhaps also a mere dogma of empiricism as Davidson claims. Baghramian challenges this rejection of pluralism. The issue is how we interpret the scheme/content dualism. She shows that there are several versions of this distinction that fall foul of Davidsonian and other arguments and argues that the wholesale dismissal of the scheme/content distinction leaves us with the problem of accounting for the ways in which the world is understood and conceptualised by different cultures, epochs, and languages. Following a suggestion of John McDowell, she argues that there is a defensible 'innocent' version of scheme/content that saves a degree of conceptual pluralism, without committing us to the pernicious dualism of thought and unconceptualised world, or leading us into an offensive type of cognitive relativism. In this version, the scheme/content distinction is introduced to explain how there can be different accounts, both true and false, of what the world is like. Conceptual schemes or perspectives are embodied in languages or cultures but these do not float unrestricted by the role of the world in shaping conceptualisation – the point that the content end of the distinction keeps in play. This version of scheme/content dualism does not involve any commitment to unconceptualised experience or any denial of direct access to the world. It is simply the thought that our life experiences are from different standpoints, and that these standpoints offer us different ways of understanding and coping with

5

the world. Baghramian rests this scheme/thick content distinction on the common-sense observation that life-experiences can be differently described and even differently experienced. Different modes of conceptualisation also have different consequences for how people act in the world and conduct their lives. Alternative conceptual schemes are, in this sense, also alternative ways of life.

If the scheme/content distinction can thus be rehabilitated without the assumption of dualism, some degree of conceptual pluralism seems justified. Hostility to pluralism then focuses on its association with forms of radical relativism and irrationalism. As Philip Pettit indicates, perspectivism (the claim that there are different viewpoints/schemes/discourses) may be used to deny the possibility of any rational reconciliation between divergent viewpoints. This yields an outlook where 'anything goes'. In practice, then, which perspective is adopted becomes a function of power and interest. This leaves us with the Jamesian question: what does the fact that there can be different ways of depicting the world tell us about the nature of the world. Pettit rejects two sorts of answer: one claiming that reality is multiple; the other that there just are many irreconcilable ways of seeing things (multiple vision). Pettit argues for a third reductive type of response, one that, in his version of 'integrative' reduction, allows for the existence of a single world, while saving the irreducible multiplicity of ways of knowing. His argument is based on an analysis of the differences and relationships between indexical and non-indexical vocabularies. Indexical facts, as reported in sentences using terms like 'then' and 'now', 'here' and 'there', 'you' and 'I' and so on, can also be reported in sentences that do not use indexical terms, sentences that pick out the same facts by clocks, calendars, co-ordinates, names, and so on. From this it is clear that indexical facts can be ontically reduced to non-indexical. But they are not also heuristically reducible. If they were, Pettit argues, they would lose their potency to mediate people's interventions as agents in the world. The non-indexical perspective encompasses the facts of the narrower indexical, but it cannot capture the *way* in which those facts are presented and known in the indexical. The indexical perspective reveals patterns and background assumptions and resonances that cannot be carried over in any attempted reduction to the non-indexical. Pettit argues that the integrative model he develops for indexical and non-indexical vocabularies can be extended to divergent perspectives generally. The divide between ontic and heuristic reducibility carries over to the relationship between the figurative and non-figurative, the practical and non-practical and to affective and non-affective perspectives on things. That W. B. Yeats died on a January day in 1939 represents the fact of his death, but not what is invoked in W. H. Auden's lament, 'O all the instruments agree/the day of his death was a dark cold day'. This is not a report about the weather on a January day. As Pettit writes: 'We make of the words – we hear in the words – a figurative message of a much more gripping and suggestive kind.'

6

The three essays that introduce this volume show that conceptual pluralism is a sophisticated and plausible philosophical position. More needs to be said, of course. So we may do well to follow James, and ask, what are the consequences of pluralism? The remaining essays may be seen as colouring in some of those consequences.

Value pluralism and liberalism

In thinking about strategies for dealing with difference in our social world, the first task is to come to an understanding of the strengths and weaknesses of the view that the fact of pluralism is begotten and best addressed by liberal principles and institutions. Liberal theory addresses the potential conflicts engendered by the pluralism of individual life-plans by constructing a neutral political space and locating difference in the non-political or private realm. But as John Gray notes, that is not the pluralism that threatens human well-being in the contemporary world. The pluralism that we have to address is a strong pluralism of incommensurable goods whose conflicts concern whole ways of life. Gray argues that liberal institutions are not a reasonable solution to the conflicts of strong pluralism. Indeed, strong value pluralism, if true, defeats liberal political morality. Gray's argument is in two parts. The first defends the truth of strong value pluralism – the claim that there are many irreducible forms of human flourishing, often uncombinable in one way of life or in one life-time, and sometimes rationally incomparable. The second part of Gray's argument attacks liberalism, particularly in its Rawlsian manifestation as a defence of principles that are neutral with respect to conceptions of the good. That version of liberalism would, if coherent, regulate the terms under which the incommensurable goods of strong pluralism could be pursued. Gray argues that neutralist liberalism is an illusion. Contrary to its own claim, it rests on some understanding of the good. It cannot, therefore, avoid being part of the conflict among incommensurable goods it claims to rise above. This destroys the claim that a liberal political regime can best accommodate the pluralistic nature of values. It also disposes of liberal universalism understood as the claim that liberal principles of individual liberty are a basic ingredient of any form of good life. Gray concludes that conflicts generated by incommensurable ways of life are settled by achieving a *modus vivendi* between them. A *modus vivendi* settlement finds terms of coexistence on the basis of any interests and values that different ways of life share and the compromises they can make regarding divergent values. Liberal institutions may be the solution to coexistence in some societies. In others, different solutions are more appropriate.

Gray has thrown down the gauntlet to liberals. How can they respond? One response might be to challenge the truth of value-pluralism understood as a theory about the nature of moral value. Political liberals are disinclined to engage in this strategy. They wish to avoid commitment to substantial claims about the nature of value, precisely in order to defend liberal neutrality in politics. But how defensible is political neutrality? Susan Mendus views liberalism as the politics of a disenchanted world – a world in which moral judgements lack the authority provided by an unquestionable framework.

> The existential condition of agents in such a world is likely to consist in a lack of moral and spiritual 'anchorage', while the philosophical condition will be one in which it is difficult to justify moral beliefs and coercive political arrangements.

Mendus reminds us that political (Rawlsian) liberals do not deny the fact of pluralism. Their position is that any view about whether the sources of value are one or many is a controversial account of the nature of the good, and neutral liberalism can take no view on this. Political liberals cannot therefore explain the fact of pluralism as the outcome of objective value-pluralism. But while this version of liberalism is not committed to value-pluralism, it does claim that a liberal society can accommodate the fact of pluralism in a way that is more than a mere *modus vivendi* or accommodation of power.

For this claim to have any mileage in the face of Gray's criticisms, liberals must show how they can explain pluralism without sinking into value-pluralism. Liberal explanations of the fact of pluralism appeal to the nature of reason itself. There are different accounts – arguments from uncertainty, indeterminacy, scepticism, and reason as tending towards diversity. The diversity of reason account comes from Rawls who writes: 'Many conceptions of the world can plausibly be constructed from different standpoints. Diversity naturally arises from our limited powers and different perspectives' (Rawls 1993). Mendus favours this type of account (though she acknowledges that it may not be a complete explanation), and supports the claim that it calls for epistemological restraint – the demand that we abstract from our own convictions in deciding what can be legitimately imposed on others. This might seem a hard, even an impossible, doctrine. It may be interpreted as requiring in us a certain attitude to our convictions, a view of them as having the status of merely provisional, never unquestionable truths. This is part of what it means to live in the disenchanted world of modernity: 'disenchantment is precisely the existential condition of being unable to hold our beliefs with certainty or to see anything as beyond question'. But we may resist uncertainty. We may hold our beliefs to be true, while admitting that reason does not mandate a single moral view. Joshua Cohen distinguishes between what can reasonably be affirmed and what is true (Cohen 1993). When we are faced with persistent disagreement we may hold our belief as true, in a sectarian way, while acknowledging that it is something about which there is reasonable disagreement. The doctrine of epistemological restraint can then be seen as forbidding any imposition of our 'truth' on those who may reasonably disagree with us. In a world of multiple frameworks, views, or horizons, what really matters for the prospect of political agreement is that we sever any connection between the state of mind (certainty/scepticism) of the agent and the justification of political coercion. The existence of reasonable disagreement rather than value pluralism is the cornerstone of neutrality.

Mendus provides us with a careful analysis of a version of liberalism that responds to Gray's challenge by refusing to be drawn into the question of the truth of value pluralism. But suppose we concede value-pluralism, does it entail Gray's conclusion that liberal institutions are merely local settlements, never embodiments of universal principles? Jonathan Riley goes to Isaiah Berlin for instruction. Berlin is commonly credited with the articulation of the most far-reaching and rigorous value pluralism. His argument that pluralism and liberalism are not logically connected is widely accepted among liberals no less than non-liberals. Berlin has also stressed the incommensurability of values, and the problems of making choices, as we sometimes must, among incommensurables. If we are pluralists in Berlin's (also Gray's) sense, does it follow that we can have no reasoned justification for liberal norms, in particular, those norms we invoke under a human rights banner? Gray has argued that if pluralism goes all the way down into principles of justice and rights, as Berlin says it does, liberal values cannot be rationally justified over illiberal ones. Berlin's liberalism, Gray insists, is 'ungoverned by reason'. It is grounded in the radical choice we must make among incommensurables, not upon rational choice. Gray's reading of Berlin implies that there may be nothing unreasonable in the survival of illiberal values in a contest with liberal principles. Riley argues for an alternative reading of Berlin. He stresses the rationalistic liberalism of Berlin, and uses it to show that Berlinian liberal rationalism is a coherent doctrine, and consistent with value pluralism. The crux of the argument is whether a minimal liberalism understood as committed to equal liberty can prioritise liberty over competing values, given incommensurability. Berlin holds:

> The idea of human rights rests on the true belief that certain goods
> … freedom, justice, pursuit of happiness, honesty, love … are in the
> interests of all human beings as such … and that it is right to meet
> these claims and to protect people against those who ignore them.
> (Jahanbegloo 1992: 39)

Equal rights for all, though they may be interpreted differently, belong to the common moral horizon of human beings as they have developed in history. For Berlin this is a moral truth, no less secure than the truth of value-pluralism. Riley argues that the 'immense value' Berlin assigns to equal liberty, opens the possibility of an all-things-considered ranking of cultures in terms of the extent of equal liberty, even though pluralism reaches into the values attached to the different rights recognised in different systems. If this

9

argument is sound, it rehabilitates a minimalist liberal universalism. Restored also is a version of the claim that liberal regimes, ones committed to some version of equal liberty, offer the best (most 'decent' or 'civilised' as Berlin would say) responses to the problem of managing pluralism.

While there continues to be disagreement over the truth of value pluralism as an ethical doctrine and even the political relevance of the doctrine, everyone accepts the fact of moral, philosophical and religious pluralism. Most people also accept that any attempt to eliminate this fact in modern societies would involve an unacceptable use of state power. And some think that pluralism is, in any case, something to be celebrated and endorsed. There is broad agreement that pluralism should be tolerated and accommodated by politics. But what does it mean to accommodate pluralism? There is a familiar liberal model that situates diversity in a private realm distinct from the common public realm of the state. This model asserts the state/civil society distinction in a particular way, one that can be represented by drawing an even line between the two realms. Strong pluralists reject this neat line between the state and civil society. For them, politics cannot be hemmed in by a non-negotiable framework. Value pluralism entails the impossibility of any set of non-conflictual rules for politics.

Iseult Honohan identifies an alternative to the standard liberal pluralist model. Her model encourages the public/political expression of differences. It pluralises the public realm, and calls for a politics of continuous negotiation of the terms of common life. Honohan recognises the interpenetration of state and civil society and locates the dispute between liberal and certain radical pluralists over the nature of the public sphere in their acceptance of a too narrow identification of the public sphere as the domain of the state. This excludes a public space for deliberative politics in which interests and values may be expressed and argued out. Her republican conception of an enlarged public sphere makes space for difference without entailing that difference automatically translates into either a rainbow of publicly entrenched values, or the political dominance of majority cultural values. This approach proposes a pluralised public sphere disengaged from full identification with the state. In this space substantive moral and cultural values are not excluded as they are in the neutral public sphere of liberalism. Through engaging with each other as bearers of different views and identities, citizens are facilitated to achieve a better understanding of each other in their differences, an appreciation of the transformative character of reasoned debate about values, and, to some degree, a common understanding of the public good. Republican politics is based on interdependence rather than commonality, and is grounded in deliberation and ongoing openness to change, rather than prepolitical commitments to a fixed common good based on nature or culture. State actions are interpretations of common goods, filtered by the deliberations of multiple publics.

Honohan's pluralised public sphere promises an emancipatory politics in which there is a great deal of social inclusion and participation. But deliberative politics cannot guarantee consensus on government action. Sometimes, law will not be in harmony with our considered views. Yet, there is a common philosophical assumption that we have a prima facie obligation to obey the law, and that there is some single general ground for that obligation. In other cases the rights of minorities and the impact of cultural traditions on the correct conceptions of these rights pose special problems for pluralist conceptions of public policy. Section three of the book examines some of the issues facing those who attempt to accommodate the ideal of pluralism within a legal and cultural framework.

Accommodating pluralism

Jonathan Wolff explores the possibility of a pluralistic theory of political obligation. He argues for a multiple plurality model which holds that: (1) an obligation to obey a particular law may have more than one ground; (2) the obligation to obey different laws may have different grounds; (3) certain grounds of obligation may apply only to a subset of citizens. The model relies on differentiating various functions of government and maps the place of standard accounts of the sources of political obligation on to obligations required under different branches of government action. Thus obligations to obey law connected to the provision of security can be justified under a self-interest (rationality) account of political obligation, while obligations falling under the provision of public goods function of government are justified by a reciprocity (fairness) account, i.e. an account tying the receipt of benefits to contribution. Obligations under a broadly redistributive function of government are handled under a reasonableness (justice) account. Wolff claims that under multiple plurality the largest group of citizens will have obligations generated under all three headings of self-interest, fairness, and justice. But the account allows for variability in political obligations, and opens a way of thinking that promises to relieve some of the political tensions that the fact of pluralism can generate.

The final two papers in the collection discuss two public policy issues raised by cultural pluralism and help illustrate some of the general issues and practical problems raised in earlier articles. Martha Nussbaum discusses approaches to the goals of public policy in light of a number of examples of the way cultural traditions pose obstacles to women's quality of life. As she notes, on the measures of life expectancy, educational attainment, and GDP per capita used by the 1996 UN Human Development Report, there is no country in the world in which women's quality of life is equal to that of men. The situation of women in developing countries is particularly distressing overall, despite some achievements. Nussbaum argues that the current leading theoretical approaches to quality of life assessment are based on faulty models of satisfaction (organic family models or utilitarian approaches) which cannot provide an accurate measure of the real well-being of women and children. The problem, as Nussbaum sees it, is that customs and political arrangements have an important bearing on women's misery and death. We need an approach that deals with the relationship between tradition and women's equality.

A new approach that many workers on development issues are turning to is 'the capabilities approach'. This approach to quality of life assessment and the goals of public policy focuses on the question: what are the people of this group or country actually able to do and to be? The capabilities approach inquires into 'the varying needs individuals have for resources, and their varying abilities to convert resources into functioning. In this way it strongly invites a scrutiny of tradition, as one of the primary sources of such unequal abilities'. In the body of her article, Nussbaum develops a detailed account of central human functioning, which does not need rehearsing here. The implications of this account as they revive themes of earlier chapters are worth noting briefly. First, the account revives a form of universalism that is sensitive to pluralism while resisting relativism and moral and political quietism. Second, the universalism that Nussbaum defends is grounded in historical experience of ideas of the human, an approach that has much in common with Berlin's account of the idea of human rights quoted earlier. Third, while the capabilities approach is indeed a universalist project, Nussbaum shows that it has robust responses to the standard attacks on universalism. Her list of basic human capabilities is very general and she insists that this allows room for the fact that individuals and groups face problems of needs and capacities in highly concrete contexts. These contexts shape the detailed specifications of the various components on the list of human capabilities. Moreover, the capabilities approach allows for concrete understanding not only of the depth and pervasiveness of local traditions but also of the depth of longing among individuals, especially women, for choice and autonomy both as means to their own survival and as means to self-hood. Finally, Nussbaum argues, the capabilities approach is monistic with respect to the norms of human functioning. It offers grounds for resisting two kinds of claim that reinforce the subordination of women: claims that men and women should exercise the basic functions in different spheres; and claims that there are different norms of human functioning for men and women.

One key implication of Nussbaum's approach is that space can be found for cultural pluralism within a universalist framework. Our responses to pluralism need not divide into unrelenting universalism or uncritical endorsement of cultural traditions. The issue is transformed into a matter of how to combine universalism with respect for cultural diversity.

This is how Will Kymlicka and Raphael Cohen-Almagor approach the issue of accommodating the claims of minorities in broadly liberal democratic countries. Their focus is on the difficulties that arise in North America and in Israel when the minority seeking accommodation is illiberal. Liberal democracies historically recognise a set of basic individual rights and assume that these are sufficient to accommodate ethnocultural minorities. But this assumption is increasingly challenged by demands for group-differentiated rights seen as mechanisms for reducing the vulnerability of minorities to majority decisions. Claims to group rights raise two quite different sets of issues depending on whether the group rights are seen as a matter of the relationship between groups, or as a matter (also) of the relationship between groups and individual members. These different claims are distinguished by Kymlicka and Cohen-Almagor as claims to 'external protections' and claims to 'internal restrictions'. The former claims are often consistent with liberal democracy and may be defensible as necessary for putting different groups in a society on an equal footing. The latter claims are inherently more problematic. Internal restrictions are often sought to protect a group from the destablising impact of internal dissent – refusals to abide by traditional practices and customs. In some cases, this type of group right is sought to protect religious orthodoxy or cultural traditions that have heavy costs for the health and lives of some members, especially women. Internal restrictions that would allow the murder of women, for example, for 'family honour' are clearly unjust, and beyond the tolerance of liberal democracies.

Of course, many of the internal restrictions that groups impose on their members are not so dramatic. Groups may deny some or all of their members certain educational and economic opportunities. They may discriminate on grounds of religion or sexual orientation. Are such restrictions always impermissible? Liberals are divided on the answer to this question as well as on mechanisms for addressing violations of rights in a non-coercive way. One way of characterising this division is in terms of rival accounts of what is the fundamental principle of liberalism itself. For some, the fundamental principle is tolerance, including tolerance of illiberal groups. To reduce the danger of injustice within groups, the tolerant liberal democratic state may insist on a right of exit for group members. But it will not seek to impose liberal principles on these groups. Rather, it will seek a *modus vivendi* type of accommodation that secures the widest possible basis for its own legitimacy. For other liberals, the fundamental principle is some conception of individual freedom. This entails a state that secures the same liberties and resources for all citizens, including the right to learn about ways of life different from one's own, to question and revise traditional practices, norms, and customs. Kymlicka and Cohen-Almagor argue that this divide between tolerance and liberal autonomy is faulty. Liberal tolerance is individual freedom-based, not group-based. It follows that decisions in favour of certain group claims that limit individual freedom of conscience, (or other freedoms) are in fact departures from liberal tolerance. So, it seems that the appeal to tolerance cannot resolve the conflict between liberal principles and illiberal minorities in liberal democracies. What does this entail?

A point of great importance here is that the issue of identifying a defensible liberal theory of minority rights is separate from imposing that theory. Kymlicka and Cohen-Almagor insist that while internal restrictions may be inconsistent with liberal principles, it does not follow that liberals should impose their principles on illiberal minorities, except in cases of egregious human rights violations. This is especially clear in the case of involuntarily incorporated groups, who may have their own systems of government and courts, and where imposition of an alternative system would both denigrate the indigenous system and continue the experience of aggression and colonial paternalism. Still, liberals do not have to stand idly by. They have a responsibility to speak out against illiberal practices, and to support internal attempts at liberalisation. Moreover, there are many types of incentives that the state can use to reduce the health risks to individuals of certain traditional practices (like female circumcision) as long as intervention to restrict such practices altogether is not legitimated by, for example, a rise in complaints about coercion. There are also ways of developing agreed and effective mechanisms for protecting human rights in minority communities – acceptance of international declarations and international review of charges of rights violations, for instance.

If Kymlicka and Cohen-Almagor are right, liberal democracies can and must develop strategies for living with cultural pluralism that combine principle and prudence, individual and group rights, universalism and particularism. Doubtless, we will all have different views about what sort of combination we should support.

Notes

1   W.V.O. Quine has been the main proponent of ontological relativity, while Nelson Goodman has advocated a sophisticated form of conceptual pluralism.

Part I

PHILOSOPHICAL SOURCES OF PLURALISM

1

SOURCES OF PLURALISM IN WILLIAM JAMES

James R. O'Shea

William James held that the 'difference between monism and pluralism is perhaps the most pregnant of all the differences in philosophy' (James 1979: 5), and he himself came down firmly on the side of a thoroughgoing philosophical (epistemological, metaphysical, and value) pluralism. A century later discussions of pluralism are now infused with a sense of political urgency, which makes it all the more important to step back and reflect critically on the fluency with which our current discussions of pluralism, whether in political philosophy or general epistemology, have come to be conducted in the language of 'alternative conceptual frameworks'. No single figure merits a more prominent place in any such intellectual history than William James, who was one of the first thinkers to articulate a comprehensive philosophical vision incorporating what we would now find it natural to call a *conceptual scheme pluralism*. In doing so he introduced conceptions that have since become the mother tongue of our philosophical thought.

In this essay I propose to examine the nature and sources of James's wide-ranging pluralism by focusing in particular on the account he offers of the role of *concepts* within perceptual experience. What view of the nature of concepts separated James from his monistic philosophical opponents and underpinned his own attempts to defend a general philosophical pluralism? In addition to its intrinsic historical interest as a prime mover in the development of pluralist conceptions throughout the twentieth century, the case of James will also serve to underscore the fact that some of the most difficult and important issues raised by the concept of pluralism have their sources in the seemingly more arcane question of how exactly it is that concepts enable us to grasp *any* truths at all.

In the first section I offer an exposition and analysis of what I see as James's functionalist account of the nature of conceptual representation. In the second section I then examine the *limits* of conceptual understanding established by James's critique of 'vicious abstractionism' and his account of the 'perceptual flux', and I show how on the basis of these limits James mounted important criticisms of various monistic theses and arguments, thereby providing support for his own fallibilist and empiricist hypothesis of pluralism. In the final section I then turn to James's own constructive account of the alternative conceptual schemes by means of which we apprehend reality, and conclude by distinguishing and briefly commenting upon four different Jamesian lines of response to the problem of *conflicting* schemes that is raised (and continues to be raised) by this pluralist outlook.

The function of concepts within experience

Percepts and concepts

Throughout his writings James operates with a fundamental epistemological distinction between *percepts* and *concepts*. Roughly synonymous terms for the percept side of the distinction, he tells us, are 'sensation', 'feeling', 'sensible experience' and the 'immediate flow of conscious life'; and for 'concept' he indicates that he freely substitutes 'thought', 'idea' and 'intellection' (James 1996: 48n). By means of percepts we are said to enjoy knowledge by *acquaintance* with particular sensible realities, while concepts enable us to signify or represent those same realities in thought and thus have knowledge *about* them (James 1975b: 18–20, 35). James regards both percepts and concepts as indispensable throughout all human experience. 'The world we practically live in is one in which it is impossible, except by theoretic retrospection, to disentangle the contributions of intellect from those of sense' (James 1996: 108); and we 'use both perception and conception in philosophy as we use both blades of a pair of scissors' (James 1978: 273–4).

While James thus highlights the essential interplay between concepts and percepts he also argues in favour of what we might call *the primacy of percepts*. In the first place he defends the strong empiricist-abstractionist thesis that all human concepts are 'abstracted and generalised from ... perceptual instances' (James 1996: 52; cp. 68–9). 'All conceptual content is borrowed' from the perceptual flux, he holds, and this 'applies as much to concepts of the most rarefied order as to qualities' (James 1996: 79–80). He then argues further that conceptual understanding can in principle never fully adequately represent perceptual experience itself, and that in fact conception by its nature tends to 'falsify' the immediate flux (more on this below). In sum, he writes, 'concepts are secondary formations, inadequate and only ministerial; and ... they falsify as well as omit, and make the flux impossible to understand' (James 1996: 79).

These limitations on conception will form an important part of James's overall defence of philosophical pluralism, but in order to see how this is so we shall have to take a closer look first at just what a concept *is*, according to James, and at the indispensable and beneficial role that concepts play in human knowledge. James himself suggests that in order 'to understand the nature of concepts better, we must now go on to distinguish their *function* from their *content*' (James 1996: 58). What does he mean by this distinction?

James's functionalist theory of conceptual content

'The perceptual flux as such … *means* nothing', writes James, 'and is but what it immediately is … [It] contains innumerable aspects and characters which conception can pick out, isolate, and thereafter always intend' (James 1996: 49). The stream of experience during any given passing moment is an indefinitely complex presentation of aspects and characters potentially available for conceptual isolation and generalisation. As to their *origin*, concepts arise from our attending to such aspects and (as James puts it) 'naming' them, thereby adding to 'the store of nouns, verbs, adjectives, conjunctions, and prepositions by which the human mind interprets life' (James 1996: 52). Thus arise the various conceptual 'worlds', as he calls them, of commonsense 'things', of mathematical forms, of ethical propositions, and so on, 'all abstracted and generalised from long forgotten perceptual instances … . By those *whats* we apperceive all our *thises*. Percepts and concepts interpenetrate' (James 1996: 52).

More important for James than this question as to the origin of concepts, however, 'is that as to *their functional use and value*' (James 1996: 55–6, italics added), and in particular the 'question of whether the whole import of the world of concepts lies in its relation to perceptual experience, or whether it be also an independent revelation of reality' (James 1996: 63). It is toward answering this question that James develops his broadly functionalist account of the nature of concepts.[1]

James puts forward the view that the concept of an *F* (his example is 'man') 'is three things': (1) 'the *word* itself'; (2) the mental *image* or picture (perhaps vague) that one might form of an *F*; and (3) the *functional* aspect of the concept as 'an instrument for symbolising certain objects' (James 1996: 58; cp. James 1976: 28–9). James refers to the mental image as the 'content' or 'the substantive part of the concept' (James 1996: 59, 61). The term 'content' in *this* context refers not to what we would call the 'intentional content' of the concept (though it may have a part to play in generating such content) but rather to the 'static' (James's term), non-relational properties of whatever mental images or pictures might regularly accompany our conception of an *F*. Years earlier in *The Principles of Psychology* he had similarly distinguished 'between two *aspects*, in which all mental facts without exception may be taken; their structural aspect, as being subjective, and their functional aspect, as being cognitions' (James 1983: 452n).[2] As James's analysis proceeds, it becomes clear that on his view the meaning or intentional content of a concept derives from its functional role as a sign or symbol capable of standing in for certain objects and representing them as standing in various relations.[3] Although the purposes of this essay preclude a full treatment of the issue here, this interpretation demands at least a bit more spelling out.

James claims that in the case of some concepts (e.g. 'God', 'number', 'substance') 'their whole value seems to be functional': they 'suggest no definite picture' and 'their significance seems to consist entirely in their *tendency*, in the further turn which they may give to our action or our thought' (James 1996: 59). In cases where there *are* definite pictures or images associated with a concept, James argues that their 'value' is primarily aesthetic (in a broad sense), and that this is a less important part of the concept's significance than are its relational or functional 'consequences':

> [H]owever beautiful or otherwise worthy of stationary contemplation the substantive part of a concept may be, the more important part of its significance may naturally be held to be the consequences to which it leads. These may lie either in the way of making us think, or in the way of making us act. Whoever has a clear idea of these knows effectively what the concept practically signifies, whether its substantive content be interesting or not.
>
> (James 1996: 59)

Immediately after this passage, James calls upon his general pragmatic 'method of interpreting concepts', which he here calls '*the Pragmatic Rule*' (James 1996: 60; cp. James 1975a: 27–30), and the result is that what he has just called 'knowing what the concept practically signifies' in terms of its functional consequences comes finally to be *identified* with the meaning of a concept:

> The pragmatic rule is that the meaning of a concept may always be found, if not in some sensible particular which it directly designates, then in some particular difference in the course of human experience which its being true will make... . In obeying this rule we neglect the substantive content of the concept, and *follow its function only.*
>
> (James 1996: 60, 61; italics added)

He concludes that 'particular consequences are the only criterion of a concept's meaning, and the only test of its truth' (James 1996: 62). What needs to be further clarified, then, is what James means by the 'functional consequences' that constitute the meaning of a concept.

For James the most basic function of conception concerns what he calls the 'exclusively practical use' of concepts, which he conjectures to have characterised 'the earliest stages of human intelligence':

> Men classed their sensations, substituting concepts for them, in order to 'work them for what they were worth', and to prepare for

what might lie ahead. Class-names suggest consequences that have attached themselves on other occasions to other members of the class – consequences which the present percept will also probably or certainly show. The present percept in its immediacy may thus often sink to the status of a bare sign of the consequences which the substituted concept suggests.

(James 1996: 63–4)

I take James's overall functionalist theory of conceptual content to be something like the following. For a person S to have the concept of a given kind of thing K is for S to be so habituated (paradigmatically, if not necessarily,)[4] through social linguistic training) that S's utterance or mental-tokening of 'this is a K' will be associated in S's mental set with a general pattern of ready-to-be-triggered inferences involving the term 'K' (or involving the relevant 'substantive' mental imagery – whatever the particular 'structural' realisation of the concept happens to be in any given case). As a result of the linguistic training and other continuing modes of social inquiry S's patterns of inferences will to a large degree become 'adapted' (James's term) to S's environment in the sense that those patterns will have come to systematically reflect or 'map' the regularities exhibited by Ks both in S's own experience and according to the generally shared testimony of others. (The 'practical adaptation' and 'mapping' here are discussed by James [1996: 63–74].)

To have the concept of a *knife*, for instance, is not a matter of one's adroitness in forming clear mental images of knives (although images may form a part of the substantive, structural realisation of the concept in any given instance), nor is it a matter of a supposed ability to 'reach out mentally and intend' or 'mentally point to' knives with the 'mind's eye' (to take two timehonoured but, for James, ultimately unsuccessful ways of explaining the intentionality of concepts).[5] Rather, to put it baldly, for S to have the concept of a knife *just is* for S to be one whose perceptual responses, inferences, actions concerning knives can be relied upon (*ceteris paribus*) to satisfactorily reflect the characteristic 'habitudes' or properties of knives, and consequently for S to be one whose inferences and actions generally lead to successful dealings (both theoretical and practical) with knives. Whatever subjective 'psychic body or structure' concepts and images may genuinely possess for an experiencer at any given time, then, the idea of their having a *general signification* 'only has a meaning when applied to their use, import, or reference to the kind of object they may reveal' (James 1983: 452–3n). In sum, particular linguistic items or particular mental events have their meaning, intentional content, or '*representative function*' (James 1983: 452n) constituted solely by their regular pattern-governed relationships (including various mediating chains of inference) ultimately in relation to the objects we perceptually encounter and act upon.[6]

21

On this general view we can now understand more clearly James's statement (quoted earlier) that 'the present percept in its immediacy may thus often sink to the status of a bare sign of the consequences which the substituted concept suggests' (James 1996: 63–4; cp. James 1983: 954 on 'recepts'). As we have seen, James holds that human experience is a combination of percepts and concepts working together. In his philosophy of *radical empiricism* (with its crucial and difficult doctrine of *pure experience*) James wants ultimately to defend the directly realist view that in perceptual acquaintance with a given physical object K we are capable of being directly aware of K itself in a manner that requires no intermediary 'idea-images' in the classical empiricist or indirect realist sense (James 1976: 8, 27; James 1983: 450). This is perfectly consistent with that same perceptual experience's being at the same time 'mediated' by the lawlike experiences or regularities that are implicated in one's having acquired a general concept of the kind of thing K (as we have seen, the intentional content of the concept is constituted by just this mediating function). In short, James's functionalist account of conceptual representation is quite compatible, it seems to me, with his directly realist theory of sense perception.

Truth and interest-relativity

The 'conceptual map-making' (James 1977: 123) James has been describing 'adapt[s] us to an immense environment' precisely by representing or symbolically mapping in 'a topographic system' the lawlike relationships that (we take to) hold among the sensible things themselves (James 1996: 66–7).[7] Having this account of conceptual representation as 'adaptation' before us we can at least hint at how one ought to understand James's famous pragmatic account of *truth*. In particular, it seems to me (although I cannot attempt the task here) that the above account provides a way of lending some plausibility to James's notorious view that the epithets '*true*' and '*useful*' are interchangeable (James 1975a: 98). For we ascribe truth to our ideas when they are actually and potentially useful in the way that maps and other symbol systems are actually and potentially useful, namely, in *guiding* us successfully (both theoretically and practically) among the things themselves, 'leading us up to them' by (among other things) symbolically representing their properties and tracking their relationships.

There is, finally, a crucial further point to be brought out in relation to James's views on the 'functional use and value' of concepts. Throughout his career James was concerned to stress that all our conceptualisation is teleological in the sense of being relative to certain interests or purposes. In 'The Sentiment of Rationality' he wrote:

> Every way of classifying a thing is but a way of handling it for some particular purpose. Conceptions, 'kinds', are teleological instruments.

No abstract concept can be a valid substitute for a concrete reality except with reference to a particular interest in the conceiver. The interest of theoretic rationality, the relief of identification, is but one of a thousand human purposes. When others rear their heads, it must pack up its little bundle and retire till its turn recurs.

(James 1978: 56, 62)

James does not mean by this, of course, that we may simply ignore the theoretical facts in those cases where we have a strong practical interest in doing so.[8] In contending that all our concepts are teleological instruments, rather, James is arguing that (1) all our conceptions are *selective*: even when we simply 'look and see', we are always attending to some particular *aspect* of the full reality that presents itself to us at any given time; and (2) the selected aspects or kinds that we thus select will always be selected for some purpose or 'subjective end', even if it be only our need to have a simple map of reality enabling successful predictions:

[O]ut of an infinite number of [relations in presented reality] we call certain ones essential and lawgiving, and ignore the rest. Essential these relations are, but only *for our purpose*, the other relations being just as real and present as they; and our purpose is to *conceive simply* and to *foresee*. Are not simple conception and prevision subjective ends pure and simple? They are the ends of what we call science; and the miracle of miracles ... is that the given order lends itself to the remodelling.

(James 1978: 96)

As James puts the same point later in *A Pluralistic Universe*:

There is no really inherent order, but it is we who project order into the world by selecting objects and tracing relations so as to gratify our intellectual interests. We carve out order by leaving the disorderly parts out.

(James 1977: 10)

What is likely to provoke controversy here are not so much the claims regarding the concept-dependence and interest-relativity of all our dealings with reality (for here James is developing notions that have since become part of the fabric of our philosophising), but rather the idea that '*there is no really inherent order*' apart from the various orders we impose upon reality. We shall confront this issue again as we now attempt to put the above understanding of the function of concepts to work in exploring James's philosophical pluralism.

23

Monism, pluralism and the limits of conceptual understanding

Vicious abstractionism and the 'insuperability of sensation'

James holds that philosophers are especially prone to a particular kind of misunderstanding of the function of concepts that he calls *vicious abstractionism* or *vicious intellectualism*:

> Let me give the name of 'vicious abstractionism' to a way of using concepts which may be thus described: We conceive a concrete situation by singling out some salient or important feature in it, and classing it under that; then, instead of adding to its previous characters all the positive consequences which the new way of conceiving it may bring, we proceed to use our concept privatively; reducing the originally rich phenomenon to the naked suggestions of that name abstractly taken, treating it as a case of 'nothing but' that concept, and acting as if all the other characters from out of which the concept is abstracted were expunged... . [M]ore than half the trouble that metaphysicians and logicians give themselves over the paradoxes and dialectic puzzles of the universe may, I am convinced, be traced to this relatively simple source. *The viciously privative employment of abstract characters and class names* is, I am persuaded, one of the great original sins of the rationalistic mind.
>
> (James 1975b: 135–6)

Vicious abstractionism thus generates paradoxes through a use of abstract terms as 'positively excluding all that their definition fails to include' (James 1977: 36). Philosophers of both the rationalist-metaphysical and atomistic-empiricist varieties have in this way been led to portray our perceptual experience as in various ways *defective* as far as the prospects of genuine human knowledge are concerned:

> From difficulty to difficulty, the plain conjunctive experience has been discredited by both schools, the empiricists leaving things permanently disjoined, and the rationalists remedying the looseness by their Absolutes or Substances, or whatever other fictitious agencies of union they may have employed.
>
> (James 1976: 26)[9]

James's metaphorical way of expressing the abstractionist misunderstanding of the function of concepts that underlies both errors is in terms of the following schematic argument: (1) the concepts that make up our conceptual schemes are 'discontinuous' and 'static'; but (2) sensible reality, by contrast, is 'continuous' and 'changing'; therefore (3) any 'conceptual scheme ... can only cover the perceptual flux in spots and incompletely' (James 1996: 81). This principled limitation on the adequacy of *any conceptual scheme* in relation to the perceptual flux is one important source of James's pluralism (see below), so it will be worth our while to attempt to cash out the governing metaphor of 'discreteness vs. continuity' with which James is operating here.

While James was well aware that we do have concepts of aspects of the flux that are continuous and changing – we have the concepts of sensible *change* and of spatio-temporal *continuity* for instance – he argues nonetheless that what he calls the 'practical' or 'scientific-theoretical' knowledge afforded by such concepts necessarily falls short of a grasp of the essential nature of the sensible flux itself. James articulates this contrast in greater detail in *A Pluralistic Universe*:

> [M]y own experience with 'pragmatism' makes me shrink from the dangers that lie in the word 'practical', and ... I am quite willing ... to ascribe a primarily theoretical function to our intellect, provided you on your part then agree to discriminate 'theoretic' or scientific knowledge from the deeper 'speculative' knowledge aspired to by most philosophers, and concede that theoretic knowledge, which is knowledge *about* things, as distinguished from living or sympathetic acquaintance with them, touches only the outer surface of reality.
>
> (James 1977: 111)

As we have seen, our conceptual schemes give us knowledge that is of tremendous practical utility, but James holds that there is a deeper sense in which even the 'map' provided by atomic physics, for example – however realistically construed – would give us knowledge only of the surfaces of things (James 1977: 123n). The operative contrast between 'surface' and 'interior' is in this case between, on the one hand, a (supposed) *non-conceptual metaphysical insight into the nature of the perceptual flux*, by direct acquaintance or 'intuitive sympathy', and on the other hand the conceptual knowledge 'about' the properties and relations of things that our conceptual maps afford us. James's general thesis is that our 'conceptual knowledge is forever inadequate to the fullness of the reality to be known ... "The insuperability of sensation" would be a short expression of my thesis' (James 1996: 79).

To take just one of James's many examples, the intellectual vice of abstractionism has led philosophers to the view that '*activity and causation are incomprehensible*, for the conceptual scheme yields nothing like them. Nothing happens therein: concepts are "timeless", and can only be juxtaposed and compared. The concept "dog" does not bite' (James 1996: 85). The suggestion here is that the philosopher who focuses on the analytic entailments of isolated concepts will never (to use Hume's terms) discover either in the ideas or the impressions any necessary connection between matters of fact. The dogged pursuit of this sort of conceptual analysis, according to James, ultimately leads either to Humean scepticism or else to an appeal to 'transempirical' realities of the Platonic, Leibnizian, or transcendental idealist varieties (as James understands 'transcendental idealism', at any rate). In each case that James considers (e.g. self, substance, qualities, change, novelty, tendency, freedom: [James 1996: 97]) he argues that a commonplace of ordinary experience has been rendered conceptually problematic by philosophers, and his diagnosis is that:

> Many of the troubles of philosophy come from assuming that to be understood (or 'known' in the only worthy sense of the word) our flowing life must be cut into discrete bits and pinned upon a fixed relational scheme.
>
> (James 1996: 85)

In contrast, James holds that our references to activity and to necessary connections (to continue with this example) reflect not only our 'practical' conceptual mapping of lawlike connections between kinds of event, but also at a deeper metaphysical level such references allegedly derive their meaning from a *direct non-conceptual acquaintance* with the perceptual reality of *activity* itself ('in our own personal activity-situations'), (James 1996: 210). In the end, I take the suggestion to be, we must recognise that there are no satisfactory *conceptual* resolutions of such classic philosophical puzzles forthcoming, and that the most important truths concerning reality are directly apprehended in such a way that we can give no sufficient conceptual account of them (or worse, the conceptual account of which leads to deep misunderstanding: [James 1976: 25]). The general conclusion is that our conceptual schemes by their very nature must always fall short of the reality to be known:

> [I]t is enough to recognise this fact, that altho by means of concepts cut out from the sensible flux of the past, we can re-descend upon the future flux and, making another cut, say what particular thing is likely to be found there; and that altho in this sense concepts give us knowledge, and may be said to have some theoretic value ... yet in the deeper sense of giving us *insight* they have no theoretic value, for they quite fail to connect us with the inner life of the flux.
>
> (James 1977: 110)

Concepts, in short, 'are always insufficient representatives' of the sensible flux of life itself (James 1996: 97). I will return again to this notion of the 'insuperability of sensation' (or equivalently, the *insufficiency* of conceptual schemes). First, however, it is time to apply the lessons just learned to the question of monism versus pluralism.

Pluralism, abstractionism and fallibilism

The doctrines concerning both the function and the limits of conceptualisation discussed above provide the key to understanding the grounds for what James variously calls his 'radical pluralism' or his 'pluralistic pragmatism' (James 1977: 26; 1975a: 125). The following passage provides a convenient starting point:

> The alternative ... between pluralism and monism ... is the most pregnant of all the dilemmas of philosophy. Does reality exist distributively? Or collectively? – in the shape of *eaches, everys, anys, eithers?* or only in the shape of an *all* or *whole?* An identical content is compatible with either form obtaining... Pluralism stands for the distributive, monism for the collective form of being ... [Pluralism] at the outset ... only has the negative significance of contradicting monism's thesis that there is absolutely *no* disconnection [between things]. The irreducible outness of *any*thing, however infinitesimal, from anything else, in *any* respect, would be enough, if it were solidly established, to ruin the monistic doctrine.
>
> (James 1996: 114–15)

The initial task described here of demonstrating merely that there exist *some* respects in which *some* things are independent in *some* respectable sense of the term 'independent' might strike us as a job for a philosophical rookie, but I think that James's denial of monism even in this form has a generalisable significance and is of broader interest.

In the chapter on 'Monistic Idealism' in *A Pluralistic Universe* James examines specific monistic arguments against the possibility of what he has referred to in the above quote as 'disconnection' between things. James reads the monist (e.g. Lotze) as arguing that if, on the one hand, we admit *any* connection between things (for example, that A and B *interact*), then we are led inevitably to the conclusion that all things are necessarily interrelated in an absolute unity; if on the other hand we admit the slightest 'independence' between any two things, then we are led to a universe of complete chaos (James 1977: 30–2). I will not attempt (as James does) to rehearse any of the monists' specific arguments for such views. James's central contention is that there are fallacies involved in all of the monists' attempts to demonstrate a priori that all things are *necessarily* interrelated or unified (the characterisation of the overarching unity differs for different monisms); in particular he argues that what makes this sort of monism seem necessary is precisely the vicious abstractionist misunderstanding of the function of concepts (James 1977: 31–3, and *passim*). For the abstractionist error consists in treating the mere definition of a given concept as if it were a full equivalent for the things that fall under that concept, and on this basis James offers detailed (and often convincing) diagnoses of the gradual slide of the Hegelian monists into an intellectualist equation of 'the real' with the domain of conceptual abstractions.

What the various considerations examined so far suggest is that James's pluralism at its core rests upon a distinction between two senses – one legitimate and the other fallacious – in which a concept may be said to 'substitute' for a thing.[10] In the first sense, concepts serve as proper functional substitutes for or symbolic representatives of the things themselves (as argued earlier), while in the second sense concepts are used in the vicious abstractionist manner that illegitimately substitutes only the *definition* of some aspect of the thing for the thing itself. The fallacy arises, as I understand James's view, when the vicious abstractionist dips back into the particulars of experience and then (knowingly or unknowingly) tries to insinuate upon us a simultaneous acceptance of two incompatible understandings of the same term. On the one hand, we are to preserve in the background the (correct) notion that the given concept is the very concept that it is solely because of its experience-mediating function. On the other hand, and at the same time, we import the abstractionist notion that the given concept *cannot* be applied to any item that possesses a property that is not *entailed* by (included within the 'analysis' of) that concept. What James's arguments on the whole suggest, I think, is that the uncritical use of both formal and informal *conceptual analyses* has been a main source of support for the (often inexplicit) denial that philosophical pluralism represents even a *possible* outlook on the ultimate nature of things.

Having thus criticised the general form of a priori argumentation employed by the monists, the way now lies open for James to consider monism and pluralism simply as competing explanatory *hypotheses* as to the nature of reality. James understands 'pluralism's doctrine' as the 'hypothesis, of a world imperfectly unified still, and perhaps always to remain so' (James 1975a: 79). In various places where he discusses the problem of 'the one and the many' and considers the manifold senses in which philosophers and common sense have considered the world to be a *unity*, his main contention is that in no case are we (at present) warranted in holding that reality is either completely or necessarily unified by any of the suggested unifiers.

Philosophers typically attempt to present 'some one vehicle of conjunction ... as all-inclusive, like one origin, one purpose, or one knower' (James 1975a: 74). For example, while James grants that *space and time* are two comprehensive 'vehicles of continuity by which the world's parts hang together' (James 1975a: 66), he rejects the general Kantian claim that such an all-comprehensive spatio-temporal unity in experience is in any way a priori necessary (James 1977: 98, 106–8). Similar remarks hold in relation to the *causal* relations that unify the experienced world (James 1975a: 66–8). 'No one single type of connection runs through all the experiences that compose [the universe]. If we take space-relations, they fail to connect minds into any regular system. Causes and purposes obtain only among special series of facts' (James 1976: 24; cp. 1975a: 67). As it thus rejects both a priori epistemological legislation and essentialist metaphysics, James holds generally that pluralism must incline us toward empiricism (James 1975a: 79; more strictly, to 'a revised empiricism': James 1977: 9).

We are now perhaps in a position to understand the meaning of James's statement quoted earlier that in the debate between pluralism and monism an 'identical content is compatible with either form obtaining' (James 1996: 114–15). For the crux of the dispute does not primarily concern whether or not certain entities *exist*. Rather, the more fundamental dispute concerns the epistemic and modal status of what are for the most part agreed facts. James is arguing that the various claims made by philosophers to the effect that the realities to be accounted for must be related in certain systematic ways all amount only to fallible hypotheses.[11] His defence of pluralism, as the hypothesis that the 'unfinished' universe is and may always remain 'imperfectly' or 'incompletely' unified (James 1977: 25; 1975a: 79), thus builds upon the negative thesis (as supported by the general critique of the abstractionist mishandling of concepts) that none of the various all-comprehensive ontologies or alleged epistemological necessities defended by monistic philosophers represents a more reasonable hypothesis than its denial. As opposed to monism, therefore, pluralism 'leaves us with the common-sense world, in which we find things partly joined and partly disjoined' (James 1975a: 79). 'What pluralists say is that a universe really connected loosely, after the pattern of our daily experience, is possible, and that for certain reasons it is the hypothesis to be preferred' (James 1977: 39).

Having climbed our way back toward the 'manys' of ordinary experience, then, let us take up finally the question of pluralism in relation to our manifold knowledge of the sensible world. If the story as outlined so far is accepted, then James will have succeeded in defending a philosophical pluralism broadly characterisable as a fallibilist and non-reductive empiricist outlook, one that is capable of giving us principled grounds for resisting a variety of perennially tempting monistic positions and attitudes. Pluralism understood in these general terms has become so thoroughly ensconced in our philosophical consciousness that we may have difficulty appreciating the significance of James's hard-earned victory less than a century ago. In the final section I want to examine the various ways in which James's pluralism cut deeper still and bequeathed to us some of the main lines of approach to the problems that continue to resurface in current discussions of pluralism.

Pluralism and the problem of conflicting conceptual schemes

The conceptual schemes of common sense and its competitors

In the *Pragmatism* lecture entitled 'Pragmatism and Common Sense' James suggests that our inherited common sense understanding of the world embodies a conceptual scheme constituted of such concepts as the following: 'Thing; The same or different; Kinds; Minds; Bodies; One Time; One Space; Subjects and attributes; Causal influences; The fancied; The real' (James 1975a: 85). He puts forward a variety of reasons to support the hypothesis that our common sense conceptual scheme was itself probably at one time a discovery or invention. He also argues that the common sense scheme has been shown to be of increasingly *limited application*, both in relation to scientific advances and when reflecting philosophically on certain non-paradigmatic cases (Is a magnetic field a 'thing'? Is a disassembled artefact 'the same'?). Such considerations as these are put forward by James to support the idea that even our most basic and practically indispensable common sense conceptual scheme ('the mother-tongue of thought', [James 1975a: 88]) is only one among several imperfect human attempts to conceptually *sort things out*, as it were.

In fact, James argues not only that there are aspects of sensible reality that are not accounted for within the general conceptual scheme of common sense, but also that some of these other aspects are in prima facie *conflict* with those isolated by common sense. In particular, he outlines conflicts between the following four conceptual schemes: '(1) Common sense, (2) common science or corpuscular philosophy, (3) ultra-critical science, or energetics, and (4) critical or idealistic philosophy' (James 1975a: 93–4, numbering added). What are these alternative conceptual schemes? In what sense do they conflict? And how does James attempt to address the resulting difficulties concerning a pluralism of apparently *conflicting truths*?

By 'common science' James refers to a straightforwardly scientific-realist construal of such postulated 'hypersensible entities' as atomic particles and ether-vibrations (James 1975a: 93). It is important to recognise that he interprets common science in such a way that there is a conflict between science and common sense. 'If common sense were true, why should science have had to brand the secondary qualities … as false, and to invent an invisible world of points and curves and mathematical equations instead?' (James 1975a: 92). Or as he put the same basic point years earlier in the *Principles of Psychology*:

> Sensible phenomena are pure delusions for the mechanical philosophy. The 'things' and qualities we instinctively believe in do not exist. The only realities are swarming solids in everlasting motion …

The modern mechanico-physical philosophy of which we are all so proud ... begins by saying that the *only* facts are collocations and motions of primordial solids.

(James 1983: 1258–9)

Concerning the new 'ultra-critical science', for its part, James comments as follows:[12]

Just now, if I understand the matter rightly, we are witnessing a curious reversion to the common-sense way of looking at physical nature, in the philosophy of science favoured by such men as Mach, Ostwald and Duhem. According to these teachers no hypothesis is truer than any other in the sense of being a more literal copy of reality. They are all but ways of talking on our part, to be compared solely from the point of view of their *use*. The only literally true thing is *reality*; and the only reality we know is, for these logicians, sensible reality, the flux of our sensations and emotions as they pass. 'Energy' ... is the collective name (according to Ostwald) for the sensations just as they present themselves ... when they are measured in certain ways.

(James 1975a: 93)

Ultra-critical science[13] has the great advantage of theoretical *simplicity*, according to James, but it is important to note his concession on the same page that 'the hypersensible entities, the corpuscles and vibrations, hold their own with most physicists and chemists, in spite of its appeal' (James 1975a: 93). The philosophical debate concerning scientific realism, as we currently refer to it, is in James's eyes an open question as to the overall best philosophical hypothesis on the matter; it is *not* one decidable ahead of time, for example, on the basis of a verificationist or anti-realist restriction on the meaningfulness or possible reference of theoretical terms.[14] While it is true that James lays his own bets on the overall theoretical advantages that he thinks are emerging in connection with the ultra-critical interpretation of science, he grants that common scientific realism has the undeniable advantage of straightforwardly embracing all the different kinds of entities that scientists think they have discovered; seen in this light, he remarks, the hyper-critical account 'seems too economical to be all-sufficient. Profusion, not economy, may after all be reality's key-note' (James 1975a: 93).

Note, furthermore, that although James in the quoted passage describes ultra-critical science as a 'curious reversion to the common-sense way of looking at physical nature', in this case, too, he holds that there is a *conflict* between the two schemes: ultra-critical science conflicts with common sense in its rejection of the ordinary notion of 'causal influences'. And when we add the fact, finally, that the conceptual scheme of 'critical or idealistic

31

philosophy' is seen by James as threatening to undermine the claims put forward by the schemes of both common sense and science, we have before us the view that while each of the four conceptual schemes is useful for certain purposes, they are nonetheless in conflict in the sense that basic claims in each scheme *contradict* basic claims in the others. The question then naturally arises as to which of the conflicting pictures of reality presented by these alternative conceptual schemes is ultimately *true*, and according to James this is a deep and difficult question to answer:

> The whole notion of truth, which naturally and without reflexion we assume to mean the simple duplication by the mind of a ready-made and given reality, proves hard to understand clearly. There is no simple test available for adjudicating offhand between the divers types of thought that claim to possess it.... . [The four schemes] all seem insufficiently true in some regard and leave some dissatisfaction. It is evident that the conflict of these so widely differing systems obliges us to overhaul the very idea of truth.
>
> (James 1975a: 93–4)

I will close by distinguishing four different strains in James's overall response to this fundamental issue of the apparently conflicting truths presented by the plurality of our conceptual schemes. Although I cannot attempt an adequate assessment of these strategies here, I hope to convey a sense of the live possibilities that were in many ways first opened up by James.

A plurality of Jamesian responses to the problem of conflicting schemes

The four Jamesian lines of response to the conflict I have in mind may crudely be labelled as (1) *instrumentalism*, (2) *scheme-relativity*, (3) *truth-convergence*, and (4) the *plenitude of the given*. The last mentioned strategy is the least familiar, though it arises out of the Jamesian themes discussed earlier. Each of the first three strategies is at least hinted at in the passage with which James closes the lecture we have lately been examining:

> Ought not the existence of the various types of thinking which we have reviewed, each so splendid for certain purposes, yet all conflicting still, and neither one of them able to support a claim of absolute veracity, to awaken a presumption favorable to the pragmatistic view that all our theories are *instrumental*, are mental modes of *adaptation* to reality, rather than revelations or gnostic answers to some divinely instituted world-enigma? ... Certainly the restlessness of the actual theoretic situation, the value for some purposes of each thought-level, and the inability of either to expel the

others decisively, suggest this pragmatistic view ... . May there not after all be a possible ambiguity in truth?

(James 1975a: 94)

Let us turn, first, to the instrumentalist strategy.

Instrumentalism

On its usual interpretations, instrumentalism does offer the theorist a way of responding to the problem of conflicting conceptual schemes. For on such a view the reference of the 'theoretical' terms incorporated in our various conceptual schemes (including common sense!) is not at issue, but only whether such theories (however interpreted, or as 'uninterpreted calculi') enable the successful prediction and control of our sensory experiences. If the only realities we need strictly countenance are our own sensations, for instance, then there would appear to be no conflict represented by the fact that both our common sense talk and our scientific abstractions enable us to predict the course of those sensations. The instrumentalist strategy has been much exploited throughout the twentieth century, and it is well-known that James presents pragmatism as itself a generalisation from the new 'ultra-critical' philosophy of science:

> [S]o many rival formulations are proposed in all the branches of science that investigators have become accustomed to the notion that no theory is absolutely a transcript of reality, but that any one of them may from some point of view be useful. Their great use is to summarise old facts and to lead to new ones. They are only a man-made language, a conceptual shorthand, as someone calls them, in which we write our reports of nature; and languages, as is well known, tolerate much choice of expression and many dialects ... Riding now on the front of this wave of scientific logic Messrs. Schiller and Dewey appear with their pragmatistic account of what truth everywhere signifies. Everywhere, these teachers say, 'truth' in our ideas and beliefs means the same thing that it means in science ... This is the 'instrumental' view of truth ... .

(James 1975a: 33–4)

Such passages as this naturally lead one to suppose that James holds that *all* our alternative conceptual schemes are simply devices for predicting the course of our subjective sensations; in which case *there are no* facts of the matter concerning which there may be genuine conflicts, apart from questions concerning the most useful and economical predictor of the flux of our sensations.

This, then, is one time-honoured strategy for coping with a plurality of apparently conflicting truths. Nevertheless I would suggest that this interpretation is in danger of misrepresenting James's views. Instrumentalism in the philosophy of science generally rests upon the notion that there is a basis of theoretically *neutral observations*. For it is the latter's (alleged) freedom from conceptual commitments that makes possible the view of 'conflicting' conceptual schemes (*including* the scheme of common sense 'things') as simply alternative tools for calculating the flow of our more basic sensory experiences. As we have seen, however, James's view of perception is that our perceptual responses are concept-laden through and through: the direct objects of perception for James are the objects *as intentionally conceived* (for example, as *that chair*), not a stream of subjective sensory qualia. If there are respects in which James ultimately falls into the myth of the given (see below), I do not think it is primarily at *this* level.[15]

Admittedly James's doctrine of 'pure experience' has been interpreted along lines favourable to the generalised instrumentalist strategy, and here I can only register my grounds (based partly on the first section above) for having difficulty with such a reading.[16] As I understand his *radical empiricism*, James articulates his direct realism – basically, that there are no 'intermediaries' separating the knower from the known – in the following way: all knowledge (and intentionality in general) involves the conceptualisation or functional sorting of a neutral given content (the 'pure experience', a bare posited 'that') into both objective terms (that *chair*) and subjective terms (*my sensation of* that chair). On this view our awareness of our own subjective stratum of sensations is as much a *product of conceptualisation* as our awareness of independent objects; and it is this wider aspect of James's view that I find uncongenial to classical instrumentalism. The tight connection here between percepts and concepts is indeed ultimately broken apart by James, but this (as we have seen) occurs primarily at the supposedly deeper level of an *ineffable and speculative metaphysics* (see the section on the plenitude of the given below and my earlier discussion of monism, pluralism and the limits of conceptual understanding).[17]

But if I am right about this, in what sense *is* pragmatism, as James suggests, to be taken as the 'view that all our theories are *instrumental*'? We might recall how James himself stated the matter in the passage quoted above: our theories are 'mental modes of *adaptation* to reality, rather than revelations or gnostic answers to some divinely instituted world-enigma' (James 1975a: 94). The general analogy James draws with instrumentalist philosophy of science, it seems to me, is that just as (for instance) the new ultra-critical science upholds 'alternative geometries' as against the metaphysical essentialist view that 'God geometrizes' (James 1975b: 40), so pragmatism holds quite generally that the truths revealed by our concepts are mutable and partially created by our own active contribution, rather than being 'eternal and fixed'. If this anti-essentialist yet realist interpretation of James's view is correct, however, it brings us straight back to our original problem of conflicting conceptual schemes: granted that we have alternative 'instruments' for coping with reality, if these conceptual schemes are realistically construed how then do we cope with the fact that such schemes present us with *conflicting* conceptions of the world's realities?

Scheme-relativity

A second, equally influential line of approach to the question of conflicting schemes is to be found throughout James's writings. One might argue that, properly understood, there really is *no conflict* at all, even when the relevant propositions are straightforwardly and realistically interpreted, but rather each proposition may be held true 'relative to' or 'from the point of view' of its own framework. As P.F. Strawson argued in 'Perception and its Objects', we may regard the admittedly ostensibly conflicting common sense and scientific accounts of the world, for example, as 'two discrepant descriptions, each valid from its own viewpoint'.

> I acknowledge the discrepancy of the two descriptions, but claim that, once we recognise the relativity in our conception of the real, they need not be seen as in contradiction with each other. Those very things which from one standpoint we conceive as phenomenally propertied we conceive from another as constituted in a way which can only be described in what are, from the phenomenal point of view, abstract terms.
>
> (Strawson 1979: 58–9)

We have seen James stress that each conceptual scheme is 'splendid *for certain purposes* but not for others (James 1975a: 94), and that our acquiring concepts is a matter of *selecting out* aspects of the chaotic flux of perception that are salient *relative to certain of our interests*: 'we have so many different businesses with nature that no one of them yields us an all-embracing clasp' (James 1977: 19). Like Strawson, James makes liberal use of the metaphor of alternative *points of view* (e.g. James 1975b: 55). In the context of discussing pragmatism as a theory of *truth*, as we have seen, he contends that even in the sciences 'no theory is absolutely a transcript of reality, but … any one of them may from some point of view be useful' (James 1975a: 33) – which, given the nature of the connection in James between utility and truth (see above), certainly seems to entail that *truth* is relative to points of view or standpoints, perhaps in something like Strawson's sense of a 'relativity in our conception of the real.'

Again, Strawson argues that in the relevant cases of conflict we 'shift our standard' and that such shifts do not 'condemn us to internal conflict. The appearance of … conflict vanishes when we acknowledge the relativity of our "reallys"' (Strawson 1979: 57).

James, too, emphasises the relativity of our assertions to a multiplicity of standards when, defending the humanist doctrine that truth consists in satisfactoriness of belief, he argues that 'satisfactoriness has to be measured by a multitude of standards' (James 1975b: 40).[18] The following passage from 'The Sentiment of Rationality' presents one of the more striking indications of this general line of response in James's writings:

> There is nothing improbable in the supposition that analysis of the world may yield a number of formulae, all consistent with the facts. In physical science different formulae may explain the phenomena equally well – the one-fluid and the two-fluid theories of electricity, for example. Why may it not be so with the world? Why may there not be different points of view for surveying it, within each of which all data harmonize, and which the observer may therefore either choose between, or simply cumulate one upon another? A Beethoven string-quartet is truly, as some one has said, a scraping of horses' tails on cats' bowels, and may be exhaustively described in such terms; but the application of this description in no way precludes the simultaneous applicability of an entirely different description.
>
> (James 1979: 66)

There are certain difficulties, however, with the idea that the 'scheme-relativity of truth' constitutes a sufficient response to the problem of conflicting schemes, both in general and as an interpretation of James. The general difficulty with such 'quietist' views (to borrow a term from Simon Blackburn),[19] is that it is hard to see how a benign acquiescence in each of several conflicting schemes really resolves the apparent conflict, especially if we admit (as both James and Strawson do) that the meanings of the terms are to be straightforwardly construed in such a way that there really is at least an ostensible conflict in the first place. James's suggestion that we may 'either choose between' the alternative points of view 'or simply cumulate one upon another' is likely to lead to the accusation that he is committed to an objectionably strong form of *relativism* concerning truth and reality. And in fact it is partly in response to such accusations (for example, in 'Abstractionism and "Relativismus"', James 1975b: 141–5) that James makes use of a third general line of response to the problem of conflicting truths, invoking a distinction perhaps more familiar in relation to its more developed use by C. S. Peirce. Without intending to deny the presence and importance of the scheme-relativity strategy in general and in James, then, I turn now to the question of 'absolute truth'.

Truth-convergence

I gave some indication in the first section as to how we might plausibly understand what James means by equating truth with 'usefulness', 'satisfactoriness', 'adaptation', and so on, in terms of his functionalist account of concepts and intentional content. However plausible a non-reductive and realist reading we might offer of the general idea that 'truth is what works', we are still going to run into the difficulty that there are bound to be cases in which the particular account of objective reality found satisfactory on the whole to one person, period, or culture will generally not be found thus satisfactory (or will be found unsatisfactory) to some other person, period, or culture. For terminological convenience, let us say that what is true is what is on the whole 'acceptable', where acceptability must be understood as what is acceptable *to* some particular person, *from* some viewpoint, *within* some conceptual scheme, and so on.[20] James is initially pulled in two different directions when he considers such questions as the following: was the ancient belief that the earth is flat *true* for those to whom this belief was acceptable (James 1975a: 107)? Since what is true is what is the case, and since *we* take it to be objectively true that the earth is not flat, accepting the previous assertion would seem to have the objectionable consequence that the earth both is and is not flat (or that the earth *changed* from being flat to not being flat). But how can James avoid that consequence, if he holds (as he does), both that being true is a matter of being acceptable overall from some standpoint, and also that such standpoints render *conflicting* assessments both over time and across persons and cultures?

Appealing to the fallibilist idea that our opinions by their very nature are always open to correction, James contends that to 'admit, as we pragmatists do, that we are liable to correction (even tho we may not expect it) *involves the use on our part of an ideal standard*' (James 1975b: 142).[21] Thus James introduces the notion of an 'absolute truth' or 'an ideal set of formulations towards which all opinions may in the long run of experience be expected to converge' (James 1975b: 143). In the *Pragmatism* lecture on 'Pragmatism's Conception of Truth' James applies this distinction to the issue of ostensibly conflicting truths in the following way:

> *'The true', to put it very briefly, is only the expedient in the way of our thinking* ... [e]xpedient in almost any fashion; and expedient in the long run and on the whole of course ... The 'absolutely' true, meaning what no farther experience will ever alter, is that ideal vanishing-point towards which we imagine that all our temporary truths will some day converge... . Meanwhile we have to live to-day by what truth we can get to-day, and be ready to-morrow to call it falsehood. Ptolemaic astronomy, euclidean space, aristotelian logic, scholastic metaphysics, were expedient for centuries, but human

experience has boiled over those limits, and we now call these things only relatively true, or true within those borders of experience. 'Absolutely' they are false; for we know that those limits were casual, and might have been transcended by past theorists ... . When new experiences lead to retrospective judgments, using the past tense, what these [later] judgments utter *was* true, even tho no past thinker had been led there... . [The earlier ones] may have been truth-processes for the actors in them. They are not so for one who knows the later revelations of the story.

(James 1975a: 106–7; cp. 1975b: 45, 48–9, 55, 105, 114n, 129–1, and especially 142–5)

On this view, truth is still understood (basically) as acceptability relative to some perspective or other, but the 'regulative notion of a potential truth to be established later, possibly to be established some day absolutely' (James 1975a: 107) brings in the *idea* of what would be acceptable from a maximally corrected perspective, a set of opinions that would withstand the test of all relevant experiences in the long run. The postulation of this ideally corrected standard enables us to assert not only that the flat-earth view is and was *false*, but (allegedly) also to assert that there is in general *one objective truth* toward which we may be expected to converge in the long run. In relation to the justification for thus hypothesising that there *is* such an ideal truth 'towards which all opinions may in the long run of experience be expected to converge', James at one point offers the rather subtle defence that (to state here only its concluding sentence) the 'hypothesis [of one absolute truth] will, in short, have worked successfully all round the circle and proved self-corroborative, and the circle will be closed' (James 1975b: 144).

Any reader familiar with the tradition of American pragmatism as continued in the writings of Quine, Sellars, Putnam, and Rorty will recognise that the notion of truth-convergence continues to be a hotly disputed resource in the pragmatist's arsenal.[22] On the one hand, to the extent that the idea of a final truth (to be reached in the limit by ideal inquiry, etc.) is made more precise, to that extent one would certainly have to devote more argument than we find in James for the conclusion that we can know that we are bound to converge to any such final scheme. On the other hand, if James's idea of an 'absolute truth' is softened merely to our grounds for believing that there will always be room for improvement in our schemes, then we are essentially back with the second, scheme-relativity strategy. There is, however, at least one further line of response to the problem of conflicting schemes to be found throughout James's writings.

The plenitude of the given

What I am calling James's 'plenitude' response to the problem of conflict derives in large part from doctrines discussed earlier in relation to the 'insuperability of sensation' and the insufficiency of conceptual schemes. For obvious reasons, both the scheme-relativity and the truth-convergence strategies focus upon the role of conceptual schemes in constituting our various points of view on the world. Consequently such approaches usually explicitly reject the myth of the given; this is certainly the case with such thinkers as Strawson, Sellars, Kuhn, Rorty, and Putnam, and we have seen that in most respects this holds in the case of James's account of percepts and concepts as well. As we also saw earlier, however, an important part of James's general defence of pluralism consisted in arguing for the thesis that 'conceptual knowledge is forever inadequate to the fullness of the reality to be known' (James 1996: 78). In certain crucial respects James thus defends a position that is quite unlike what we find in most present-day conceptual scheme pluralists, for in this case it is the *conceptually unrepresentable richness of the given* to which James ultimately appeals in support of the intelligibility of his own conceptual scheme pluralism.

We have seen that the function of concepts for James is to '*carve out* order by leaving the disorderly parts out', which James understands after the analogy of a block of marble from which 'statues may be produced by elim-inating irrelevant … chips of stone' (James 1975a: 10). The scheme-relativ-ity, truth-convergence, and even the instrumentalist strategies tend to focus on the alternative ways in which these various *orders* are produced. The non-conceptual insight that the Jamesian metaphysician is supposed to grasp, however, is that all of the alternative and often conflicting ways in which we conceptualise the flux were, so to speak, *already contained 'in solution' in the flux itself* (see e.g. James 1996: 199; 1983: 277; 1977: 127–9):

> Look where you will, you gather only examples of the same amid the different, and of different relations existing as it were in solution in the same thing. *Quâ* this an experience is not the same as it is *quâ* that, truly enough; but the *quâs* are conceptual shots of ours at its post-mortem remains, and in its sensational immediacy everything is all at once whatever different things it is at once at all … Of course this *sounds* self-contradictory, but as the immediate facts don't sound at all, but simply *are*, until we conceptualise and name them vocally, the contradiction results only from the conceptual or dis-cursive form being substituted for the real form.
>
> (James 1977: 120, 121)

This appeal to 'raw life as more of a revealer' of the nature of reality than any of our *conceptions* of reality (James 1977: 121) is a veritable celebration of the myth of the given – here put forward not as myth, of course, but as the deepest of metaphysical insights into the nature of reality. The conclusion seems to be that we are entitled both to realistically construe the meanings of our terms in the way explained in section one, *and* to accept that our conceptual schemes present intrinsically conflicting pictures of reality. This will always appear objectionable to the intellectualist, who will quite reasonably wonder how we can get away with ascribing contradictory features to reality. The thrust of James's overall argument, however, is that the intellectualists, on the negative side, have failed to understand the limits of conceptualisation, and on the positive side, have failed to achieve the relevant (non-conceptual) insight that the given chaos of sensible reality is the primordial repository for whatever contradictory aspects our various 'post-mortem' conceptual 'shots' may succeed in abstracting from it.[23] That variants on such a view were held by James not only in the later 'Bergsonian' stage of his career but also from his earliest writings is suggested by this striking passage taken from the end of the famous 'Stream of Thought' chapter in *The Principles of Psychology*:

> [T]he mind is at every stage a theatre of simultaneous possibilities. Consciousness consists in the comparison of these with each other, the selection of some, and the suppression of the rest ... . The mind, in short, works on the data it receives very much as a sculptor works on his block of stone. In a sense the statue stood there from eternity. But there were a thousand different ones beside it, and the sculptor alone is to thank for having extricated this one from the rest. Just so the world of each of us, howsoever different our several views of it may be, all lay embedded in the primordial chaos of sensations, which gave the mere *matter* to the thought of all of us indifferently. We may, if we like, by our reasonings unwind things back to that black and jointless continuity of space and moving clouds of swarming atoms which science calls the only real world. But all the while the world *we* feel and live in will be that which our ancestors and we, by slowly cumulative strokes of choice, have extricated out of this, like sculptors, by simply rejecting certain portions of the given stuff. Other sculptors, other statues from the same stone! Other minds, other worlds from the same monotonous and inexpressive chaos! My world is but one in a million alike embedded, alike real to those who may abstract them. How different must be the worlds in the consciousness of ant, cuttle-fish, or crab!
>
> (James 1983: 277)

In general, to the extent that the plenitude response goes beyond the scheme-relativity strategy it seems to me to be highly problematic. It is difficult to see, for example, in what sense James can maintain (James 1977: 120–1, italics added) that '*all living language conforms*' to the flux of 'sensational life' when the latter is thus understood as a 'primordial chaos' in the way required by the plenitude strategy; for James contends that we must turn a 'deaf ear' to 'discursive thought' in order to achieve the relevant metaphysical insight here. 'As long as one continues *talking*', he insists, 'intellectualism remains in undisturbed possession of the field' (James 1977: 131). Such a blanket appeal to the ineffable given is unlikely to carry weight with philosophers concerned to clarify the problem of a pluralism of apparently conflicting truths. As long as we continue *talking*, at any rate, we seem to be faced with a difficult dilemma once again. For if, in the metaphor exploited by James above, the alternative statues are to be conceived as *actually* in the marble, then we seem to be left with an incoherence that no appeal to ineffability will appease; but if the alternative statues are understood as merely *possible* constructions out of the marble, the deeper problems concerning our actually conflicting schemes would seem to be left unresolved.

The coherence of this fourth aspect of James's pluralist philosophy is therefore questionable. If past experience is any guide, however, then perhaps even this last Jamesian idea somewhere harbours insights for those struggling to make some uniform sense of our multiform conceptual schemes.

Notes

1 For a reading of James along similar lines, see the comparison of James's views with Brian Loar's 'functional role' account of the content of beliefs in Bird (1986: 64–5). For an alternative 'phenomenological' reading of James on intentionality, see for example Wilshire (1968: 7–8); and Wild (1969). Sprigge (1997) offers an instructive comparison of James with 'contemporary externalism about mental content'; see also Sprigge (1993).

2 This passage was quoted by James from his own earlier article (1884).

3 The philosopher perhaps most responsible for developing the contemporary functional role account of intentional content is Wilfrid Sellars, who sees his own view as building on certain aspects of Kant and the later Wittgenstein. For a start, see Sellars (1963, 1969, 1974, 1981). See also Rosenberg (1986) and Brandom (1994).

4 James holds the view that '*thought is possible without language*' (James 1983: 256–8). I refrain from engaging that controversy here.

5 For James's apparent rejection of the second approach to intentionality, see his 'The Function of Cognition' and 'The Tigers in India' (the latter taken from 'The Knowing of Things Together'), collected in (James 1975b). Resistance to the functionalist account of the 'aboutness' of concepts sketched above is likely to mirror precisely the sorts of resistance James encountered in relation to his pragmatic account of truth: to his opponents, all of this talk about the 'workings' of our ideas will seem to miss out on *the intentional relation itself, the truth relation itself*, and so on. My sympathies lie with James here. For a consideration of this general line of objection to James, see Bird (1986: chapter 10).

6 In 'A World of Pure Experience' James characterises the overall picture this way: 'The towering importance for human life of this [conceptual] kind of knowing lies in the fact that an experience that knows another can figure as its *representative*, not in any quasi-miraculous "epistemological" sense, but in the definite practical sense of being its *substitute* in various operations, sometimes physical and sometimes mental, which lead us to its associates and results' (James 1976: 31).

7 The practical consequences and advantages that our 'conceptual map-making' (James 1976: 122–3n) affords us, according to James, are made possible by the fact that our concepts succeed in *getting things right* in the sense of (at least to some degree) correctly representing general aspects and relationships that hold true of things in the sensible world. Contrast Rorty's (1997) non-epistemological reading of James. Hilary Putnam's article in the same volume (1997) provides a useful corrective to Rorty's view.

8 In relation to the famous 'will to believe' doctrine, for example, it is well-known (if not always sufficiently borne in mind) that the main issue concerns only the sort of question '*that cannot by its nature be decided on intellectual grounds*' (James 1979: 20).

9 Though I do not explore the matter further here, James's metaphysics of 'conjunctive relations' is crucial to his overall 'radical empiricist' account of the flux of experience.

10 On James's notion of 'substitution' here, see also Bird (1986: 109–10).

11 This holds true, incidentally, even for the various a priori '*necessary* truths' that, according to James, concern only 'relations among our ideas' in Locke's sense. See James (1983: final chapter) and (1975a: 119).

12 For further discussions by James on the interpretation of science, see for example, James (1979: 33–4, 93, 103–4; 1983: 1230–2, 1250, 1258–62; 1996: 70, 90n; 1977: 112–3n; 1976: 40–1; 1975b: 44–5.

13 I will continue to use James's term, leaving aside consideration of distinctions between instrumentalism, conventionalism, fictionalism, constructive empiricism, etc.

14 For an overview of current debates on this issue, see Leplin (1984).

15 Wilfrid Sellars's attack on 'the myth of the given' is basically a criticism of the notion that there exist states of the knower that are somehow both (a) basic knowings and yet (b) are not dependent in an essential way upon the acquisition of concepts. Foundationalist sense-datum theories are classic examples of the Myth, but so is, for example, any view (such as Plato's or Chisholm's) that endows *the intellect* with a power of 'directly grasping truths' in a way that is not at bottom *derivative* from our *linguistic* practices. I briefly indicate below the level at which I suspect James is in danger of falling prey to the Myth. See Sellars's classic (1997), with a helpful study guide by Robert Brandom.

16 In a similar vein see Bird's critical assessment of Ayer's phenomenalist reading of James's doctrine of pure experience (Bird 1986: 118–20; Ayer 1968: 302–3). Russell, of course, characterised James's account of pure experience as a 'neutral monism' (1956: 138–59). I cannot do justice to the notion of pure experience here, but the reader should note James's qualification of that doctrine in James (1976: 14–15).

17 See the discussion of the latter distinction in the second section of this chapter, concerning 'the insuperability of sensation', as well as the discussion of the 'plenitude of the given'. Note, by the way, that I do not mean to suggest that James's doctrine of pure experience is free from all difficulties concerning the myth of the given. On the contrary, the main difficulties with that doctrine stem from the fact that since on James's own reckoning the 'pure experience' itself cannot in any way be *described* (since to do so is already to conceptually sort the experience in the ways just discussed), it will always remain unclear just what a pure experience *is*.

18 Compare also James on the different levels, dimensions and varieties of rationality (for example, James [1977: 54–5, 144–5]).

19 See Blackburn's objections to 'quietism or dismissive neutralism' (which he attributes to the later Wittgenstein), in Blackburn (1984: 146); see also

Blackburn (1993). For an objection to Strawson on this issue, see Hacker (1987: 198–204).

20 I should mention that there is an important issue as to whether James is ultimately guilty of confusing the question of the experiential consequences following from the truth of a given proposition with that of the satisfactory consequences (e.g. emotional) following from one's belief in that proposition. See Lovejoy (1963: chapter 1), and compare a related criticism by Bird (1986: 188). Meyers (1971) attempts a defence of James on this issue, following Perry (1958).

21 For one possible way of cashing out James's inference here (namely, from 'liability to correction' to 'involving the appeal to an ideal standard'), see Simon Blackburn's interesting discussion of Hume's 'Of the Standard of Taste' in Blackburn (1984: 197–201).

22 Quine argues against the idea of convergence in (1960: 23). Sellars argues in favour of convergence in (1968: chapter 5), and this Sellarsian outlook is further developed in Rosenberg (1980) and (1988). Putnam at times argued in favour of a conception of convergence, e.g. (1981: 56), but he has since come to abandon it.

23 On conceptual distinctions as 'post-mortem' see also James (1996: 99), 'Properly speaking, concepts are post-mortem preparations, sufficient only for retrospective understanding'.

2

ON THE PLURALITY OF
CONCEPTUAL SCHEMES[1]

Maria Baghramian

Philosophy at the end of twentieth century is marked with a preoccupation with ideas of pluralism, relativism and multiplicity of perspectives. Pluralism, or the view that the natural and normative domains can be conceputalised, described, perceived and evaluated variously and in non-convergent ways, has a long historical pedigree. One important element in the philosophical background to the idea of pluralism is the Kantian distinction between the content of our experiences and the conceptual schemes that we use in order to organise and make sense of these experiences; or the doctrine of scheme content dualism (SC). Kant saw SC as a corrective measure to Leibniz's intellectualisation of sensations and Locke's sensualisation of concepts (Kant 1929: A 21/B 327) and a crucial step in establishing a comprehensive account of how objective and universal knowledge is possible. However, once it was accepted that there was a distinction to be drawn between the data of experience and the conceptual principles for organising and conceptualising them, it was easy to accept that there could be more than one system or scheme of organisation. Kant's grand scheme was turned on its head and conceptual relativism became the commonly accepted by-product of SC. This turn of events did not deter philosophers from adopting one of the many versions of the distinction in their explanations of the mind/world relationship – C.I. Lewis, for instance, believed SC to be an almost self-evident philosophical truth and Quine embraced it wholeheartedly.

In recent years, however, SC has fallen out of favour. For one thing, conceptual pluralism, primarily through the work of Kuhn, Feyerabend and the linguistic theories of Whorf, has become identified with more pernicious types of cognitive relativism. Furthermore, SC has been seen as yet one more instance of the various unhelpful dualisms that are part of the Cartesian and empiricist philosophical legacies.

The onslaught on the very idea of conceptual schemes has been spearheaded by Davidson, with Richard Rorty bringing up the rear. Davidson develops two main lines of attack on the idea of SC. Firstly, there is the charge of incoherence. According to Davidson, the very idea of a conceptual scheme is incoherent because we can entertain the possibility of there being an alternative conceptual scheme only if such a scheme is untranslatable into our language. However, translatability into a familiar tongue is a criterion of languagehood. So:

> If translation succeeds, we have shown there is no need to speak of two conceptual schemes, while if translation fails, there is no ground for speaking of two. If I am right then there never can be a situation in which we can intelligibly compare or contrast divergent schemes, and in that case we do better not to say that there is one scheme, as if we understood what it would be like for there to be more.
>
> (Davidson 1980: 243)

If we cannot speak of alternative conceptual schemes then we cannot make sense of SC either.

Secondly, he offers the charge of dogmatism, making the claim that the very idea of a conceptual scheme is 'a dogma of empiricism, the third dogma of empiricism. The third, and perhaps the last, for if we give it up it is not clear that there is anything distinctive left to call empiricism' (Davidson 1984: 189).

Davidson is not explicit on why the idea of a conceptual scheme should be seen as a dogma of empiricism and not just a philosophical error. Most commentators have focused on the argument from incoherence and have ignored the second aspect of Davidson's attack on SC. In this paper I explore the question of the sense(s) in which the dualism of scheme and content can be construed as a dogma of empiricism, within a Davidsonian framework. I then make use of the answers to this question to construct a version of SC which is immune from Davidsonian criticisms. The paper falls into three sections. The first outlines some of the ways in which the dualism of scheme/content can be set out; the second utilises the results obtained to explore the connections between SC and empiricism and argues that two versions of SC are linked with aspects of empiricism. I then argue that there is a third version of SC that cannot in any interesting sense be seen as a 'dogma of empiricism' and can act as 'the innocent version' of SC that John McDowell has recently exhorted us to adopt. Such an 'innocent version' of SC might, I believe, afford us the opportunity to allow for a degree of conceptual pluralism without alienating us from the world or threatening us with a promiscuous type of cognitive relativism.

The scheme content distinction

SC distinguishes between two elements in our thinking: the conceptual apparatus or scheme, and that which we think about – that is, the content.

However, this seemingly simple distinction has been formulated in a variety of ways.

Schemes

According to Davidson, conceptual schemes are languages which do either or both of two things. Conceptual schemes (S1) organise something – that is, systematise and divide up content. They are the categories we use for identifying and classifying objects, and the principles of classification which we use to group things together. They also provide us with criteria for the individuation of what there is. Alternatively, conceptual schemes (S2) may be construed as the means of fitting, that is facing, predicting and accounting for content (Davidson 1984: 191). In this sense, they are systems of representation (Searle 1995: 151) or alternative ways of describing reality. They are the set of central beliefs, the basic assumptions or fundamental principles (Popper 1994: 34) that people hold.[2] These formulations are not mutually exclusive. In particular S2 can, and often does, include elements of S1 because representing or fitting reality is not incompatible with ordering, individuating and categorising it.

The linguistic tools used by S1 are the referential apparatus of language, such as predicates, while in the case of S2 the linguistic unit is the set of whole sentences that a speaker holds true. A variety of metaphors has been used to convey the role that conceptual schemes play in shaping the content of our thoughts. Conceptual schemes, it has been claimed, are like the principles we might use in order to organise and rearrange a closet.[3] They are the cookie cutter we use to cut and shape the malleable dough of the content. Or even more graphically, they 'carve up nature at its joints'. The carving may be done with 'a rapier' or a 'blunt instrument'.[4] In the case of S2 it has been claimed that conceptual schemes provide a framework for our pictures of reality, a framework which also gives structure to the ways in which reality is conceptualised (Popper 1994: 33).

Content

We can find four accounts of content in Davidson:[5]

(C1) The content of a conceptual scheme may be something neutral, common, but unnameable, which lies outside all schemes: the Kantian 'thing in itself' or alternatively what William James calls the 'absolutely dumb and evanescent, the merely ideal limit of our minds'; that which we 'may glimpse ... but never grasp ...' (James 1977).

(C2) The content is the world, reality, nature or universe which is either unorganised or open to reorganisation. The world is found and not made, but it is, in Schiller's words, 'plastic'; that is, it has a certain degree of malleability.

(C3) The content may be sense-data, surface irritations, sensory promptings, the 'sensuous', or what in the seventeenth and eighteenth century vocabulary was known as 'ideas' or 'impressions'. In other words it is the stuff that falls under the by now pejorative term 'the given'.

(C4) The content is our experiences, broadly conceived: what C.I. Lewis, following James, has called the 'thick experience of every-day life' rather than the 'thin experience of immediate sensations' (Lewis 1929: 30).

These formulations of 'content' are not equivalent. It is tempting to identify C1 with either C2 or C3. William Child, for instance, thinks that the neutral content could be seen as the uninterpreted, theory-neutral reality or alternatively as the uncategorised content of experience (Child 1994). But this is clearly wrong. The world is not the unnameable, nor are our sense-data, since we have already named them. As Rorty in his defence and elaboration of Davidson has pointed out:

> The notion of 'the world' as used in a phrase like 'different conceptual schemes carve up the world differently' must be the notion of something *completely* unspecified and unspecifiable – the thing in itself, in fact. As soon as we start thinking of 'the world' as atoms and the void, or sense-data and awareness of them, or 'stimuli' of a certain sort brought to bear upon organs of a certain sort, we have changed the name of the game. For we are now well within some particular theory about how the world is.
>
> (Rorty 1982: 14)

So, C1 should be seen as an independent account of content and for Davidson, as for Rorty, probably an incoherent one.

C3 and C4 are not equivalent. C4 is the 'thick experience of the world of things' (Lewis 1929: 54) it is the world of trees and houses, it is the experiences of love and hate and disappointment. C3 is the 'thin given of immediacy', it is the patch of colour, the indescribable sound, the fleeting sensation, '"the buzzing, booming confusion" on which the infant first opens his eyes' (Lewis 1929: 30). The difference between C2 and C4 can be expressed as the distinction between the world and the world as it is experienced by us, the view from nowhere versus the perspectival view of the world. William Child has ably shown that C2 and C3 are not equivalent either, and the scheme/world dualism does not necessitate the acceptance of scheme/sense data dualism (Child 1994).

Davidson has something to say on all four versions of content. In his earlier work he had argued that 'the entities that can count as the content of our schemes are either reality (the universe, the world, nature) or experience' (Davidson 1984 : 192).

In more recent work, on the other hand, the emphasis has been on 'the unsullied stream of experience being variously reworked by various minds or cultures' (Davidson 1989: 161). According to this version, the uninterpreted given, sense-data, precepts, impressions, sensations, appearances and adverbial modifications of experience are the content of conceptual schemes. Consequently, various commentators have argued that the real target of Davidson's attack is the dualism between concepts and experiential intake or the 'dualism of scheme and Given' (McDowell 1994) and that only recently has Davidson 'realised more fully the purely epistemological character of the dualism he wishes to reject' (Levine 1993: 19).

A closer look at the relevant texts sheds a different light on Davidson's position. In 'The Myth of the Subjective' (Davidson 1989), he argues that conceptual relativism rests on a mistaken analogy with having an individual perspective or position on the world; a direct parallel with scheme/world distinction. He refers the reader to his earlier article 'On the Very Idea of a Conceptual Scheme' (Davidson 1984) and his argument about the incoherence of this position presented there. The remainder of 'The Myth of the Subjective' is then devoted to the discussion of scheme/sense data distinction. In what follows I will proceed on the assumption that Davidson allows for both C2 and C3. The role of C4 will be discussed later.

Scheme content dualism and empiricism

Davidson is not explicit about his reasons for calling scheme/content dualism a dogma of empiricism. In this section I shall examine some possible reasons for thinking that SC constitutes a dogma of empiricism.

Empiricism, simply put, is the view that our knowledge of the world is obtained through our sense experiences. One philosophical consequence of this rather minimal claim is the notorious distinction between analytic/synthetic statements, or the first dogma of empiricism. Further philosophical by-products of empiricism are also of importance to discussions of SC. Empiricism can be formulated either as a theory about mental content – in this sense it is also presented as a theory of truth – or it may be seen as a theory of knowledge, justification and evidence. Each of these formulations carries a philosophical baggage that has proved unpopular with a number of contemporary philosophers, including Putnam, Rorty and McDowell, as well as Davidson.

Empiricism, when formulated as a theory of how the mind acquires its content, has been associated with representational accounts of mind, whereby the human mind is seen as a vehicle for mirroring or picturing reality. 'Our ideas', to use Locke's idiom, or our mental states, in more modern terminology, represent, stand for, or picture, aspects of reality. The correspondence theory of truth, with its ontology of facts and states of affairs and the metaphor of mirroring or picturing, and the copy theory of reference, have been used to explain how the content of our mental states can represent, or fit the world. Empiricism as a theory of justification, on the other hand, was shaped by its encounter with scepticism. The empiricist reaction to scepticism was to result in the claim that sense-data can act as the ultimate evidence for our knowledge of the world, and hence as the foundation of empirical knowledge. In doing so, empiricism gave rise to the notorious problem of explaining how the mind can transcend beyond the veil of ideas or senses and gain access to the external world. SC may be seen as a dogma of empiricism either if it is a direct consequence of one or of more of the above three philosophical by-products of empiricism, or if it acquires its philosophical motivation and justification from them. I shall examine each in turn.

SC and the analytic/synthetic distinction

It has been suggested that SC relies on, and is also motivated by, the suspect notion of a priori truth and hence that the third dogma of empiricism should be seen as a variant of the first dogma. Robert Kraut, for instance, has argued that SC is intimately related to:

> The dichotomy between analytic and synthetic truths; sentences guaranteed true by the structure of the scheme are true purely on the basis of meaning, rather than on the basis of empirical fact. But this is an untenable dualism, and thus any other dualisms which embraces it is thereby tainted.
>
> (Kraut 1983: 401)

Richard Rorty has also made connections between the scheme/content and analytic/synthetic dualisms. According to Rorty:

> The notion of a choice among 'meaning postulates' is the latest version of the notion of a choice among alternative conceptual schemes. Once the necessary is identified with the analytic and the analytic is explicated in terms of meaning, an attack on the notion of what Harman has called the 'philosophical' sense of 'meaning' becomes an attack on the notion of 'conceptual framework' in any sense that assumes a distinction of kind between this notion and that of empirical theory.
>
> (Rorty 1982: 5)

There is some historical justification for this view. The origins of the idea of conceptual schemes can be traced to Kant's distinctions between spontaneity and receptivity on the one hand and necessary and contingent truths on the other. Together with these distinctions we have also inherited the view that the mind is divided into active and passive faculties. The world imposes its impressions on the passive faculties and these impressions are in turn interpreted by the active, concept-forming faculty (Rorty 1982: 3). Further support for this position can be mustered from the fact that one of the direct targets of Davidson's criticism, C. I. Lewis, constructs his version of SC on the back of the dualism of a priori/a posteriori, and in that sense the analytic/synthetic distinction. According to Lewis:

> The two elements to be distinguished in knowledge are the concept, which is the product of the activity of thought, and the sensuously given, which is independent of such activity ... . The concept gives rise to the a priori; all a priori truth is definitive, or explicative of concepts ... .The pure concept and the content of the given are mutually independent; neither limits the other.
>
> (Lewis 1929: 37)

Conceptual schemes, then, are truths by definition, while their contents are the empirical data of senses. Thus, the very idea of SC seems to presuppose the analytic/synthetic distinction.

Despite its initial plausibility, this cannot be the correct account of the third dogma. Davidson allows that the 'analytic/synthetic distinction is explained in terms of something that may serve to buttress conceptual relativism, namely the idea of empirical content' (Davidson 1984: 189), but in his subsequent article adds: 'the scheme-content division can survive even in an environment that shuns the analytic-synthetic distinction' (Davidson 1989: 161). The reason for this view becomes clear once we bear in mind that Davidson's main target when rejecting SC was Quine. Quine explicitly identifies conceptual schemes with languages, but famously rejects the suggestion that we can ever draw a clear boundary between the a priori and non-a priori elements in language. SC, for Quine, is part of the holistic story he tells about our attempts to give an account of what there is. Quine's holism disallows the sharp contrast between synthetic sentences, with their purely empirical content, and analytic sentences which are supposed to have no empirical content. The organising role that was attributed to analytic sentences and the empirical content that was supposedly peculiar to synthetic sentence, according to Quine, are shared and diffused by all sentences of a language. But this diffusion does not obliterate the distinction between the scheme elements and the content elements of the system.

> The interlocked conceptual scheme of physical objects, identity, and divided reference is part of the ship which, in Neurath's figure, we cannot remodel save as we stay afloat in it. The ontology of abstract objects is part of the ship too, if only a less fundamental part. The

ship may owe its structure partly to blundering predecessors who missed scuttling it only by fools' luck. But we are not in a position to jettison any part of it, except as we have substitute devices ready to hand that will serve the same essential purposes.

(Quine 1960: 123–4)

Thus, at least within a Quinean framework, we can retain the dualism of scheme and content even when we have abandoned the analytic/synthetic distinction. And in so far as Davidson's arguments are conducted within this framework, then the third dogma of empiricism cannot simply be a variant of the first dogma.[6]

Empiricism as a theory of content and SC

Conceptual relativism, as Davidson has noted, is often expressed in terms of scheme/world or scheme/reality distinction. Searle, for instance, has argued that conceptual schemes are the different ways and the different vocabularies and sets of concepts used to carve up a language-independent reality. Conceptual schemes, he argues, are a sub-species of 'systems of representation'. Representations are the variety of interconnected ways in which human beings have access to and represent features of the world to themselves. It is possible to have any number of different, and even incommensurable, systems of representations for representing the same reality. Furthermore, systems of representation are influenced by cultural, economic, historical and psychological factors; they are human creations and to that extent they are also arbitrary.

In what sense could this conception of SC be seen as a dogma of empiricism? Different replies can be given depending on which version we are examining. One possible reply can be found when we look at empiricism as a theory of content, and the version of SC that emphasises the role of conceptual schemes as the medium or framework for facing or fitting or representing reality or the totality of evidence (S2/C2 or S2/C1).

The beginnings of this reply can be found in Quine's reaction to Davidson's criticisms (Quine 1981). Quine distinguishes between empiricism construed as a theory of truth and empiricism as a theory of evidence. According to Quine, SC is a useful theory when taken in its epistemological sense, as a theory of evidence and justification. But he agrees with Davidson that the duality of sentences that fit facts is pernicious. According to him:

If empiricism is construed as a theory of truth, then what Davidson imputes to it as a third dogma is rightly imputed and rightly renounced. Empiricism as a theory of truth thereupon goes by the board, and good riddance.

(Quine 1981: 39)

Davidson, as part of his overall philosophical project, wishes to do away with
the legacy of empiricism which imposes intermediaries such as facts, conceptual schemes, paradigms, or world-views between us and the world. Searle's
'system of representation' is yet another example of such intermediaries. For
Davidson the attempt to characterise conceptual schemes in terms of the
notion of fitting or representing the world or the totality of our experiences
comes down to the idea that something is an acceptable conceptual scheme
if it is true. However, he adds, 'the truth of an utterance depends on just two
things: what the words as spoken mean, and how the world is arranged.
There is no further relativism to a conceptual scheme, a way of viewing
things, a perspective' (Davidson 1990: 122). Searle's defence of conceptual
relativism depends on postulating systems of representation that also act as
ways of viewing things. But if Davidson is right, we do not need to introduce
a distinction between reality and our conceptual scheme which would fit or
face that reality. We should do away with such intermediaries for two reasons.
First, no satisfactory account of what these entities may be is available to us;
and second, the introduction of intermediaries threatens our hold on the
world and reality. Consequently, Davidson's preferred account of the deter-
minants of the content of our thought is causal and holistic, where the link
between the world and mind is direct and unmediated.

A different set of considerations come into play when we look at S1/C2.
Once again Searle can act as a handy foil. He argues:

> Any system of classification or individuation of objects, any set of cat-
> egories for describing the world, indeed, any system of representation
> at all is conventional, and to that extent arbitrary. The world divides
> up the way we divide it, and if we are ever inclined to think that our
> present way of dividing it is the right one, or is somehow inevitable,
> we can always imagine alternative systems of classification.
>
> (Searle 1995: 160)

But he goes on to add:

> From the fact that a *description* can only be made relative to a set of
> linguistic categories, it does not follow that the *facts/objects/states of
> affairs/etc., described* can only *exist* relative to a set of categories.
>
> (Searle 1995: 166, emphasis in the original)

One problem with Searle's argument is that if there is any truth to conceptual relativity or scheme/world distinction then facts, objects or a state of
affairs would have to be individuated by the conceptual tools available within
that conceptual scheme. It simply does not make sense to talk about different conceptual schemes representing the same fact or object differently when
what counts as the same object or fact cannot be decided prior to and inde-

pendently of the way in which it is to be defined or individuated by a conceptual scheme. To speak of a 'scheme/world' or a 'scheme/reality' distinction, in the manner that Searle does, is to presuppose that we can understand, and hence individuate, the already existing world or reality and then impose our conceptual schemes on it. If 'the world' is a name for the objects that our world view or conceptual scheme individuates, then it cannot play the role which Searle assigns it in his defence of scheme/content dualism.

This is the lesson learned from Putnam's 'mereological sum' example of conceptual relativity. Putnam proposes a scenario 'where one and the same situation can be described as involving different numbers and kinds of objects' (Putnam 1989: 180). He asks: faced with a world with three individuals, does the question 'how many objects are there in this world?' have a determinate reply? The answer is no, because any reply would depend on how we interpret the word 'object'. From an atomist perspective there would be three independent, unrelated objects in this world, while from a mereological standpoint the reply is seven objects (or eight, if we include the null object as a part of every object). The point is that if we are to take conceptual relativity seriously then we have to accept that what counts as an object or a fact or even existence will be decided internally, only by the criteria available within the given conceptual scheme.

It might be argued, as Thomas Nagel and Bill Child have done (in a slightly different context) that even if we may not be able to:

> Form a *detailed conception* of the world without using our concepts
> ... it does not follow from this that we cannot form the *bare idea* of
> the world as it is in itself without reading a structure into it, [and]
> we just do understand the idea of the world as it is in itself.
> (Child 1994: 57, emphasis in the original)

We can have the bare idea of what counts as the same world or the same object across various conceptual schemes, and so we can speak of different schemes representing them in different ways. It's not at all clear, however, what 'the bare idea of the world' in this context can be. I have the bare idea of chemistry in so far as I know what the subject matter of chemistry is, and also a vague notion of what sort of experiments and formulae are used in that field and scant knowledge of the entities involved in these experiments and formulae. But what does it mean to say that I have a bare idea of the world? If the world is the totality of what there is, then a bare idea of the world would be a bare idea of the totality of what there is and not of something else. But the problem was to give some meaning to the suggestion that we can talk about the world, to give meaning to 'world', outside all conceptual schemes. To suggest that we can have a bare or a vague idea of what there is, rather than a detailed one, does not in any way help us to solve the original problem.

53

We might be able to make sense of the Nagel/Child suggestion if we think that the world presents itself to us pre-labelled, so to speak; that is, the world has an intrinsic structure which makes itself manifest to us. In so far as empiricism, at least in some versions of it, relies on the idea of the world possessing certain inherent features, we can detect a connection between SC and the empiricist conception of the world. Davidson is not explicit on this point, but I think the rejection of such a position will be in line with his anti-empiricist sentiments.

Alternatively we might wish to resort to James and claim that the unconceptualised world is what we may glimpse, but never grasp (James 1977). But the question 'what entitles us to call that which we glimpse "the world"?' remains intact. If there is any truth to conceptual relativity then both what we glimpse and what we grasp are mediated by the conceptual tools available to us. It might be argued that the world is *that* (whatever it might be) which we glimpse. But this tautological reply is more applicable to the infamous thing in itself rather than to the world in any intelligible sense of 'world'. To take this route is to plunge back into the habit of talking about what cannot be talked about, and the incoherence of it all looms large.

Empiricism as a theory of content, then, introduces a pernicious form of SC by turning schemes into intermediaries between us and the world. The dualism also relies on an incoherent notion of 'same world' and 'same object' which cannot sustain the type of conceptual relativity envisaged by its defenders.

Empiricism as a theory of justification and SC

SC has frequently been presented as a response to the epistemological worries about the relationship between the mind and the world. If we approach the mind/world relationship by privileging the contribution of the human mind, then, in order to secure our grip on the world, we need to introduce some empirical constraints on what is conceptually warranted. The sceptical challenge intensifies the worries about our ability to retain our hold on the world and underlines the need to have some unassailable source for justifying our claims about the connections between our minds, with their conceptual apparatus, and the external world. As John McDowell has argued:

> The point of the dualism is that it allows us to acknowledge an external constraint on our freedom to deploy our empirical concepts ... The putatively reassuring idea is that empirical justifications have an ultimate foundation in impingements on the conceptual realm from outside.
>
> (McDowell 1994: 6)

The target of the accusation of dogmatism, in this instance, is specifically the scheme/sense-data distinction within the context of empiricism as a theory of justification, or evidence (*pace* Quine). According to Davidson, 'the idea that there is a basic division between uninterpreted experience and an organizing conceptual scheme is a deep mistake born of the essentially incoherent picture of the mind as a passive but critical spectator of an inner show' (Davidson 1989: 171). Davidson feels the need to pursue the issue of scheme/given dualism further because, as we saw, although Quine accepts Davidson's criticisms of scheme/world dualism he continues to support a version of scheme/sense data dualism.

Empiricism, as an epistemological theory, Davidson argues, is based on the view that the subjective is the foundation of objective empirical knowledge. However, he denies that empirical knowledge either has an epistemological foundation or needs one. What motivates foundationalism is the thought that it is 'necessary to insulate the ultimate sources of evidence from the outside world in order to guarantee the authority of the evidence for the subject' (Davidson 1989: 162). McDowell, who lends his voice to the rejection of the scheme/sense data distinction, has pointed out that one main problem with this approach is that:

> Even as it tries to make out that sensory impressions are our avenue of access to the empirical world, empiricism conceives impressions in such a way that they could only close us off from the world, disrupting our 'unmediated touch' with ordinary objects.
>
> (McDowell 1994: 155)

Once we begin characterising the mind/world relationship in terms of the distinction between conceptual schemes and unsullied streams of experience or the given, then the next, almost inevitable, step is the claim that all we can have access to through our experiences of the world are the immediate contents of our senses, our impressions, or ideas. Thus, instead of finding any solace for our epistemological anxieties, this particular version of empiricism saddles us with further philosophical worries about our hold on reality.

Once again, what Davidson objects to is the view that construes conceptual schemes as intermediaries between the human mind and the world. The aim is to find ways in which we can be directly in touch with the world, without any further need for incorrigible or otherwise privileged and foundational epistemic items. A naturalistic account of knowledge, Davidson argues, that makes no appeal to such epistemological intermediaries as sense-data, qualia, or raw feels, would give us that unmediated hold (Davidson 1989: 171). Once we accept that sensations do not play an epistemological role in determining the content of our beliefs about the world, then we are giving up the third dogma of empiricism (Davidson 1989: 166).

Empiricism as a theory of justification, as well as empiricism as a theory of content, motivate versions of SC that distance us from reality and prevent us from having an unmediated contact with the world. The scheme/sense data distinction imposes elements from the content side of dualism as intermediaries between us and the world. The tertiary entities introduced by the scheme/world distinction, on the other hand, are the unwelcome contributions of the scheme side of dualism. To think that these intermediaries are either necessary or desirable in our account of the relationship between our mind and the world is to fall prey to the third dogma of empiricism.

The alternative

The scheme/world dichotomy is often introduced in order to account for the different ways in which the mind can mediate reality. The intuition behind this move is that although we can assume that there exists, at most, one world, we can give various and at times not wholly compatible accounts, both true and false, of what that world is like. The scheme/world distinction helps to explain how we can maintain our belief in the uniqueness of the world while allowing that there can be different representations of it. It is an attempt to find a place for the contributions of the human conceptual apparatus and the restrictions put on those contributions by the world or 'how things are anyway'. To deny the impact of the world on our conceptual and cognitive processes is to fall prey to the greatest excesses of idealism. To deny a role to human conceptualisation, to overplay the idea of direct unmediated contact with the world, on the other hand, leaves us unable to account for error and false belief. If the mind/world relationship was not mediated by conceptual schemes, the story goes, if the world had a direct impact on our minds, then we would be unable to explain how error is possible. C.I. Lewis, for instance, defends the idea of SC by arguing that 'if there be no interpretation or construction which the mind itself imposes, then thought is rendered superfluous, the possibility of error becomes inexplicable, and the distinction of true and false is in danger of becoming meaningless' (Lewis 1929: 39).

SC, then, can be formulated to solve specific philosophical problems which are independent from empiricist considerations. The scheme/world distinction, in particular, is motivated by the need to explain the prevalence of differing conceptions of the world, including the erroneous ones. Davidson does admit that his approach to the question of the relationship between the mind and the world poses problems for explaining the nature of error, how to identify it or explain it (Davidson 1989: 166). The wholesale dismissal of SC as the third dogma leaves us with the problem of finding an account for the variability of the ways the world is understood and conceptualised by different cultures, epochs, and languages.

If we accept that there is use for some version of SC, the scheme/world division, even shorn of its representationalist presuppositions, would be incapable of helping us. For, as we saw, we cannot make sense of the suggestion that the world, as the content of our conceptual apparatus, is not already contaminated by our concepts. Furthermore, to entertain the idea of an uncontaminated reality is to invite the type of alienating dualism that was the target of Davidson's attack.

McDowell has suggested that there might be an 'innocent' version of SC that does not commit us to dualism. He argues: 'Conceptual schemes or perspectives need not be one side of the exploded dualism of scheme and world. Thus innocently conceived, schemes or perspectives can be seen as embodied in languages or cultural traditions' (McDowell 1994 : 155). In this approach, languages and traditions can figure as constitutive of what he calls 'our unproblematic openness to the world'. If the third dogma of empiricism is indeed located in the empiricist's attempt to introduce various intermediaries between us and the world, be it on the side of scheme or content, then an innocent version of SC would not hamper our direct contact with the world or reality.

The making of such an innocent version of SC is implicit in Davidson. C4, or the version where the content of the conceptual scheme is the thick experience of our lives, the rich variety of lived experiences and encounters with the world that constitute the very fabric of our existence, may provide us with an approach to SC which avoids the pernicious dualism under attack. Davidson himself introduces this possibility only to dismiss it with other varieties of SC. He says:

> The notion of organisation applies only to pluralities. But what every plurality we take experience to consist in – events like losing a button or stubbing a toe, having a sensation of warmth or hearing an oboe – we will have to individuate according to familiar principles. A language that organises such entities must be a language very like our own.
>
> (Davidson 1984: 192)

Stubbing a toe or hearing an oboe are instances of what I have called 'thick experiences' rather than the thin, contentless sensations of pain or sound. As this passage shows, Davidson allows for the abstract possibility of scheme/thick experience distinction but blocks it by recourse to his incoherence argument. I am not going to rehearse the arguments against Davidson's position on translatability. The relevant point is that Davidson believes that conceptual relativity rests on the assumption that 'conceptual schemes and moral systems, or that languages associated with them, can differ massively – to the extent of being mutually unintelligible or incommensurable, or forever beyond rational resolve' (Davidson 1989: 160). But my suggestion here is neutral on the question of the limits on how removed from ours an alternative conceptual scheme can be. Rather, the view towards which I am gesturing gives us the means of talking about different ways of conceptualising our lived experience in the world. It is a way of permitting space for the intuition, shared by some philosophers, that there are no non-perspectival and unconceptualised views of things. It is one with the view that our dealings with the world, whether through our perceptual experiences, thoughts or feelings, are always from within a perspective and are permeated by our concepts and by our interests and are informed by our location within a specific culture, history and language. This approach does not prevent us from having direct access to the real world, so we are not ending up with intermediaries between us and the world. With McDowell, we can deny that there can be a purely unconceptualised content to our experience. Experience itself, as McDowell has argued, is already equipped with conceptual content. For instance, to experience colour we must be equipped with the concept of visible surfaces of objects, and the concepts of suitable conditions for telling what a thing's colour is by looking at it (McDowell 1994: 27). But the experience of colour can be conceptualised in widely different ways, as cross-cultural studies of colour terms amply demonstrate. What is being emphasised is that all our life-experiences are from a standpoint and each standpoint is richly endowed with conceptual inputs. These standpoints are also the means of making sense of experiences and coping with the world (in the broadest sense possible) by conceptualising them in different ways.

The scheme/thick content distinction receives its philosophical justification not from empiricism, but from the common or garden observation that our life-experiences can be variously described and to that extent, one could even say, 'variously experienced'. The different modes of conceptualisation also have consequences for the ways in which people act and conduct their lives. So conceptual schemes are individuated by looking at their consequences on how people engage with the world in their day to day lives, as well as on purely abstract grounds. The presence of different conceptual schemes manifests itself most dramatically when we come across unfamiliar ways of conceptualising what, in a rough and ready fashion, can be called 'the same experience'. To take just one, rather striking example, in Dyirabil, an aboriginal language of Australia, all objects and experiences in the universe are classified into four groups:

1 *Bayi* chiefly classifies human males and animals; but also the moon, storms, rainbows and boomerangs.

2 *Balan* classifies human females; but also water, fire, fighting, most birds, some trees, etc.

3 *Balam* classifies non-flesh food, but also cigarettes.

4 *Bala* everything not in the other categories including noises and language, wind, some spears, etc.[7]

This fourfold classification provides us with a rather striking instance of how familiar experiences such as noises, as well as pre-individuated objects such as food and animals, can further be conceptualised in ways that make them seem strange and unfamiliar to non-Dyirabil thinking. Furthermore, this alternative way of conceptualising and categorising their lived world also has consequences for how Dyirabil-speaking people conduct their lives and react to various events and experiences involving these categories. In this sense then, alternative conceptual schemes are also alternative ways of life.

With McDowell we can reassure Davidson that there is no gap between thought and the world and hence avoid the myth of the Given, without renouncing the claim that experience can act as a rational constraint on thinking or the claim that our content-full experiences can be made sense of in differing ways. I'm not sure with how much of this Davidson would disagree. But by his sweeping dismissal of SC. Davidson disregards the role played by the very idea of conceptual in explaining our cognitive architecture. We know, both intuitively and on empirical evidence, that there are different possible views of the world and our place within it. The above account of a rough idea of a conceptual scheme, shorn of any empiricist presuppositions, attempts to accommodate this intuition and allow a philosophical space for conceptual pluralism without threatening us with a promiscuous relativism.

Notes

1 An earlier version of this paper was given at the meeting of the Aristotelian Society, June 8, 1988 and appeared as 'Why Conceptual Schemes?' in the Proceedings of the Aristotelian Society, XCVIII, Part 3: 287–306. I would like to thank those present for their helpful comments and criticisms.
2 This interpretation has been proposed by Quine and echoed by Rorty.
3 This is Davidson's favourite metaphor.
4 Quine (1961) and Whorf (1956), respectively, have used these particular metaphors.
5 The distinction between C2 and C3 is more explicit in Davidson's work and has been discussed frequently by other commentators. However, both C1 and C4 also are present in Davidson's discussion of SC.
6 And if the first and the second dogma are in essence one, then the same considerations would apply to the latter as well.
7 The case study originally analysed by R.M. Dixon can be found in Lakoff (1987: 92). Similar examples are plentiful in anthropological literature and are often employed in discussions of conceptual schemes by psychologists and cognitive scientists. To take an example from a somewhat different domain, Levy reports that Tahitians categorise sadness with sickness, fatigue or the attack of an evil spirit and do not have a separate word, or an independent concept for it. He does not claim that the Tahitians do not experience sadness; rather, they conceptualise their experiences differently from the way Europeans do.

3

A
SENSIBLE PERSPECTIVISM

Philip Pettit

Perspectivism is associated with the work of Nietzsche in the nineteenth century and it is frequently invoked nowadays as a theme in postmodernist writings; in particular as a ground that justifies radical forms of relativism and irrationalism. There is no prospect of rational reconciliation between divergent viewpoints, under the picture that perspectivism allegedly delivers. Anything goes in principle, and what goes in practice is a function of where the power and the influence lie.

The core perspectivist idea is that all claims to knowledge bear the marks of the contingent circumstances and assumptions of those making the claims, so that it is deeply mistaken to privilege any particular perspective and treat it as providing the ultimate heuristic standpoint. I find the core perspectivist idea attractive but I do not think that it leads towards the iconoclastic position with which it is associated. This essay is an attempt to identify what is right in the idea and to provide an overall framework for making sense of it.

The essay does not look at the political implications of the sort of perspectivism defended, but these are hardly going to be iconoclastic either. The moderate perspectivism envisaged fits naturally with a pluralist, tolerant attitude towards divergence in modes of inquiry and evaluation – indeed it suggests that any other attitude would be seriously out of place – and for that reason it encourages the pluralist vision of a society and polity where different viewpoints can be fostered. But it does not associate such pluralist sentiments with the rampant irrationalism that usually goes under perspectivist colours.

The paper is in five sections. First I present a simple case for perspectivism, explaining what exactly I mean by the doctrine. Then I chart three possible responses to it, only one of which looks attractive: the belief that perspectives can be integratively reduced. I provide a model of integrative reduction – the reduction of the indexical to the non-indexical – in the third section; and then in the fourth I try to make plausible the claim that this model can be extended to make sense of discursive, perspectival cleavages in general. The paper concludes with a section in which I discuss the significance of perspectivism, as it is understood and accommodated here, for philosophy in general; I argue that it gives a new slant on what we should expect philosophy to try, and to be able, to accomplish.

A case for perspectivism

The core perspectivist idea is familiar to contemporary analytical philosophers from Thomas Nagel's claim that there is no such thing as the view from nowhere (Nagel 1986). All representations of what there is are affected in one way or another by contingencies, roughly, of position. They are marked by the sensory organisation, cognitive processing or linguistic articulation on which they rely, by the theoretical assumptions and cultural associations that they embody, or by some such contingently variable influences. All forms of representation are perspectival and there is no hope of transcending those perspectives in a god's-eye depiction of things (see too McDowell 1983; Nagel 1986; Price 1992; Strawson 1985; Williams 1978).

I am happy to go along with this story of multiple viewpoints or perspectives. The reason is that a relatively straightforward line of argument seems to me to support the position. I will sketch that argument briefly in this section, drawing on work that I have done elsewhere (Pettit 1990, 1991, 1994). The argument is Wittgensteinian in character but I do not try to detail or establish its Wittgensteinian credentials.

The argument can be presented in seven steps.

1   Any discursive form of knowledge presupposes semantic competence in the terms of the discourse.

2   Some of the terms within any subject's competence must be semantically basic: that is, understood ostensively, without theoretical definition.

3   No finite set of ostended exemplars instantiates just one potential semantic value – just one referent – for a term.

4   If such exemplars identify a relatively determinate value for a subject, therefore, that must be because of a contingency in how the subject is disposed to respond.

5   Thus the mastery of the basic terms in any subject's vocabulary is achieved in a response-dependent way; the unresponsive subject will lack the conditions required for non-parasitically mastering such a term or concept.

6   There are different discourses to the extent that the responsiveness required for semantic competence is tuned or primed by different clustered sets of factors.

61

7   Perspectivism is best understood as nothing more or less than the claim that there are different discourses in this sense.

Steps 1 and 2

The argument begins with two simple but irresistible steps: first, the observation that I can be possessed of a certain form of discursive knowledge only so far as I grasp the meanings and the referents of the terms in question; and second the remark that I must understand some of those terms in a basic, theoretically undefined way. Many terms will be understood on the basis of definitions, explicit or implicit, in the other terms at my disposal. But, on pain of circularity, not all terms can be understood in this way. Some of them I must master just from seeing how they are used: in particular, what they are used to pick out. I must master them on the basis of ostension, or something like ostension: that is, by having sample referents of the terms brought to my attention.

While these claims are hard to resist, it is worth adding two caveats. First, the terms that I master ostensively may not be mastered one by one, in an atomistic fashion; it may be that I can only master a number of such terms together in the sort of package deal that Quineans talk of; it may even be that I can only master some terms ostensively so far as I am already the master of certain other terms, ostensive and defined. Second, the terms that I master ostensively at any one point in time may come later to be mastered definitionally; and the terms that I master ostensively may be understood definitionally by others, and vice versa. The only claim here is that at any particular time each of us must understand some of the terms within our competence on a pretheoretical, ostensive basis.

Step 3

The third step in the argument makes the familiar point that no matter how many instances are presented to me as ostended examples of where a given term applies, those instances will fail to determine a unique semantic value for the term (Kripke 1982). Let the term in question be a predicate, so that the semantic value it is to be assigned is a property. No matter how many instances of the property are presented as examples, they will not succeed in uniquely determining that property as the semantic value ostended. The reason is that any finite set of things will instantiate an infinite number of properties: it will be a proper sub-set of an infinite number of possible property-extensions.

Suppose I am presented, for instance, with a set of regular geometric shapes. Those examples will certainly instantiate the property of regularity but they will also instantiate an endless variety of other, perhaps gerrymandered properties: properties like that of being regular-in-the-shapes-presented-or-otherwise-being-irregular, of being regular-both-in-the-shapes-presented-and-in-all-three-sided-shapes-or-otherwise-being-irregular, and so on through an open-ended set of possible variations.

Steps 4 and 5

The fourth and fifth steps draw the lesson taught by the last. We know that human beings are capable of learning the semantic value of a basic term – learning which property is to be associated, for example, with a basic predicate – from ostension. And that means that a finite set of instances can make a property salient to people and teach them which property to associate with a given predicate. Since this trick cannot be pulled off just on the basis of the instances, it must involve something happening on the side of the subject, as a result of exposure to those instances. It must be that, presented with those examples, the subject responds with an inclination to go one way rather than another in extrapolating from the set of examples and identifying things that share, and things that do not share, the ostended property. The ability to master the term and concept in question – the ability to learn which property it designates – is response-dependent. It presupposes that the subject is tuned to respond in a certain extrapolative way and thereby to latch onto the particular property associated with the extrapolative disposition. Otherwise the set of examples would leave the subject at sea, aware of too many candidates for the role of providing the semantic value of the predicate.

As we needed to enter caveats before, so it is important to mention a number at this point too. First, the response-dependent story of semantic mastery that I have sketched is not meant to be a complete account of conceptual mastery or, more generally, rule-following. At the least, it needs to be filled out by a story as to how a subject can get a property wrong – and be conscious of this possibility – if they rely on their own extrapolative inclination to identify instances (Pettit 1990, 1996).

Second caveat. The response-dependent story – say, as filled out to allow for fallibility – does not aspire to show that ostension makes a property determinate to the point of fixing the right predication in all possible novel cases (*pace* Kripke 1982; see Pettit 1996, Postscript). What it is introduced to vindicate is the capacity of ostension to fix the right predication in an open list of novel cases – not necessarily all possible cases – and thereby to give people something to talk and think about in those cases. Meaning sceptics assert that no finite set of examples determines the right application in any new case. Non-sceptics deny this, committing themselves to the claim that a relevant rule of correctness can be determined by how the subject responds to such a set of examples. But non-sceptics can think that finite sets of examples determine how a term should be applied in new cases without thinking that they can determine how it is to be applied in all conceivable new cases.

Third caveat. The response-dependent story of semantic and conceptual mastery does not entail that in using the term or concept learned people will be predicating, not the property at the source of the response – the property that unifies those instances towards which people are disposed to extrapolate from the original examples – but rather the relational property of typically arousing that response in human beings. That the predicate 'regular' is learned response-dependently does not mean that those who learn it think of the property that unifies regular shapes as one of looking a certain way to them: they may think of it as that property, the intrinsic property exemplified in such and such shapes. Of course some response-dependently mastered terms may pick out relational, in particular anthropocentric properties: the predicate 'funny', as used of jokes, surely picks out such a property. But the point is that the response-dependent story of semantic competence does not necessarily make basic terms of discourse anthropocentric in the same way (Jackson and Pettit 2002; cf. Peacocke 1993). Those who use a response-dependent term for certain items may do so in virtue of having the reference-fixing response and yet not be aware of that response; thus they can hardly be held to use the term in order to predicate the property of giving rise to that response.

Steps 6 and 7

The last two steps of the argument finally take us to the doctrine for which I want to use the name 'perspectivism'. Human discourse is not a single seamless web in which the basic terms are introduced and applied on the basis of a certain set of universally available responses, and other terms then defined by reference to those basic terms. Human discourse, rather, is a patchwork. The patchiness comes of the fact that the responses that facilitate the mastery of basic terms are driven by different, clustered sets of factors. As these factors cluster and divide from one another, so too do corresponding modes of discourse. And what perspectivism claims is precisely that in this sense there are a number of different discourses.

It is fairly obvious that human thought is structured around vocabularies, however loosely demarcated, such that we learn to master each in a manner that does not require an ability to define its terms in other vocabularies. We learn to master the language of belief and desire, and to use this language in explanation of one another's doings, without relying on definitions of its terms in the language of neuroscience – and vice versa. We learn to master the language of colour and beauty, sound and music, without relying on definitions of its terms in the language of physics – and vice versa. We learn to master the language of normative assessment, identifying justice and kindness and rightness and so on, without relying on definitions of its terms in the language of non-evaluative fact – and vice versa.

What the claim in the last two stages of the argument does is help to make sense of such palpable facts. Given the response-dependent ways in which we gain semantic mastery of basic terms, it is clearly possible that the factors tuning responses cluster in such a way that they give rise to relatively independent bodies of semantic competence and discourse. The sorts of examples given are good evidence that that possibility is realised. It is a matter of common observation that different discourses enjoy a high level of definitional autonomy in relation to one another and the response-dependent story of semantic mastery makes very good sense of that fact.

We need not consider here the question of how widespread discursive cleavages go, though we shall be suggesting further examples later. Some will think that many of the most interesting divergences occur only across different cultures, for example, while others will restrict themselves to divergences – such as those given in our illustrations – that we are as likely to find within any single culture. But I abstract from such undoubtedly interesting questions here.

One last comment. Different discourses are not only relatively independent in the sense explained; sometimes they are also mutually inhibiting. The best example is provided by the way that the use of ordinary intentional vocabulary to make sense of a psychological subject inhibits the use of neuroscientific vocabulary to do so; and vice versa. This example is nicely dramatised by Daniel Dennett (1979) when he asks us to imagine playing chess with a computer (cf. Davidson 1980; 1984). It is clear that if we are to play chess then we had better treat the computer in the vocabulary of intentional states: the language of beliefs, desires, intentions, and so on. It is clear that this is to do something different – to take a different stance, as Dennett says – from what we might do in looking at the electronic configuration of the computer and at how it is electronically configured to respond. We cannot simultaneously think of the computer in the two vocabularies: we have a choice between seeing it as an intentional subject, and playing chess, or seeing it as an electronic system and pursuing a purely predictive project.

I do not suppose that wherever we find relatively independent discourses, in the sense explained, we find discourses that are also mutually inhibiting. But it is a possibility worth keeping in mind. We shall see that it is often realised, and I suspect that many of those who think of themselves as perspectivists give it great prominence. Perspectives are mutually inhibiting or exclusive to the extent that you cannot see things from two angles at once, and so the very metaphor at the origin of perspectivist claims suggests the thesis of mutual inhibition as well as mutual independence.

Responses to perspectivism

How should we react to the fact that there are many different perspectives that we can assume, as we put ourselves under the control of different sorts of tuning factors? Sensitised to the effects of things on the senses, for example, and to the ways in which they command our emotions and desires, we can see a world of colour and beauty and value. Sensitised to the ways in which they fit and interact with other things – our bodies included – we can see a world of shape and volume and mass and causation. What does it say about the nature of the world that it can be depicted – and, we presume, accurately depicted – in such different ways?

One salient answer would say that the reason why representations are multiple is that reality itself is multiple. Corresponding to different forms of representation, so the picture would go, there are different realms of reality that relate in the manner of Cartesian mind and Cartesian matter, or the Platonic realm of sense and the Platonic realm of intellect, or perhaps Nelson Goodman's (1978) many worlds.

But the multiple-reality story will not attract many contemporary adherents. Some will refuse to endorse it on the grounds that it would make sense only if we had access to an external, god's-eye depiction of the things represented in different perspectives (Price 1997). Most will reject it, as I reject it, on the grounds that it fails to explain the intuitive fact that properties in the supposedly different realms are often superveniently connected: aesthetic properties supervene on perceptual, for example, evaluative properties supervene on descriptive and, according to most accounts, mental properties supervene on physical. There is no variation possible in supervenient properties without variation in the subvenient; and this sort of connection, however it is further articulated, is hard to square with a hypothesis of multiple, distinct realms.

A second salient answer would say that reality can be multiply represented without itself being multiple in the envisaged sense, because representation is constructive in character. Spelt out in cruder terms than adherents may favour, the idea is that reality is relatively indeterminate and that our more determinate representations vary as we choose to construct an image of it, now with this purpose in mind, now with that. Each image will be too determinate to be a faithful reflection of what there is and the different images can be seen as different constructions that we impose, for different pragmatic reasons, on the relatively unconstraining data that we confront in experience and experiment. There may not be a multiple reality, then, but there is multiple vision. There are many ways of seeing things – ways of seeing things that may not be easily reconciled (Nagel 1986: 88) – but there are not many ways things are.

This second alternative is most readily associated with Nietzsche's so-called perspectivism, at least on the received reading of that doctrine under which it posits an indeterminate nature (Leiter 1994). The alternative can be given different glosses, too, some idealist in character, some Kantian, some pragmatist, but no matter how it is presented, the approach is too mysterious for my own tastes. It offends against a natural sense of how representations ought to track reality, even if it does not violate intuitions in the outrageous manner of the multiple-reality account.

The third salient answer to the question of how the world can allow of multiple representations is reductivist in character. It refuses to multiply either reality or vision, arguing that some representations are more fundamental than others and that it must be possible, in principle, to identify a single form of representation that is the most basic of all those available. The reductivist idea is that we can think of reality as answering to this encompassing scheme of representation and make sense, at the same time, of how other, more specialised forms of representation are also possible.

I favour this third, reductivist answer to the question of how the world can allow itself to be multiply represented – but not in the stock versions. In stock versions of reductivism, the claims that we make within a special form of representation are analysed in such a way, so it is alleged, that we can see in principle how to construct equivalent and equipotent claims – if you like, translations – within a more comprehensive scheme; that, or they are explained away as the product of intelligible error. I do not think that reduction is always either translational, in any straightforward sense, or eliminative, as indeed many contemporary philosophers acknowledge (see Papineau 1995; Jackson 1998). I believe that once we recognise the multiple, perspectival nature of representation, we can identify a third variety of reduction that is neither translational nor eliminative. I shall call this third variety of reduction 'integrative'; integration is not as good as translation but it is a lot better, of course, than elimination.

The metaphor of visual perspective already points us towards the possibility of integrative reduction. It is possible for one visual perspective to be more encompassing than another in the sense that everything visible from the encompassed perspective will be visible from the encompassing but not vice versa; think, for example, of the balcony view of the front of the theatre and of the way in which this encompasses the view from the stalls. The encompassing perspective in such a case will deliver to us everything that is delivered in the encompassed, though not at the same angle and not perhaps at the same level of resolution; the ontology of the narrower scene will be included in the ontology of the wider. Consistently with this ontic reduction, the narrower perspective may retain a certain visual autonomy. It may be that you have to occupy that perspective in order to experience, or even vividly imagine, how things present themselves there. Although it is ontically reduced, as I shall say, the perspective remains heuristically indispensable; it is associated with a way of knowing how things are at the front of the theatre that is not available from the balcony.

By analogy, the idea in integrative reduction is that it may be possible to reduce one perspective to another in an ontic sense while allowing a certain autonomy – a heuristic autonomy – to the reduced perspective. The sort of representation available at the reduced perspective may not be capable of being replicated at the reducing; it may incorporate a way of knowing things that is lost at the reducing. The ontic reduction may be effected without a heuristic reduction.[1]

So far as there is ontic reduction, what is offered in the exercise envisaged is something more than elimination. But so far as it is not a form of heuristic reduction – so far as it loses the way of knowing associated with the reduced discourse – what is offered is something less than translation. The eliminative exercise involves neither ontic nor heuristic reduction; the translational exercise involves both. Integrative reduction is a half-way house, offering reduction of an ontic but not of a heuristic kind.

A model for the integrative reduction of perspectives

Consider the different representational perspectives associated with a purely non-indexical vocabulary, on the one hand, and a vocabulary that includes indexical terms on the other. Indexical terms identify times by reference to time of utterance as 'then' and 'now'; identify places by reference to place of utterance as 'there' and 'here'; identify people by reference to the identity of the utterer as 'I' and 'you'; and so on. Non-indexical terms can identify those very same times and places and persons but will do so without relying on the utterance in which they figure; they will pick them out by names, co-ordinates, calendars, clocks, and the like.

There is an obvious sense in which indexical facts – the facts which can be truly reported in sentences that use some indexical terms – reduce ontically to non-indexical; and yet in an equally obvious sense indexical facts remain heuristically irreducible. There is a clear sense, that is to say, in which the indexical perspective can be integrated with the non-indexical in a manner that parallels the way in which the view from the stalls can be integrated with the view from the balcony.

The ontic reducibility of indexical to non-indexical facts can be expressed as follows. Think of all the non-indexical facts that actually obtain, including facts about which speakers are at which venues at which times. Imagine now that we exactly replicate the actual world in these non-indexical respects, adding nothing on the way (Jackson 1998). Will the replicated world display all and only the indexical facts that obtain at the actual world? Of course it will. Let the non-indexical facts be carried over to the replica, and the indexical will travel at no extra expense. They will travel for free, because they depend on the non-indexical.

If there is any doubt about this, a little reflection will put it to rest. In replicating the non-indexical facts of the actual world, we replicate the positions of speakers in space and time. This is so for any indexical sentence that can be uttered by such a speaker; we ensure that things are such that it has the same truth-condition[2] and the same truth-value as the corresponding sentence in the actual world. But that is just to say that in replicating the non-indexical facts of the actual world, we replicate the indexical.

Here is another way of emphasising the ontic reducibility of indexical to non-indexical facts. Suppose that we are given complete non-indexical information on the nature of the world that we inhabit. Will that information leave open further possibilities of an indexical kind? Will it be consistent with the truth of any of a number of inconsistent indexical sentences? And will we have to wait, then, on information as to which of those sentences is true before the open possibilities are closed? Of course not. There can be no bare, indexical difference between possibilities. There are no indexical ways things can be that are fixed independently of how things are in non-indexical respects. No indexical difference without a non-indexical difference (Lewis 1990: 505).

If indexical facts are reducible in this ontic sense to non-indexical, it should be equally clear that they are not reducible in a heuristic sense. There is no way of interpreting indexical reports in non-indexical terms such that the mode of knowledge associated with the indexical reports can be equally well provided – even putting aside problems of extra complexity – by their non-indexical counterparts. The indexical perspective enjoys heuristic autonomy in relation to the non-indexical.

Consider any indexical report such as 'I am in Canberra' or 'It is 3.30 p.m. now' or 'Here is a tennis partner'. With such a sentence we can always specify when those words will express a truth. 'I am in Canberra' is true for any speaker S and any time, t, if and only if S is in Canberra at t. 'It is 3.30 p.m. now' is true for any speaker S and any time t if and only if it is 3.30 p.m. at the time of utterance. But while we can produce such biconditionals – and, as it happens, such a priori true biconditionals – we cannot claim to be able to use them in order to offer the speakers non-indexical ways of registering the things that are known, in the mode in which they are known, at the indexical perspective.

This point is made salient by John Perry's well-known argument that indexical modes of thinking are essential for agents (Lewis 1983, Essay 10; Perry 1979).[3] Take the indexically recognised facts that prompt me into action: this, in the way that my recognising that I am in Canberra prompts me to check my email or that my realising that it is 3.30 p.m. now prompts me to go to afternoon tea. Suppose that I could only recognise such facts in a wholly non-indexical mode: I could register that P. P. is in Canberra but not that I am in Canberra, and not that I am P.P.; I could register that afternoon tea is at 3.30 p.m. but not that it is now 3.30 p.m., and not that afternoon tea is now. In such a case, and regardless of the strength of my desires, my beliefs would be incapable of prompting me to action. For why should a belief about P.P.'s whereabouts lead me to do anything, short of knowing that I am P.P.? And why should a belief about what happens at 3.30 p.m. prompt me to take any initiative unless I recognise that it is now 3.30 p.m.?

The lesson is that while indexical facts reduce ontically to non-indexical ones, they are not heuristically reducible. In particular, they are not interpretable without serious loss in non-indexical language. They are not interpretable, indeed, without losing the very possibility of thinking in the manner of an intentional agent. The facts that are registered from the perspective of indexical language introduce nothing that is not encompassed by facts that are registered in the perspective of non-indexical: it is not as if indexical facts are something over and above non-indexical. Yet the indexical way of conceptualising and knowing those facts is not replaceable without serious loss by any non-indexical mode of conceptualisation or knowledge. Represent indexical facts in non-indexical fashion and they lose their normal profile and potency; they become incapable of heuristically mediating people's interventions as agents in the world around them.

In the non-indexical account of indexical phenomena, we are enabled to see from a non-indexical perspective how indexical sentences come to express truths. We can see in non-indexical terms that if the world is thus and so, then such and such indexical assertions will be true, such and such false. That is the sense in which the account offers a case of ontic reduction. But we are forced to admit at the same time that we cannot properly express or formulate those truths in non-indexical language: the indexical mode in which those truths are presented and known is not available at a non-indexical perspective. That is the sense in which the example illustrates heuristic irreducibility.

While we can offer a non-indexical reduction of what is sayable in indexical language, then, the reduction is neither translational nor eliminative. It is not eliminative, because it saves indexical truths. It is not translational, because it does not make available sentences that can serve in place of indexical sentences.

There is very little mystery, happily, about how this can be. The indexical perspective relies on a characteristic perspectival factor for the presentation of the propositions expressed in indexical sentences: this factor is the identity or whereabouts of the utterer, taken as such. Those propositions are presented either in terms that presuppose the identity of the speaker, as in talk of mine and yours and ours, or in terms that fix the speaker's location in space and time, as in talk of here and there, now and then. It is the identity of the actual speaker that fixes the reference of 'I' and 'you' and 'we', the location of the actual time and place of utterance that fixes the reference of 'now' and 'here'.

We can see from the non-indexical perspective how that factor plays a background role in the indexical presentation of potential belief contents; we see that for any speaker, for example, a sentence using 'I' will be true just in case it is true of that speaker. But we cannot put the factor into play in the same backgrounded way ourselves: we do not enjoy the appropriate speaker identity or location and, even if we did, the restriction to a non-indexical standpoint would prevent us from exploiting it. We can mention or identify the factor that serves a crucial role in indexical representation and we can explain how it serves in that role; but we cannot put the factor to any use ourselves (cf. Papineau 1995: 263).

The reduction of the indexical to the non-indexical serves as a model of integrative reduction, and as a model of how in principle perspectivism can be vindicated without recourse to the hypothesis of multiple vision or a multiple reality. What it illustrates is, broadly described, the following structure. There is a relatively narrow perspective, on the one side – the indexical perspective – at which certain patterns are salient: those expressed in the use of indexical sentences and those that must be grasped, by the Perry argument, for anyone intent on action. There is a relatively broad perspective, on the other – the non-indexical one – from which we can see how the narrow perspective operates and can recognise that it is directed to bona fide realities. But while the broader perspective enables us to recognise that the narrower is ontically reliable in this way, it does not itself enable us to represent directly the patterns – those expressed in the index-ical sentences – that are salient at the narrower perspective. It enables us to see that there are such patterns to be seen at the narrower perspective but it does not make those patterns directly visible to someone restricted to the broad: to someone stuck with using non-indexical language. What such a person can represent is not the local pattern registered by 'It is now 3.30 p.m'. but rather the global pattern whereby a person using that sentence at a certain location in space-time will be detecting a corresponding local pattern.

The possibility of extending the model

My wager is that wherever we find the discursive divergences that perspec-tivism postulates, we will be able to reduce one discourse to another, or both discourses to a third, on the integrative pattern that the indexical case illus-trates. I cannot vindicate my hypothesis definitively, of course, but I can do something to make it plausible. What I propose to do here is to show, in brisk outline, that integrative reducibility appears to be available – and to be all that is available – as between discourses that differ in a number of striking ways. I argue that figurative discourse is integratively reducible to non-figu-rative; practical representation, as I call it, to non-practical; and affective rep-resentation to non-affective.

Figurative and non-figurative representation

Some uses of language are meant only to amuse or shock or play but many, even many that are intended to elicit such effects, are representational in character: they are meant to convey a way things are. Among such linguistic representations of the world – among such conceptualisations, as I shall say – some are more or less figurative, some more or less non-figurative.

71

By non-figurative conceptualisation I mean that sort of representation in words or in concepts that relies solely on the pre-established meanings of the words used or, in the case of novel terms, on meanings that it explicitly introduces. Each referring expression picks out a determinate particular, each predicative expression a well-known property or a compound of well-known properties, each functor a familiar function, and so on, and each representational essay serves to convey something about the distribution of such properties across the universe of such particulars.

Conceptualisation is figurative precisely when the relation between the content represented – the story told, the scenario conveyed – and the meanings of the representational elements is not straightforward in this way. The words used are employed in such a way that the hearer or reader knows they are not meant literally – they are not meant in their established or stipulative senses – and knows that the content represented has to be identified on some basis other than by mere reference to those meanings.

Figurative representation may involve understatement, overstatement, insinuation, double entendre, irony, flattery or any of the many devices mapped in studies of rhetoric. But perhaps the best-known figurative form is provided by the example of metaphorical language. Here the user of the words says something so obviously false or banal that the hearer has to think twice and, relying on something more than the literal meanings of the words, has to identify a non-literal content. W.H. Auden writes in memory of Yeats: 'O all the instruments agree/The day of his death was a dark cold day'; but we do not hear in these words a banal report about the weather on a January day in Dublin, 1939. We make of the words – we hear in the words – a figurative message of a much more gripping and suggestive kind.[4]

We need not concern ourselves here with the detail of how such figurative speech is to be analysed. Without going into such detail, we can agree that there is a contrast between how it achieves representational ends and how non-figurative speech does so. Where non-figurative speech relies only on the pre-established or stipulative meanings of the words it employs, figurative – in particular, metaphorical – speech has to rely on something else besides. It puts into use, not just the literal meanings of the words, but the shared experience of the things and properties to which the words literally direct us and the shared sense of how those things and properties model items in the situation that the speaker is addressing. The dark and cold ascribed to the day of Yeats's death come to model features of the loss which his death entails. The instruments that chart the dark and cold come to stand for the indices by which we might measure that loss. And so on.

Given this dependence on experience, association and analogy we can see how the relation between figurative and non-figurative representation can fit the pattern distinctive of relations between narrower and broader perspectives. Figurative representation puts into play elements that non-figurative accounting cannot exploit in the same way, even though it can register and itemise those elements in the finest detail.

Experience, association, and analogy bring figurative speech to life for those who use and hear it; they let the language sing. There need be no mystery there from the literal perspective, since in principle the experience, association and analogy can be fully countenanced and their effects understood. But this ontic reducibility of the figurative to a literal perspective cannot be matched by anything deserving of the name of heuristic reduction. For the figurative mode of representation and knowledge requires experience, association and analogy to be put to use, not just to be given suitable mention in the ontological annals.

The point at issue here is familiar from discussions of analysis and art and the different methodologies of the two. The language of analysis, and the language of science in general, strives for exactitude and replicability and naturally embraces non-figurative modes of expression. The language of art strives for expression that is evocative rather than exact, and oriented to particularity rather than replicability. There is no end to what can be said in the language of analysis and there is no difficulty about the prospect of that language mapping all of the elements that go to make a language of art. Even if it can track the language of art in this way, still the language of analysis can never replace or exhaust it. The language of art may be worthy of celebration, indeed, for this very resistance to interpretation: for its irreplaceability. As Auden says in his lament for Yeats: 'poetry survives/In the valley of its saying where executives/Would never want to tamper'.

We argued before that, confined to a non-indexical perspective, we might be able to see exactly how indexical sentences could get to be true but we would not be able to express those truths in the same way: we would not be able to think about things in the manner required for intentional agency. We see now that the pattern is repeated in the case of figurative and non-figurative conceptualisation. Figurative representation is ontically unmysterious from the point of view of non-figurative but still it remains heuristically opaque. The discussion following will show that this pattern is repeated again and again.

Practical and non-practical representation

Imagine someone who argues regularly on these lines:

1 If every snake is timid, then that can't be a snake: look at the way it is tracking us.

2 That may have been a snake, for it certainly moved away quickly; but then again it may not, for lizards are timid as well.

3 If all snakes are timid, and this is a snake, then let's see what it does when I walk nearby: it ought to slither away into the bush.

4   You think that not all snakes are timid? OK, then show me one that is not.

5   Let's see whether there is any snake that will not be scared at the slightest sign of a human.

Imagine not just that the person argues regularly in this way about snakes, given their belief that all snakes are timid. Suppose that the person always argues on parallel lines for any belief of such a general or conditional kind. For arbitrary belief of the form 'All As are B', or 'If anything is an A, then it is also a B', they are prepared to argue from 'A' to 'B', from 'not B' to 'not A', from 'not A' to 'possibly B, possibly not B'; and from 'B' to 'possibly A, possibly not A'.

Does a person of this kind believe the principle associated in logic with *modus ponens* and *modus tollens*? They do not believe it, we suppose, in the sense of being disposed in the manner of logicians to assent understandingly and sincerely to a sentence that formulates the principle; it may even be that they lack the words required to express it. But do they believe it in some other sense? Someone may say that they believe it in the sense of acting as if it were true. But that says little or nothing, for the principle is a necessary truth and it is hard to see how anyone could fail to act as if it were true (Stalnaker 1984). The question is whether the person believes the principle in a substantive sense akin to, but distinct from, the belief that goes with sincere assent.

We must surely agree that the person does believe the principle in such a sense. The person is a reasoning subject who invokes certain considerations as grounds for drawing certain conclusions: that is, for believing the conclusions in the assenting or judgemental manner. They endorse precisely the considerations that the principle makes it right for them to endorse: or at least that is what they do when they are being clear-headed and critical. They do not believe the principle judgementally, in the sense of being disposed to assent with understanding and sincerity to a sentence that formulates it; they believe it, as I shall say, in a practice-based or practical manner (Pettit 1998a).

Three features mark this mode of belief. First, the person is capable of recognising and understanding instances of reasoning that rely on the principle: for example, 'If every snake is timid, then that can't be a snake: look at the way it is tracking us'. Second, the person believes of precisely such instances that they are valid; even if he or she does not say that a suitable piece of reasoning is valid or that the conclusion follows or anything of that kind, they treat it as valid: they are disposed to produce the premises as reasons for maintaining the conclusion. Third, having such a universal and activated disposition to believe of instances of the principle that they are valid, the person counts as believing the principle *in sensu diviso*; they manifest a case-by-case counterpart to the belief in the universal principle that all such instances are valid.

Once we see that it is possible for someone to believe and therefore to represent things in this practical manner, then it should be clear that many of the things we believe are represented for us in precisely this way. For our judgements are conducted all of the time on the basis of principles of reasoning that we rarely stop to spell out. Not just deductive principles of reasoning from judgement to judgement, as in the case of the *modus ponens* principle. Also the probabilistic principles that guide us in moving inductively from observation to observation, as we build up our picture of how things are in this or that situation. And also the principles that guide us in moving from perception to judgement and from judgement to the expectation of perception: the principle that takes us, for example, from the sensation of redness and the assumption that nothing is amiss to the judgement that something is red and from the judgement that something is red to the expectation that it will look red if nothing is amiss.

Nor is it just an accident that many of the things we believe are represented to us in a practical manner. Lewis Carroll's story of Achilles and the Tortoise shows that this is an inescapable feature of our beliefs. Achilles believes he can force the Tortoise to admit Z, given that he admits two premises, A and B, which logically imply Z. But the Tortoise insists that he needs more than A and B as premises; he also needs C: if A and B are true, Z must be true. Very well, says Achilles: you admit A and B and C, so now you must admit Z. No, replies the Tortoise, for I must also endorse another premise, D: if A and B and C are true, Z must be true. The lesson is that in order to reason from certain judgementally accepted premises to judgementally accepted conclusion, we have to believe in the practical way that such premises support such a conclusion; or if we take that as itself a premise, then we have to believe in the practical way that the new premises support the conclusion; and so on.

With our distinction in hand, it should be clear that in conceptually representing things to ourselves we may occupy either a relatively practical perspective or a relatively non-practical perspective. This distinction offers a parallel to the distinctions between indexical and non-indexical, figurative and non-figurative. If there is any contrast with those earlier dichotomies, it is simply that there is no such thing as the final, completely non-practical representation of anything: that is the lesson of Lewis Carroll's tale.

As the counterpart of those other distinctions, it should be no surprise to find that the divide between practical and non-practical conceptualisation holds out the same prospect of ontic but not heuristic reduction. It may be possible from a less practical point of view to take account of everything that shapes the practical representation of certain facts. But it is clearly not going to be possible to represent them and know them in the same way: some of the factors that the non-practical representation takes into account will be put to use in the practical representation in a way that cannot be replicated – though it may be simulated in imagination – at the less practical perspective.

Take, for example, the practical way in which most of us believe that various things follow from others. We believe them just so far as registering the entailing matters is not an inert affair; it involves seeing them as necessitating the entailed. The field of representation, as we might put it, is highly charged. These considerations, these matters of perception, just are reasons for making this or that judgement. Their status as reasons reaches out and grips our minds under the practical way of believing in the principles that countenance them as reasons. Thus the happy look on someone's face announces pleasure; the manifest weight of a load makes equally salient the strain that someone carrying it must feel; the clink of the billiard balls reveals immediately the causality at work in shifting the second, previously stationary ball; and so on. The world as practically represented is inferentially alive.

With any practical representation of things, it is clearly going to be possible to spell out the principles involved and to give a judgemental, less practical account of how things are depicted there. In this sense it is going to be possible to give an ontic reduction of the practical perspective to a perspective that is less practical. But equally clearly, it is going to be impossible at the less practical perspective to replicate the way things are seen at the practical one; it is going to be impossible to provide a heuristic reduction. For while we may be able at the less practical perspective to itemise the ratiocinative dispositions that play a role in the practical representation of things, we will not be able to put those dispositions to work in the same way. We will not be able to let the represented world come alive in the inferential manner associated with the presence of such dispositions. Someone might be quite willing to endorse in a non-practical way a variety of principles of reasoning but suffer from such an ailment that they are incapable of having those principles inform the way they see things; they might have to conduct their reasoning in a painful, step-by-step fashion.

Affective and non-affective representation

We mentioned in illustration of practical belief, that a person may believe in a principle of reasoning through being disposed to treat certain judgementally or perceptually registered contents in a suitable way: as reasons for drawing appropriate conclusions. But it is not only our judgements and perceptions that give us contents: that give us ways things seem. Our moods and emotions and desires may also give us corresponding appearances. Our gloom may make things seem hopeless, our embarrassment may make a situation excruciating, our pleasure may make a painting look beautiful, our desires may give various prospects an attractive or repulsive aspect.

Once we see this, we must admit the possibility that as people may argue from something's looking red in a situation where nothing is taken to be amiss to its actually being red, so they may argue in corresponding ways from parallel appearances. They may argue from something's looking attractive in

76

a situation where nothing is taken to be amiss, for example, to its being the sort of thing that is genuinely attractive, even perhaps desirable (see Smith 1994). This observation shows that the category of practical belief may be broader than our earlier discussion suggested.

But it also shows something else. Suppose that I ordinarily come to judge that one or another option is desirable by reliance on the principle that links what looks attractive in situations where nothing is amiss to what is desirable. If I believe that principle in practical mode, then that means that I will ordinarily come to judge that one or another option is desirable through finding it attractive – through coming to desire it – in circumstances where nothing seems to be amiss. The attraction or non-attraction of options, in the absence of a belief that things are in any way amiss, will serve as the ordinary inferential prompt for judging that something is desirable or not desirable. My evaluative judgements will generally have an affective character. They will not leave me cold. They will be non-inductively associated with the presence of corresponding desires (Jackson and Pettit 1995). There will be an internal connection between evaluation – the fact of making an evaluation – and feeling.

Our observation points us, then, to a further divide among conceptual representations, apart from those between the indexical and non-indexical, the figurative and non-figurative, and the practical and non-practical. Conceptual representations of how things are may be affective, involving the presence of mood or emotion or desire or something of that kind. Or they may be more or less non-affective.

This divide, as we would expect, conforms to the now familiar pattern. We may fully understand from a non-affective point of view how it is that those who enjoy certain affections in the presence of things may come to represent those things in various patterns. We may be able to offer an ontic reduction of the affective perspective to a non-affective one. But that is not to say that we will be able to provide a heuristic reduction of the affective perspective. For the factors – the affections – which play a background role in the affective perspective, helping to shape how things are represented there, can only be taken into account in a foreground way within the non-affective. They can be itemised but they cannot be put to work; they can be mentioned but they cannot be used. We all realise from time to time that were nothing amiss we would indeed find a certain option the attractive one and that we do not actually find it attractive, because things are amiss in a certain way: we are at a low ebb and are suffering a temporary value-blindness. Someone who was locked into that position would be able to take full ontic account of how things are registered in ordinary judgements of value but they would not be able to provide themselves with the same mode of representation and knowledge.

Philosophy in a perspectivist perspective

The discussion of the integrative reducibility of the indexical to the non-indexical, and this last sketch of how the same structure is found in other cases, should help to make plausible the central claim I want to make about perspectivism. This is that while perspectivism is sound – while there are many different discourses, each enjoying a relative independence from the others – this does not mean either that reality is multiple or that our vision of reality is multiple. The discussion should establish the robust prospect that wherever there are divergent, discursive perspectives, it will be possible to provide an integrative reduction of one to the other, or of both to a third.

Our discussion does more, however, than just support this abstract claim and this challenge to those who think that perspectivism forces us to postulate a multiple reality or multiple vision. It points us towards an important lesson for philosophy in general, though not a lesson that I can develop fully here. This is that many stock objections to philosophical, broadly reductive accounts of certain phenomena may be misplaced; they may suppose that the aim is to provide translational reduction rather than reduction of an integrative sort.

Consider the complaint, associated in particular with Kripke's Wittgenstein, that there is nothing naturalistic in which rule-following can apparently consist: nothing that could normatively guide us, and guide us in an indefinite range of cases, in the way that we are apparently guided when we follow rules (Kripke 1982). Or consider the complaint that it is necessarily impossible to provide a compatibilist, naturalistic account of free will, for no matter how much indeterminacy is left by the physical world, and no matter how sophisticated the mechanisms that I embody, still there will be nothing available to answer to my sense that I can choose to do or not to do such and such (Van Inwagen 1983). Or consider, finally, the familiar reflection that however detailed an account we offer of the cognitive architecture and processing of human beings, or indeed of their neurobiological constitution, we cannot ever hope to identify consciousness thereby: such an account will never make sense of there being something it is like to be human and to enjoy human experience; it will never take us beyond physical dynamics (Chalmers 1996: 121).

The motif that recurs in complaints like these is: keep adding wood and all you'll have is wood. Keep adding non-normative factors and all you'll have is non-normative; keep adding non-autonomous causal loops and all you'll have is non-autonomous; keep adding non-conscious scanning devices and all you'll have is non-conscious. But from the point of view developed here, this criticism does not look to be overwhelming.

It is possible to account ontically for indexical representation and indexical facts – the matters reported indexically – in non-indexical terms; and yet we shouldn't think that such accounting will offer us anything that has the heuristic presence of the indexical. And a similar message holds for attempts to make sense of the figurative in terms of the non-figurative, the practical in terms of the non-practical, and the affective in terms of the non-affective. Why then should we expect attempts to account for normativity, free will or consciousness to give us a heuristic sense of that phenomenon? We might as sensibly hope for a proof of God's existence that would bring us to our knees at the conclusion.

I have argued elsewhere that the experience of normativity which characterises rule-following involves a representation of rules – say, a representation of the properties that we seek to track in predication – that puts into play two distinct background factors (Pettit 1990; 1996). One is a disposition to extrapolate in a certain way from various sets of exemplars of the predicate and so a tendency to see those exemplars as instances of a more or less determinate pattern or property. The other is a disposition to authorise other people's (or one's other selves') predicative responses, side by side with one's own, and to identify the property as that which is guaranteed to correspond with one's response only when things are such as to facilitate convergence between authorised respondents: only when things, as we theorists might say, are normal or even ideal (Pettit 1998b). Such an account of rule-following countenances a narrower perspective – that of the subject who instantiates the two dispositions – than the explanatory perspective from which it is offered. Even if the account is successful, then, it should not be surprising that it does not make palpable for someone at the explanatory perspective the pattern – a pattern expressed in the language of 'ought' and 'right' – that is allegedly salient to the subject of the dispositions.

What is true of such an account of rule-following ought to hold also for certain accounts of free will: for example, for those that follow in the tradition of Peter Strawson's (1982) paper on 'Freedom and Resentment', but without embracing multiple vision (see Pettit and Smith 1996). These accounts would seek to make impersonal, ontic sense of what free will involves, while emphasising that the ontic matters in question present themselves very differently within an involved interpersonal perspective. The key to the approach is the idea that what is distinctive about our experience of free will is not the facts registered in that experience so much as the heuristic mode in which they are registered. That mode of registering explains the grip that the notion of free will has on our minds and hearts.

As this lesson bears on the analysis of normativity and free will, so it may also bear on the possibility of accounting for consciousness. Suppose we can ontically reduce all that is tracked in conscious experience: say, in the experience of certain things as coloured. It ought not to be an objection that someone who comes to see red things for the first time, even someone who had total knowledge of the ontically reductive facts, will learn a new fact (Jackson 1982, 1986). We will say that however new the mode of presentation, what the person registers is a fact that is no more additional to the established facts than are indexical facts additional to non-indexical. But won't the person at least learn the new fact that old fact that can be presented in a second mode (Chalmers 1996: 142)? No. The person will also have known that previously; what he or she will achieve in coming to see things as red is something akin to a practical skill (Lewis 1990): access to the second mode of presentation.

In each of these cases, we can imagine a successful reduction of the phenomenon in question that does not do the equivalent of bringing those of us putting forward the reduction to our knees: that does not give us a palpable, engaged sense of normativity or free will or consciousness. The test of the success of the reduction will be that when we try to simulate the position of someone at the relevant, narrower perspective, we find ourselves forced to acknowledge that from that perspective things would be precisely as we experience them in our everyday sense of normativity, free will or consciousness. But it will require simulation of the narrower perspective to be persuaded of this; the reduction in itself will not carry a power of phenomenological conviction.

The lessons in the cases just mentioned combine to provide hope that there may be a comprehensive, relatively neutral scheme available within which we can give an integrative reduction of different perspectives and discourses.[5] Take physicalism, for example, understanding it to be the doctrine that if we replicate the microphysical aspect of the actual world, adding nothing on the way, then we will replicate all other aspects of the actual world as well; the actual world does not involve any particulars, any properties or any laws that are not fully provided for by microphysical arrangements (Jackson 1998; Pettit 1993). If physicalism is true, then it ought to be possible in microphysical terms to account ontically for all the phenomena there are. That may seem outlandish if ontic accounts are expected to be heuristic accounts, for the language of microphysics is clearly lacking in endless respects. It is not going to be indexical or figurative or affective in character, for example; and it is not going to be as practical as many other forms of representation. But once we recognise that ontic accounting does not mean heuristic accounting, the suggestion begins to make sense.

More than that, indeed, the suggestion begins to assume the form of a really challenging programme. Think of how philosophers have worked in recent years to make sense of how a purely physical brain and organism could come to be minded in the fashion of an intentional and thinking system. If physicalism is correct – or if it represents a useful working hypothesis – then that sort of investigation exemplifies a more general programme. This would consist in the attempt to make ontic sense of a variety of phenomena – phenomena like rule-following, free will and consciousness – under the assumption that the only materials allowed are those that we can reasonably expect to populate the microphysical realm.

To conclude, an objection to physicalism suggests that the microphysical perspective is more encompassing than the various perspectives we assume in tracking colours and norms, for example, free capacities and conscious experiences. But in suggesting this, doesn't it thereby insinuate that really the phenomena tracked in those other viewpoints are chimeras? They seem to be there so long as we stick to a suitably narrow perspective but as soon as we move to a more comprehensive standpoint, they prove as elusive as the end of the rainbow: we reach out and lay our hands on nothing.

I strongly resist this objection. If physics is capable of tracking all that there is, and if it can countenance the phenomena that other narrower modes of representation track, then those other forms of representation also track realities; they can be seen as physics by other means.[6] If that does not seem to be a sufficiently elevated vocation for such ways of representing things, then we must remember that they are modes of access to the world charted in physics by means that physics itself cannot replicate. More than that, indeed, we must remember that they are modes of access to the physical world by means that are of inherent importance for creatures that are living, minded and socialised in the fashion of human beings. The world that would be fully theorised in the final physics only becomes a world fit for humans – a *Lebenswelt* – when it is presented in less encompassing perspectives.[7]

Notes

1   Some will find the word 'epistemic' more natural than 'heuristic' in this and in other contexts in the paper. But I avoid 'epistemic' for the following reason. Those who reject the 'knowledge argument' (Jackson 1982, 1986) say that there is no extra fact known by someone who experiences colour that cannot in principle be known by the person who knows all the physical facts but sees only in black-and-white. And yet such philosophers will typically stress that the person who experiences colour has a very different way of knowing some of those facts. What is different about their way of knowing can hardly be described as epistemic, given rejection of the knowledge argument, but it is readily described as heuristic.

2   I abstract from the difficulty that on some accounts of transworld identity the sentences will not refer to the same individuals and so will not in that strict sense have the same truth-conditions.

3   Ruth Millikan has made me aware that I need not endorse the detail of the Perry story – I may take a line that she herself would find more congenial – and yet use the story for my present purposes.

4   The comments I make here are probably consistent with the well-known position on metaphor defended by Donald Davidson (1978). He maintains that strictly a metaphorical sentence only has a literal truth-condition and in that sense a literal content, but he insists that by startling a hearer the sentence can serve to convey all sorts of other thoughts and reflections. But if Davidson's views are inconsistent with what I remark here, then that is probably the worse for those views. After all, it is surely manifest that metaphor does convey the sort of thing that can serve as the content of a belief. One thing that makes that manifest is that we can easily conditionalise on metaphor and that when we do so, we do not conditionalise on the literal content. If the day of Yeats's death was a dark, cold day, we can say, then he must have been a great poet. It would be a bad joke, and poor taste, to deduce instead: he must have died in winter.

5   My thanks to David Armstrong for pointing out that such a scheme may or may not be physicalist in character and so the lessons do not combine to support physicalism directly.

6   I abstract from the strategy introduced by David Lewis (1996) in his treatment of knowledge. Under this strategy claims at a narrower perspective fade into insignificance as we go to a broader, but I think that it is applicable only in very special cases – see O'Leary-Hawthorn and Pettit (1995).

7   This is the text of the Parcells Lecture, delivered at the University of Connecticut, Storrs in February 1999. I was greatly helped by comments received at the time, and later, from members of the audience, as I was helped by comments received when the paper was first presented at a seminar in the Australian National University in May 1997. My thanks for written comments to Andrew Gleeson, Michael Esfeld, Barry Hindess, Jakob Hohwy, Alex Miller, and a number of anonymous reviewers, and for separate, very useful discussions of the material to Tim Crane, Frank Jackson, Ruth Millikan, Michael Smith and, in particular, Huw Price.

Part II

VALUE PLURALISM AND LIBERALISM

4

WHERE PLURALISTS AND LIBERALS PART COMPANY[1]

John Gray

Introduction

That we cannot have everything is a necessary, not a contingent, truth.

(Berlin 1969: 170)

It is a truism of recent political philosophy that liberal regimes embody a solution to a problem of pluralism. Contemporary liberal theory has sought a ground for liberal institutions in the rational incomparability of incompatible values and conceptions of the good. It has found a solution to the conflicts they engender by locating them in the realm of voluntary association. In this familiar reasoning, a species of moral conflict characteristic of liberal cultures is resolved by the adoption of liberal institutions. The central argument of recent political philosophy moves from liberal premises about pluralism in individual life-plans to liberal conclusions about the priority of individual liberty. It is an unilluminating deduction.

The variety of pluralism that should shape the agenda of political philosophy today is not the pluralism of personal plans and ideals that preoccupies recent liberal theory. It is the strong pluralism of incommensurable goods and bads whose conflicts implicate whole ways of life. Conflicts between communities whose ways of life are incompatible are a major threat to human well-being in the late modern world. They ought to govern the agenda of contemporary political philosophy.

At present that agenda is formed by the project of formulating an apology for liberal institutions. Late twentieth-century political philosophy aimed to find bad reasons for what conventional liberals believe by instinct. In its apologetic idiom contemporary political philosophy resembles late nineteenth century moral philosophy. Its anxious conventionality of outlook is reminiscent of those nineteenth century intuitionists who treated the habits and prejudices embodied in Victorian folkways as unquestioned points in ethical theory.

The relations of value-pluralism with liberal political morality exemplify starkly the apologetic character of recent political philosophy. In the Rawlsian school it has been taken for granted that value-pluralism and liberal ethics go together. In their profoundly enlightening writings on value-pluralism Isaiah Berlin and Joseph Raz argued that liberal institutions have a foundation in values of choice and autonomy. The possibility that pluralism in values might undermine liberal political morality has been entertained only rarely.[2]

My concern here is to explore that unfamiliar prospect. I conclude that if a strong version of pluralism is true, liberalism is indefensible. I do not mean that if there are conflicts of values which reason cannot resolve there can be no reason to defend liberal institutions. There can be many reasons for defending liberal institutions. Yet, if value-pluralism is true, the core claim of all liberal political philosophies – that a liberal regime is ideally the best or most legitimate regime for all humankind – must be rejected.

There is no straight path from the truth of strong value-pluralism to the legitimacy of any regime. Value pluralists have no truck with the idea of an ideal regime. They find the very idea of perfection suspect. Some liberal regimes may be highly legitimate. So too may some non-liberal regimes. In both cases the test that value-pluralists apply is how regimes promote and protect valuable ways of life and ensure a *modus vivendi* among them.

My argument has two parts. First, I consider some of the varieties of ethical pluralism. I distinguish some weak versions of value-pluralism from the strong version that I believe to be true. Strong value-pluralists believe that there are, irreducibly, many varieties of human flourishing. Many of them cannot be combined within one way of life or realised across the lifetime of a single human being. Some of them are rationally incomparable. The human good harbours rival perfections. This is a claim in anthropology. The theory of values it articulates is not sceptical or relativistic. It is a species of objective pluralism.

Second, I argue that strong value-pluralism defeats liberal political morality. Whichever value is taken to be centrally constitutive of liberalism, it can be only one among the conditions and ingredients of the good life; it will sometimes come into conflict with others; and within any such value there will be conflicts – between different equalities, negative liberties or dimensions of autonomy, for example. Principles of rights or justice cannot be insulated from such conflicts within and between goods. Insofar as they have any determinate content principles of right embody substantive conceptions of the good. They express particular understandings of human interests and well-being. These understandings themselves generate value conflicts, some of them rationally irresolvable. Principles of justice and theories of rights cannot settle rationally irresolvable conflicts among values. They are disabled by such conflicts.

If strong pluralism is true then no value can be given a unique priority amongst the ingredients and conditions of the human good. There is no ranking or weighting of goods that can command the assent of all reasonable people. This truth subverts liberal moralities that accord a unique primacy to some good, such as negative liberty or personal autonomy. It undercuts liberal moralities that do not promote any single overriding good but instead seek to rank conflicting goods. It undermines rights-based liberal moralities that aim not to maximise or rank goods but instead to regulate their pursuit by a system of side-constraints. In every case, liberal principles break down when they meet conflicts among the values they seek to promote or regulate that no theory of rights or justice can settle.

This is not to say there cannot be better or worse settlements of conflicts among goods. Within any one way of life conflicts among incommensurables can have settlements that are better or worse in terms of that way of life. When ways of life containing incommensurable goods conflict it is reasonable to seek a *modus vivendi* between them. The terms of such *modi vivendi* will be constrained by a universal minimum morality that specifies a range of generically human goods and bads; but within the vast range of legitimate *modi vivendi* there are many that do not embody the full range of liberal freedoms. The mix of goods and bads that is embodied in liberal institutions has no unique or overriding claim on reason. To suppose that liberal institutions are always and ideally the best solution for the problems created by pluralism is not only unjustified, it is demonstrably unreasonable.

Varieties of value-pluralism

Strong value-pluralism makes three related claims. The first is what might be called *anti-reductionism about values*. The goods of human life are many and cannot be derived from or reduced to any one value. The diverse experiences, activities, options, projects and virtues that enter into good lives for humans are not tokens of a single type. Contrary to Bentham and Plato, the human good is irreducibly diverse. The goods of human life have no common denominator.

Second, goods are often incompatible and sometimes rivalrous. They may crowd one another out, exclude one another altogether, or belong to ways of life that are by necessity uncombinable. Not only valuable options, virtues and whole conceptions of the good may be incompatible; so also may be rights and the requirements of fairness. Let us call this non-harmony among values.

Third, there is no principle or set of principles that enables conflicts among values to be resolved in ways acceptable to all reasonable people. Diverse and conflicting goods and evils sometimes cannot be rationally compared or traded off. There is no *summum bonum* or hierarchy of goods in terms of which human lives can be weighed or ranked. Contrary to J.S. Mill and Aristotle, there is no one kind of life that is the best life for all humankind or for any single person. The diverse types of flourishing of which humans are capable are not only often uncombinable, sometimes they are rationally incomparable. Let us call this value-incommensurability.

It is the last of these three claims that best marks out strong value-pluralism. Many philosophers accept that goods are irreducibly diverse and often uncombinable; but they deny that their conflicts may be rationally irresolvable. Griffin and Stocker are among them (Griffin 1986, Stocker 1990). I will not discuss this weak variant of value-pluralism. This is partly because I think it uninteresting and false, but chiefly because I am concerned here with the claim that strong value-pluralism poses no threat to liberal morality or else actually supports it.

Consider some of the different ways in which values can conflict. Some goods can be embodied in a variety of combinations, but the price of promoting all of them is that none is achieved to the extent it might be if it were pursued alone. Sometimes goods exclude one another altogether. There may be valuable options within one human life or way of life that, either as a matter of fact or in virtue of how they are constituted, cannot be combined at all. The reasons why goods cannot be combined may be more or less contingent. A career of drinking absinthe for pleasure cannot be combined with the fulfilments that go with longevity; but technological advance might allow a liquor to be invented that produces the same pleasure as absinthe without its life-shortening side-effects. Here the incompatibility of goods is highly contingent. It can be overcome without altering either of the goods concerned. There is no reason in the constitution of the goods why we should not have a great deal more of both of them. Because they are not mutually dependent or partly constitutive of one another they can be pursued, perhaps even maximised, not only separately but also conjointly.

In other cases, disharmony among goods arises from deeper features of human life. No-one can hope to be both a chess grand master and a world-class ballet dancer. The brevity of the human life-span, together with the demands these activities place upon the human organism, preclude any of us achieving in both of them the level of excellence that a few can achieve in each.

If humans lived much longer than they do, and if their physical and intellectual powers were greatly augmented, then perhaps many of us could achieve what now none can hope for; but if the human life-span were to be greatly extended and our natural powers significantly enhanced much else would change in the way we live. Sometimes goods cannot be combined in virtue of the natural necessities of human life. The question whether such conflicts express regularities in human life that are contingent (though unalterable) or whether they articulate conceptual impossibilities is not always easily answerable. In considering different sorts of conflict among values, a sharp distinction between those that are matters of fact and those that express logical truths may not be helpful.

A better way of thinking about what is accidental and what is necessary in such conflicts is suggested by Wittgenstein when he writes in *On Certainty:*

> The river-bed of thoughts may shift. But I distinguish between the movement of the waters on the river-bed and the shift of the bed itself; though there is not a sharp division of the one from the other and the bank of that river consists partly of hard rock, subject to no alteration or only to an imperceptible one, which now in one place now in another gets washed away or deposited.
>
> (Wittgenstein 1974: 15, sections 97 and 99)

Wittgenstein's metaphor suggests that whether values are uncombinable as a matter of necessity may be itself a matter of degree.

Some ways of life cannot be combined because they embody alternatives that are mutually exclusive. A life of risk and adventure and a life of tranquillity and contemplation cannot both be lived by one person across an entire lifetime. Yet, within limits, most can alternate between them. Though they exclude each other as alternatives that can be adopted conjointly they can be pursued successively. But one need not be better or worse than the other.

One who has lived a life of action and adventure and then adopts a life of tranquillity and contemplation need not have found any flaw in the life he relinquishes. Both may be excellent; but the dispositions needed for an active life crowd out those required by success in a life of contemplation. Because they drive one another out – in that neither of them can be highly developed in the life of one who displays the other – some ideals of personal development are not fully realisable.

J.S. Mill's ideal of all-round individual development – 'individuality' – falls into this category. In *On Liberty*, Mill imagines that there is a form of life that is uniquely best for each of us. Mill advocates experiments in living as means whereby each of us can discover the contents of this unique life. But if some of a person's powers can be developed only at the expense of others, some of his needs met only at the cost of thwarting others, some aspects of the good life lived only at the price of altogether shutting off others, then all-round development is not a possibility.

This impossibility may apply over time as well as at any one time. Some ways of life alter their practitioners irreversibly. They thereby rule out some other ways of life forever. If both the way of life that I opt for and those that I thereby forfeit forever answer deep needs of my nature then there is no life in which my nature, can be fully realised.

The idea that the good life for humans is one in which each of us satisfies fully all the demands of his individual nature may not be wholly coherent. If some kinds of personal creativity depend upon lacks or defect, as when the creativity of a Van Gogh or Kafka expresses repressed or unresolved dilemmas, if increased self-knowledge can diminish creativity or vitality, then an ideal of personal life in which all of our individual powers are maximally developed is unrealisable.

Ethical theories in which the idea of realising our individual natures is central break down on the same conflicts that defeat an ethics whose core is a conception of the best life for the species. The ethics of Spinoza and Mill founder for the same reason that undermines those of Aristotle and Marx. For individual human beings, as for the human species, all-round development is not an option. Experiments in living cannot enable us to discover a way of life in which all our powers are developed and our needs met. There is no such life.

Some virtues belong to ways of life that are constitutively uncombinable. The Aristotelian virtues of the great-souled man cannot be mixed – in a person or a society – with the virtues of humility that are preached in the New Testament. The warrior virtues celebrated in *The Iliad* cannot be mixed with those of Socratic inquirers. These are virtues that belong to ways of life whose mutual exclusivity arises in part from the moral notions by which they are constituted. They exclude one another because they cannot be admixed without incoherence. Such virtues cannot be combined, not because of any narrowness in the constitution of the species, but as a matter of their logic or grammar.

It may not always be easy to tell the difference between generically human virtues that have been given different cultural renderings and virtues that are specific to different ways of life. For the purposes of my present argument this does not matter. Rationally undecidable dilemmas can occur both within and between ways of life. They can arise when different virtues make competing demands within a way of life and when virtues distinctive of different ways of life have incompatible implications. In the latter case whole ways of life come into conflict.

The ways of life prescribed by universalist religions are inherently incompatible. Particularist faiths enjoin practices that cannot be admixed. Practitioners of Shinto and Orthodox Judaism have ways of life that cannot be combined. Such particularist faiths are inherently exclusive of one another but, because they make few prescriptions for all humankind, they are not inevitably rivals. In contrast, Christianity and Islam are necessarily rivals. If a person gives up life as a Christian for life as a Muslim he must judge the life he lived as a Christian to be wanting. He cannot wish merely to try another style of life. He must have concluded that the claims to truth made by Christianity are in error and the way of life that is founded upon them flawed. Here the conflict of ways of life expresses a contradiction between beliefs. Christian and Muslim ways of life are not rivals in virtue of the practices they enjoin upon their believers; they are rivals in virtue of the contradictory moral beliefs by which each is partly constituted.

If value-pluralism is true then this kind of conflict between ways of life is unnecessary. It always depends on mistaken beliefs. Strong pluralism does not reject all universal moral claims. It does not deny that there are universal, pan-cultural goods and bads – it affirms their reality. It sees such universal values as marking boundary conditions beyond which worthwhile human lives cannot be lived. For those who are subject to them the practices of slavery and genocide are insuperable obstacles to a worthwhile human life; but there are indefinitely many ways of life that lack these and other practices precluded by the universal minimum of generically human values (Hampshire 1989).[3]

Strong pluralism denies that universal values are fully realisable only in one way of life. It repudiates the central claim of universalist religions to have identified the right or best way of life for all humankind. It rejects the secularisation of this claim in the universalist moralities of the Enlightenment. It therefore rejects the claim that the human good can be fully realised only in a liberal regime.

Conflicts arising from the clashing universalist claims of religious fundamentalists are founded on errors. Internalising the truth of value-pluralism within a human subject or a culture has the effect of dissolving such rivalries. In this way accepting the truth of value-pluralism can reduce conflicts among values and promote *modus vivendi*. A similar result follows for the rivalry of liberal regimes with some (non-fundamentalist) illiberal regimes. If the universalist beliefs that shape liberal regimes are mistaken then their rivalry with such non-liberal regimes is illusory. Liberal and non-liberal regimes need not be rivals – they may be alternatives. This is a result of no small consequence for liberal cultures. I return to it in the conclusion of this inquiry.

There need be nothing tragic in conflicts of values, they may bespeak the abundance of good lives that are available to humans. There is tragedy where weighty obligations conflict and the right action contains wrong. There is tragedy where virtues and excellences depend for their existence on vices or defects, as when artistic creativity depends on psychological repression or personal unhappiness. There may be tragedy when a great good depends for its existence on a great evil. Bads as well as goods may be incommensurate. The issue of what is the best mixture of goods and bads may be undecidable.

The reductive-monistic traditions of ethical thought that we inherit from Socratic and Christian sources insist that when goods (or bads) conflict they can be ranked in a hierarchy that all reasonable people will accept. Aristotle was clear that the best life was open to only a few human beings; he was in no doubt what that life was, a life of friendship and philosophical inquiry. J.S. Mill thought the best life for each of us has some unique features; but he never doubted that for all fully developed human beings the higher pleasures of the intellect and the moral imagination trump the lower pleasures of sensuous pleasure and physical activity.

Aristotle and Mill are in the central tradition of western ethical theory. They do not doubt that where good lives cannot be combined they can be ranked for the species and for its individual members in a hierarchy of value.

Strong pluralists stand outside this tradition. They deny that reason compels assent to any hierarchy among the goods that occur in flourishing human lives. They affirm that some good lives cannot be compared in value. Goods may be incommensurate in virtue of the social conventions that make them what they are. Consider friendship and justice. Someone who charges money for his company when those he knows are in trouble is not a friend. This does not mean that friendship is incomparably more valuable than money. To say that friendship and money are incommensurate goods is not to rank friendship over any amount of money. If that were what is meant by saying these goods are incommensurate, the effect of incommensurability in blocking an exchange of money for friendship would be one-way. Yet, on the contrary, those who perceive that friendship is not a marketable good will no more try to buy it than to sell it. To need to buy friendship is a tragic condition. It is tragic not because friendship is infinitely more valuable than money, but because friends, unlike psychotherapists or sexual partners, say, cannot be bought.

To affirm that goods are incommensurate is not to rank them in a lexical ordering. It is to say that they cannot be so ranked. Someone might perceive that friendship and money are incommensurables and yet, if required to choose between them, choose the good that can be bought. In so doing they may act wrongly – by defaulting on a family obligation, perhaps – but they are not exchanging something infinitely precious for something that has no value. Nor are they making a trade-off between two goods because one is worth more than the other – they are adopting a particular kind of life. There need be no loss for them in this.

Conflicts among many incommensurable goods can be dissolved by breaking down their constitutive conventions. This is what moral rebels and reformers often seek to do, sometimes with good reason. If a code of honour makes demands whose effect is to threaten the safety of loved ones, there may be reason to dispel that moral conflict by dissolving the conventions that generate it. Not all incommensurable goods promote the well-being of those entrained by the practices that engender them.

Yet we can easily imagine a society in which pervasive commensurability has impoverished human life. A world that contained neither justice nor friendship would be free of the tragic conflicts that can arise from conflicts between them; but this would be the freedom from tragedy that sometimes goes with utter poverty, not that which comes with an abundance of options.

We have here a clue as to why moral reformers sometimes establish incommensurabilities where they have not hitherto existed. When they prohibited slavery abolitionists contributed to making persons and chattels incommensurables. As a result human beings can be neither bought nor sold as property, even if they consent to the exchange.

In a world in which all goods were for sale one type of incommensurability would have ceased to exist. This would not be because goods that once were incommensurate with money could now be bought and sold. It would be because some of the goods that engender incommensurability had been destroyed. Like friendship, justice is constituted by certain conventions, among these are conventions blocking the exchange of trial verdicts for money. When we say that there are countries in which justice can be bought we mean that in those countries there is no justice. One of the goods that engendered incommensurability has been destroyed.

Some ethical theories shatter incommensurability in a similar way. Classical utilitarianism and more recent split-level, indirect utilitarian theories aim to make incommensurables comparable by developing a calculus or metric enabling them to be traded off against one another and the result assigned an aggregate value. A value-pluralist does not deny that such a metric can be constructed. Goods that are irreducibly different can always be made comparable as tokens of a single type of value. It is not impossibly difficult to render the goods of a happy human life into the jargon of preference utilitarianism.

The objection a value-pluralist makes to all such accounts is that they displace the evidences of ethical life for the sake of a theory. What is the authority of moral theory when it has this result? It is a matter of common experience that some practical and moral dilemmas are undecidable. Theories that purport to solve these dilemmas do so at the price of dissolving or compromising the goods that generate them. The task of theory in ethics is to track coherence in ethical life where it can be found, not to invent it. Ethical theories that achieve consistency at the price of disregarding the evidences of ethical life have little claim on reason.

Incommensurable goods are not always constituted by social conventions. They are not confined to ethical contexts. They are not peculiar to humans. Some may be found in the lives of other animals. They do not always depend on differences amongst cultures. Some incommensurable values – some goods, some bads, some virtues, some vices – are anthropological universals.

To be at risk of a violent death at the hands of one's fellows is, as Hobbes contended, a great threat to any kind of human flourishing; but it cannot be, as he supposed, the *summum malum* of human life. Lifelong under-nourishment can be no less of an obstacle to human well-being. It may be impossible to judge a non-liberal regime in which press freedom is restricted but no one is undernourished as better or worse than a liberal regime that contains a malnourished underclass. A non-liberal regime that protects its citizens against the Hobbesian evils of crime and civil strife by limiting freedom of religion may not be better or worse than a liberal regime in which religious freedom is protected but citizens are unsafe from crime and civil disorder.

There are generically human goods and bads. They are often competitive. Sometimes there is no single best mixture of them. Any ethical theory that denies the reality of such rationally undecidable dilemmas among anthropologically universal values is flawed. Theories of natural law, Kantian philosophies of right and all liberal political theories are flawed in this way.

To say of goods that their worth is not rationally comparable does not mean that one is incomparably more valuable than the other. It means that no such comparative judgement is possible. That does not mean that incommensurable goods are incomparable in value with any other good. When we judge goods to be incommensurables we mean that they cannot be compared as to value with one another, not absurdly, that their value cannot be compared with that of any other good. Judgements ascribing incommensurability are not admissions of indeterminacy. Indeterminacy may sometimes be a mark or symptom of incommensurability, but then it is evidence of incommensurability, not a criterion for it.

Judgements of incommensurability track relational properties among goods and bads. We can judge the life of a crack addict to be a poorer human life than that of either a carer in a leprosarium or judicious *bon viveur* without being able to rank the carer's against the hedonist's. Incommensurability can be a transitive relation. If the life of a carer is incommensurate with that of a *bon viveur* and the life of a *bon viveur* with that of a creative artist such as Gauguin, then the carer's life and Gauguin's will also be incommensurate. Incommensurability need not be an impediment to practical or moral reasoning.[4]

Strong pluralists claim knowledge of the human good. They claim that the varieties of human flourishing cannot be contained within any one life or one way of life and that some of them cannot be compared in value. There need be no single reason why the worth of goods cannot be rationally compared. Incommensurability may have many sources – I offer no general account of it here. Wherever it exists, it is not a result of any imperfection in human understanding but it is a fact of ethical life. When it occurs amongst generically human goods and bads it is a final truth about the human world.

For strong pluralists, as for C.S. Peirce, truth is what inquirers are fated to converge upon; but in ethics we are destined to come to a consensus that humans flourish in divergent forms of life whose worth cannot be compared. As Raz has put it: 'where there is incommensurability it is the ultimate truth. There is nothing further behind it, nor is it a sign of imperfection' (Raz 1986: 327).

How strong pluralism defeats liberalism

There is an extremely familiar argument that the kinds of conflicts among goods which strong pluralism tracks cannot threaten liberal values. It tells us that liberal political morality consists of principles of right that do not presuppose any particular conception of the good. If liberal principles do depend on a conception of the human good, it is so parsimonious that it cannot spawn conflicts among incommensurables. Liberal principles regulate the terms within which substantive goods may be pursued. If these goods are, that does not affect the principles. John Rawls puts this conventional view canonically: '... liberal principles can be applied following the usual guidelines of public inquiry and rules for assessing evidence.... Hence applying liberal principles has a certain simplicity' (Rawls 1993: 162).[5] If strong pluralism is true, no political morality can be sealed off from conflicts of goods in this way. To suppose that liberal principles can be so insulated makes sense only if they do not themselves engender conflicts among incommensurables. Yet the principles of liberal morality acquire a definite application only insofar as they regulate specific goods. Each of these goods – negative liberty, personal autonomy, or whatever – itself generates conflicts among incommensurables.

Liberal principles founder where the goods they regulate encompass conflicting values and rational inquiry cannot yield a judgement as to how these conflicts are rightly settled. Principles of right cannot arbitrate conflict among divergent conceptions of well-being. Their content varies according to that of those conceptions. In Rawls, as in Nozick and Dworkin, liberal principles are meant to be sheltered from the kinds of conflict that can arise between ways of life partly constituted by incommensurable goods. This protection is illusory if such conflicts enter into the content and application of liberal principles themselves.

The belief that intractable disagreements about the human good can be resolved for the purposes of law or public policy by a theory of rights or basic liberties is not an inadvertence in recent political philosophy. It expresses the quintessential illusion of liberalism. In political philosophy claims about rights are always conclusions, never foundations. The bottom line is always an understanding of the good. Theories of the right cannot circumvent deep divergences concerning the good. The project of a rights-based political morality is incoherent (Raz 1994).

Consider Rawls's account of the basic liberties. Rawls developed this in response to Herbert Hart (1975). Hart showed that Rawls's requirement that each person have the maximum liberty consistent with every other person having the same liberty, was disabled by an indeterminacy. He argued that judgements about what constituted the greatest liberty embody assessments of the relative importance of the human interests they protect. Judgements about what is the greatest liberty will vary along with these comparative assessments of human interests. There is no value-neutral method of judging the greatest liberty. Different ideals of life will support divergent accounts of human interests. They will thereby yield conflicting judgements about maximal liberty. Hart's argument demonstrates that comparative judgements about greater and lesser liberty cannot be insulated from controversial ideals of the good life. Indeed we can make such judgements only by deploying some such ideal. If, however, ideals of the good life are rationally incommensurable, then so are the values of conflicting liberties. Judgements about the greatest liberty avoid indeterminacy only at the cost of ranking human interests according to ideals that may be rationally incomparable. Here, as elsewhere, the indeterminacy of liberal political principles is a mark of the incommensurabilities they conceal.

Rawls responded to Hart's criticism by proposing an account of basic liberties that (he hoped) did not necessitate contested judgements about the greatest liberty. It stipulated that when basic liberties come into competition they were to be 'contoured'. Their scope was reconceived so that their conflicts were defined away. Basic liberties were to be shaped so that they formed a system of compossible claims. Rawls's aim was to avoid the troublesome necessity of making on-balance judgements about the greatest liberty.

Rawls hoped to evade the conflicts of substantive goods that competition among (and within) particular basic liberties commonly reveals. His manoeuvre was a sleight of hand. If freedom of expression clashes with freedom from racial abuse, if the liberty of privacy comes into competition with the freedom of expression demanded by investigative journalists, if the freedom of association claimed by Catholics, Muslims and Orthodox Jews in setting up schools in which gay teachers are not hired impinges on the freedom of gays from homophobic discrimination, there is a conflict of ways of life. It cannot be conjured away by 'contouring' the liberties that are at stake when the competing interests and rival ideals that the different ways of life express make incompatible demands on law and government. Rawls's principles of fairness have a definite content only insofar as they protect weighty human interests; but human interests do not compose a harmonious system. They engender conflicts that can be resolved only by ranking them in accord with some specific conception of human well-being. How the claims of the basic liberties are balanced will vary according to their impact on human interests. That will be assessed variously according to different conceptions of human well-being. Yet no such conception can command the assent of all reasonable people. Even an agreed conception may generate intractably divergent judgements on how conflicts among the ingredients of well-being are to be resolved. Such differences will govern the relative importance accorded to different options and translate into differences about what is the greater liberty. The necessity of making controversial judgements about comparative liberty has not been avoided. It has merely been obscured.

Liberal theories of rights that seek to avoid a commitment to the maximisation of any value cannot avoid the necessity of such judgements. This is as true of Nozick's theory of side-constraints as it is of Rawls's account of basic liberties. Nozickian side-constraints derive whatever determinacy they have in their scope and contents from their contribution to definite human interests. Judgements about what counts as coercion invoke the impact of different kinds of restrictions of options on human interests. Judgements about degrees of coercion depend on rankings of human interests. They will vary as these interests are accorded a different weight in different conceptions of human well-being.

Any understanding of what is encompassed in a right to self-ownership is bound to refer to the interests served by that right. Otherwise the right is contentless. As soon as a side-constraint has a definite content, however, its demands conflict with those of some others. Applying the theory of side-constraints in such cases of conflict involves according some of them greater weight than others. The strategy of 'contouring' side-constraints in order to show that any conflict is illusory fails for the reasons Rawls's account of the basic liberties fails. In any application of a theory of side-constraints, invoking controversial judgements about relative priorities amongst human interests cannot be avoided. Nor is this result restricted to liberal theories in which some version of liberty is the central value. A similar necessity applies in Dworkin's account of the fundamental right to treatment as an equal. All rights-based liberalisms founder on this necessity.

When we judge that one society or person is freer than another we are presupposing a ranking of human interests that articulates a particular conception of well-being. It is only that conception that allows us to weigh, even perhaps to individuate and enumerate, the options we assess. There can be no calculus of liberties whose results are neutral regarding rival conceptions of the good. Liberty cannot be measured because the interests that are opened or closed by different options are often incommensurate. It cannot be maximised because what counts as the greatest liberty varies with different conceptions of the human good.

Liberal theories that aim to avoid maximisation of their central values, such as Nozick's theory of side-constraints, Dworkin's theory of equality and Rawls's theory of the basic liberties, must still appeal to conceptions of human interests to give their principles a definite content. They cannot avoid taking a stand in controversies about what is most important for the human good. Such controversies are sometimes rationally intractable. We are a long way from the simplicity in the application of liberal principles which Rawls envisaged.[6]

Mill's harm principle has an analogous disability. The celebratedly misdescribed 'one very simple principle' prescribes that individual liberty may be restrained only when harm to others is at issue. It cannot be applied in any simple or mechanical way. Applying it involves making judgements of comparative harm. Such judgements will vary according to the content of different accounts of the human good. This is not a mere indeterminacy in the application of Mill's principle. If it was only that it would not be a serious objection to the Millian account. Unlike Rawls's basic liberties, Mill's principle is not meant to protect a fixed set of liberties. It rules out restraint of liberty in the self-regarding area; but that states only a necessary condition of justified restraint. The scope of the liberties Mill's principle protects is determined by applying the principle of utility. What these liberties are will vary with circumstances (Gray 1996, postscript).

By comparison with Rawls's doctrine, this indeterminacy in Mill's principle is not a weakness but an advantage. It relieves Mill of the necessity of attempting to circumvent conflicts amongst liberties. Unlike Rawls, Mill does not imagine that the agenda of political philosophy is set by the legalist project of drafting an ideal constitution. Mill's goal is not to specify any fixed or final list of basic liberties. He aims to offer advice to legislators. His principle of liberty fails to perform this service. It fails not because of any indeterminacy in it but by virtue of the incomparability of the harms and benefits it requires us to assess.

There is no one settlement of conflicting liberties, or rights that any reasonable person is bound to accept. Reasonable people make divergent judgements as to how different structures of rights will contribute to human well-being. There are many ingredients of the good life; none has a weight that always overrides any other. The good life for humans demands a clean and healthy environment, a stable and cohesive society and a distribution of benefits and burdens that is accepted as fair. It requires many other goods as well. There can be no complete or definitive list.

It may be that in a society lacking some of these ingredients no good life can be lived. Yet even among such ingredients of the good there will be conflicts such that if one amongst them waxes others will wane. Depending on their histories and circumstances, different societies will have reason to opt for different mixes even of goods without which no good life can be lived. To impose any single ranking or weighting on the ingredients of the good is unreasonable. This will be so even if – impossibly – reasonable people agree in their judgements as to what are the ingredients of the good. The fact of reasonable divergences in judgements of the relative importance of the various ingredients of the human good undermines all liberal moralities.

It does not follow from the truth that the ingredients of the human good may be incommensurate that there are not better and worse settlements of their conflicts. What follows is only that what makes a settlement of their conflicts better or worse is a local affair. There are no universal principles that rank or weigh generically human goods. Judgements of the relative importance of such goods appeal to their role in a specific way of life. When we ask how the claims of free association are to be balanced against those of collective action in framing trade union law, say, we are asking which settlement of this conflict best embodies a specific way of life. The answer may well be different in societies whose ethical life is highly individualist from those in which it is more solidaristic.

A reasonable balance can be struck among conflicting goods and bads that are incommensurate by considering how different mixes of them contribute to the renewal of a valuable way of life. The content of such a balance will vary with the way of life it expresses. Within a way of life, there are often agent-relative reasons for resolving conflicts among incommensurable values in particular ways. They invoke the mix of incommensurate goods and bads that shapes the way of life. It is this mix of values specific to a particular way of life that allows values whose conflicts cannot be subject to an arbitration acceptable to all reasonable people to be resolved. Such resolutions are internal to particular ways of life. There is no presumption that they will conform to liberal principles. Where they do it is because the way of life they presuppose is that of a liberal culture.

Conclusion

Can it be that Socrates and the creators of the central Western tradition in ethics and politics who followed him have been mistaken, for more than two millennia, that virtue is not knowledge, nor freedom identical with either? That despite the fact that it rules the lives of more men than ever before in its long history, not one of the basic assumptions of this famous view is demonstrable, or, perhaps, even true?

(Berlin 1969: 154)

The problem of pluralism faced by late modern societies is not primarily that created by the existence of incommensurate ideals of personal life. It is finding terms of coexistence for ways of life animated by divergent and incommensurate conceptions of the good. I have argued that a balance can sometimes be struck among conflicting incommensurables by invoking the mix of values characteristic of a particular way of life. But how are conflicts between incommensurate ways of life to be resolved?

Conflicts between incommensurate ways of life are settled by achieving a *modus vivendi* between them.[7] *Modus vivendi* is a reasonable implication of strong pluralism. If strong pluralism is true, no way of life has reason to impose itself on any other, save perhaps when the other violates a minimal morality that is binding on all, and every way of life has reason to seek terms of coexistence with others in which their distinctive goods are preserved. In a *modus vivendi*, ways of life find interests and values they have in common and reach compromises regarding those in which they diverge. Their pursuit of *modus vivendi* is governed by a universal minimum morality that specifies universal goods and bads that mark the boundaries of a worthwhile human life. I have said little about this morality. Here I say only that it works as a constraint on the reasons that practitioners of different ways of life can invoke when they seek a *modus vivendi* between them. Its content overlaps with that of liberal morality in that both proscribe such practices as genocide and slavery; but it underdetermines liberal morality in that it does not dictate distinctive liberal freedoms of the press, religion or autonomous choice.

Liberal institutions are only one solution to the problem of coexistence amongst diverse ways of life. There have been and are others no less legitimate. Among non-liberal institutions that have framed a *modus vivendi* between communities and traditions, the Roman practice of recognising several non-territorial jurisdictions and the Ottoman *millet* system of communal autonomies are notable. In India today Muslim law and secular law apply to different communities. Such institutions are rejected by liberals because they allow insufficient freedom of exit from communities; but freedom of exit is only one good that a regime may have reason to protect. The avoidance of war, the protection of the environment and the maintenance of valuable forms of common life make no less valid claims. Where its exercise endangers such goods individual choice has no automatic or overriding priority.

Sometimes conflicts among communities can be avoided only by policies that restrain individual freedom of choice. Ethnic strife has been avoided in contemporary Singapore by policies some of which could not be implemented in liberal cultures. Policies that discourage the formation of ghettos by limiting freedom of choice in housing are an example. Yet the good such policies protect, for example peace among ethnic communities, is a great good in which some liberal regimes have long been notably deficient. This does not mean that liberal regimes should adopt illiberal policies. It means that liberal regimes sometimes do less well than non-liberal regimes in the *modi vivendi* they engender among communities.

Political choices are sometimes tragic. The ordinary business of government is commonly a quasi-utilitarian enterprise. Framing and implementing economic and social policies often involves an effort at rendering incommensurate goods comparable. That enterprise is a necessary evil in all governments, however liberal they may be. One of the many evils of modern war is the all-encompassing commensurability it imposes on its protagonists. No good escapes the lethal calculus. A similar pressure in the direction of commensurability pervades contemporary health-care. We are often unable to respect incommensurabilities whose reality we do not doubt.

The choice of a regime may incur irreparable losses for those subject to it. This may be no less true of liberal regimes than of others. Sometimes a non-liberal regime may do better than some liberal regimes in enabling and sustaining a *modus vivendi*. At other times liberal and non-liberal regimes may both do well while being incommensurate. At yet others liberal regimes may do best by all relevant criteria. All *modi vivendi*, liberal or non-liberal, close off some paths to the human good. Even in the best *modus vivendi* there is loss.

If strong pluralism is true there is no avoiding loss. Yet loss is not always tragic. If regimes are alternatives rather than rivals then their differences can enrich human life. Human flourishing shows itself in an exfoliation of incompatible ways of life of which none can claim that it uniquely embodies the human good. To be sure, liberal regimes that assert that their freedoms are universal human rights make precisely that claim. Their practices express the belief that negative freedom and personal autonomy are values in the absence of which no worthwhile human life is possible. From this conviction it follows that any way of life or regime in which they are not prized is illegitimate.

100

Liberal polities animated by such universalist beliefs are bound to treat all other regimes and ways of life as rivals or enemies rather than legitimate alternatives. Liberal morality is not a formula for coexistence among regimes that embody different ways of life. So long as the world contains a diversity of regimes it is a prescription for conflict. But if strong pluralism is true, the diversity of regimes, some liberal, some not, need not be a sign that some are illegitimate. It may be an expression of the human good, whose nature it is to be plural.

Pluralism and liberalism are rival doctrines. The political implication of strong pluralism is not liberalism. It is *modus vivendi*. Sometimes *modus vivendi* is best fostered by liberal institutions. But liberal institutions are merely one variety of *modus vivendi*, not always the most legitimate. Where repressive regimes make *modus vivendi* unattainable liberals and pluralists can march together. Where liberal institutions claim universal authority liberals and pluralists must part company.

Liberal regimes are formed partly by a belief in the universal legitimacy of their institutions. In this they resemble the fundamentalist regimes that are presently their defining enemies. Strong pluralism undermines the fundamentalist belief in the universal authority of any single way of life. It thereby undermines the core claim of fundamentalist liberalism. Strong pluralism supports the perception of liberal institutions as local settlements, not embodiments of universal principles. It is bound to subvert the self-understanding of contemporary liberal cultures.

Contemporary philosophers are inclined to hold that the truth of pluralism can be acknowledged fully only in liberal cultures. Bernard Williams has written that 'it is an argument for the liberal society that that society expresses more than any other does a true understanding of the pluralistic nature of values' (Williams 1980: xviii). Richard Rorty has suggested that an awareness of the local character of liberal values enhances their universal appeal: 'To see one's language, one's conscience, one's morality, and one's highest hopes as contingent products, as literalizations of what were once accidentally produced metaphors, is to adopt a self-identity which suits one for citizenship of a liberal state' (Rorty 1989: 61).

If I am not mistaken, the contrary is a more faithful rendering of the matter. Strong pluralism is a subversive truth. It cannot coexist with the articles of faith of any universalist creed. For that reason it is bound to undermine the local certainties of liberal societies.

Notes

1   A draft of this paper was presented to a meeting of the Royal Irish Academy. I am grateful for the comments of Tony O'Connor, Jonathan Riley and Loren Lomasky. I am indebted to Henry Hardy for his written comments on an early draft of this paper and conversation over several years on the subject of pluralism.

2   John Kekes is one of the few who has done so (Kekes 1993; 1997). In earlier
    writings of my own I developed an historicist argument for the near-universal
    legitimacy of liberal institutions that appealed to strong value-pluralism (Gray
    1993: 322–6). I think now that this argument establishes a good deal less than I
    hoped for it.
3   Stuart Hampshire (1989) provides an account of a universal minimum morality
    that deserves wider discussion.
4   The claim that incommensurability entails a breakdown in transitivity seems to be
    made by Joseph Raz (Raz 1986: 325) where he states: 'The test of incommen-
    surability is failure of transitivity.' I endorsed this claim in (Gray 1995a: 56). I
    now think it needs amendment.
5   I have commented on the anti-political character of Rawls's 'political' liberalism
    in (Gray 1997: chapter 3).
6   I develop an early version of this argument in (Gray: 1989: 141–6).
7   I have argued for *modus vivendi* between communities in (Gray 1995b: chapters
    8 and 9).

5

PLURALISM AND SCEPTICISM IN A DISENCHANTED WORLD[1]

Susan Mendus

Introduction

It is a commonplace that the late twentieth century western world was a disenchanted realm – a world in which we can no longer rely upon the existence of God, or teleological conceptions of human nature to justify our moral beliefs and political arrangements. Some have taken this condition to be a cause for celebration, and have argued that it represents man's liberation from myth, superstition and false dogma. Others have seen it as a source of regret and have argued that without the authority of something 'beyond ourselves' we are left aimless and rootless in a world ultimately devoid of moral meaning. Whatever the evaluative conclusion, the philosophical question remains the same: how can we ground morality and politics in a world without metaphysics, theology or teleology?

In this chapter, I do not aspire to provide a complete answer to that question, but only to respond to one set of difficulties alleged to be inherent in justifying morality in conditions of disenchantment. These are the difficulties posed by the claim that without external validation our moral beliefs and political arrangements must be grounded in moral pluralism and scepticism. Again, evaluations differ, and while some embrace pluralism and scepticism, others believe them to be the harbingers of meaninglessness and moral incoherence. However, my aim is to show that, whatever valuation is put on them, they are not the inevitable recourse of the philosopher in disenchanted times, nor are they the only foundations for liberalism understood as the politics of disenchantment.

The next section explains more fully what disenchantment is and what its inconveniences are. I then go on to argue that liberalism, as the politics of a disenchanted world, need not be implicated in either moral pluralism or scepticism. Finally I consider whether liberalism, understood as having no necessary commitment to pluralism and scepticism, nevertheless contains sufficient resources to sustain us morally and politically in the conditions of modernity.

The nature of disenchantment

At the most general level, a disenchanted world is usually characterised as a world bereft of God. This, however, is shorthand for a whole array of circumstances that are alleged to be consequent upon, or associated with, the demise of religious and metaphysical belief. I shall concentrate on two of these: loss of moral authority and loss of moral coherence.

The concern that the modern world is one in which we lack moral authority is given clearest expression by Charles Taylor in *Sources of the Self*. Referring back to his earlier article, 'What Is Human Agency?', Taylor argues that in conditions of modernity questions about what makes life meaningful involve 'strong evaluation', that is:

> They involve discriminations of right or wrong, better or worse, higher or lower, which are not rendered valid by our own desires, inclinations or choices, but rather stand independent of these and offer standards by which they can be judged.
>
> (Taylor 1989: 4)

Taylor expresses this in the language of 'frameworks' and he is insistent that human beings, as strong evaluators, need frameworks within which to situate their actions and make sense of their lives. However, frameworks are problematic in the modern world, where it is no longer possible to see any particular framework as unchallengeable or beyond question. There may be (indeed there are) some people who hold a particular framework unquestioningly. Religious believers presumably fall into this category. They, however, do not represent modernity, but merely one strand of modernity – a strand, moreover, which is highly disputable, even if not disputed by them – and in a world where all frameworks are disputable, questions about the meaning of life become simultaneously unavoidable and unanswerable. Thus, Taylor notes that we are in:

> A fundamentally different existential predicament from that which dominated most previous cultures and still defines the lives of other people today. That alternative is a predicament in which an unchallengeable framework makes imperious demands that we fear being unable to meet. We face the prospect of irretrievable condemnation or exile, of being marked down in obloquy forever, or of being sent to damnation irrevocably ... the form of danger here is utterly different from that which threatens the modern seeker, which is something close to the opposite: the world loses altogether its spiritual

contour, nothing is worth doing, the fear is of a terrifying emptiness,
a kind of vertigo, or even a fracturing of our world and body-space.
(Taylor 1989: 18)

The disenchanted world, then, may be characterised as a world without God,
but its more general nature is that it is a world in which moral judgements
lack the authority provided by an unquestionable framework. The existential
condition of agents in such a world is likely to consist in a lack of moral and
spiritual 'anchorage', while the philosophical condition will be one in which
it is difficult to justify moral beliefs and coercive political arrangements.

This loss of authority hints at a second characteristic of modernity, one
that is given expression by Alasdair MacIntyre. This is that the modern world
lacks moral coherence. For MacIntyre, the rejection of teleological and the-
ological frameworks has resulted in our inhabiting an emotivist culture where
moral disagreement masquerades as argument, but is in fact no more than
the clash of individual wills:

> From our rival conclusions we can argue back to our rival premises;
> but when we do arrive at our premises argument ceases and the
> invocation of one premise against another becomes a matter of pure
> assertion and counter-assertion. Hence perhaps the slightly shrill
> tone of so much moral debate.
>
> (MacIntyre 1985: 8)

For MacIntyre, then, the rival sources are not simply sources of emptiness in
our lives, they are also sources of incoherence in moral argument. Despite
the rejection of foundations, horizons or unquestionable frameworks, we
continue to believe that moral argument is possible, and that it can be conducted on the basis of reason alone, which will adjudicate between rival
frameworks. This, however, is a mistake, for the very possibility of *argument*,
as distinct from mere assertion and counter-assertion, depends upon there
being an accepted framework within which alone things can count as reasonable or unreasonable.

The understanding of disenchantment therefore proceeds in stages: first it
is the loss of any sense that the world has a single and meaningful order independent of us. Second, and at the 'existential' level, that loss raises a (hitherto non-existent) question about what invests our lives with meaning and
legitimises our moral beliefs. Thirdly, but at the philosophical level, it makes
problematic the criteria by which we justify our moral and political beliefs.
Characteristically, what is invoked here is the power of reason, and while
optimists claim that this invocation is one which substitutes rationality for
superstition and dogma, pessimists contend that at best it will 'fail to satisfy',
and that at worst it will convert moral argument into nothing more than a
cacophony of conflicting voices. So the loss of an unchallengeable framework

is loss of moral authority, the recognition of disparate frameworks poses a problem of moral coherence, and the invocation of reason raises the question of how much can be justified in a disenchanted world.

The description of disenchantment provided by Taylor and MacIntyre is in large part a description of the existential condition in which 'we' moderns are likely to find ourselves in a world bereft of God and thus devoid of external authority. At best, we may have certainty within ourselves, but this certainty is constantly jeopardised by the knowledge that others do not share it. There is no unquestionable framework even for those who do not, as a matter of fact, question the framework they adopt. Nor is there any obvious way of reconciling the different demands made by the different frameworks. How, then, can politics accommodate these facts and what conceptual assumptions are necessary for that accommodation?

Two claims are frequently made about the philosophical assumptions that underpin political liberalism as the politics of a disenchanted world. The first is that it implies value pluralism; the second is that it is premised on scepticism. It is these claims that I wish to question, but before discussing them in any detail it will be important to say a bit more about pluralism and scepticism as the philosophical concomitants of liberalism, and about how they are related to disenchantment at the existential level. The examination of the relationship between existential condition and philosophical justification will in fact be a central task of this chapter and I hope that its significance will become clear by the end. I begin, however, with a discussion of pluralism and scepticism as philosophical theories, and of the role they play in the justification of liberalism.

Liberalism, pluralism and scepticism

In the Introduction to *Political Liberalism* John Rawls explains that the book attempts to address a 'serious difficulty' which was unresolved (or unsatisfactorily resolved) in *A Theory of Justice*. The serious difficulty is this:

> A modern democratic society is characterised not simply by a pluralism of comprehensive religious, philosophical and moral doctrines, but by a pluralism of incompatible yet reasonable comprehensive doctrines. No one of these doctrines is affirmed by citizens generally. Nor should one expect that in the foreseeable future one of them, or some other reasonable doctrine, will ever be affirmed by all, or nearly all, citizens.
>
> (Rawls 1993: xvi)

These, famously, are the 'facts of pluralism', and Rawls makes it clear that his central aim in *Political Liberalism* is to indicate how a liberal society can accommodate these facts in a way which is more than a mere *modus vivendi* or accommodation to power. Thus *Political Liberalism* takes as given the fact that we live in a world of disparate and conflicting frameworks, a world in which no single framework or horizon can be taken for granted or accepted unquestioningly. The problem that then needs to be addressed is how we can provide a politics for such a world, and the facts of pluralism provide the premise from which that politics is to be constructed.

It might be concluded from this that liberalism is inevitably committed to pluralism, since it takes as its premise the facts of pluralism. However, before leaping to this conclusion it is important to bear in mind a distinction between pluralism as a statement about the way the modern world is, and pluralism as a theory of moral value. Charles Larmore draws the distinction in the following way:

> What Rawls (and others) call pluralism is the expectable inability of reasonable people to agree upon a comprehensive conception of the good. What Berlin has so memorably described as pluralism, however, is precisely a deep and certainly controversial account of the nature of the good, one according to which objective value is ultimately not of a single kind, but of many kinds. Doctrine and reasonable disagreement about doctrine can hardly be the same thing.
>
> (Larmore 1996a: 154)

So where the value pluralist asserts that the sources of value are many and not one, the Rawlsian simply notes that different people have different views about value – views which, as a matter of fact, are unlikely to be reconciled. Whether this is because the sources of value are indeed many rather than one is something about which the Rawlsian liberal should remain silent. So far from being allied to pluralism, liberalism should take no view about pluralism understood as a doctrine about the sources of value.

The matter cannot, however, be left at that. Rawls's initial problem was to show how the facts of pluralism are to be accommodated politically, and if they are not to be accommodated by invoking value pluralism, then how are they to be accommodated? The multiplicity of frameworks characteristic of modernity has one very obvious explanation, and that is that the sources of moral value are themselves multiple, but if, as Larmore suggests, that explanation is unavailable to Rawls, then what explanation can be provided and how can it reassure us that the inconveniences of disenchantment are not as great as the pessimists fear?

Joshua Cohen has suggested that one explanation of disagreement is to be found in an analysis of the nature and scope of practical reason itself. He advocates a distinction between what can reasonably be affirmed and what is true, and argues that although reason will not always mandate a single moral view, it does not follow from this that no single moral view contains the whole truth. So, when we are faced with persistent disagreement, it is open to us to 'affirm' our own belief while simultaneously acknowledging that belief is not fully mandated by reason. Cohen writes:

> It is permissible to take the *sectarian* route of affirming one's own view, that is, believing it as a matter of faith. And since believing is believing true, a rationally permissible (though not mandatory) response to an apparently irresoluble rivalry of evaluative conceptions is to affirm that one's own view contains the whole truth, while the truths in other views are simply the subsets of those views that intersect with one's own.
>
> (Cohen 1993: 282)

On Cohen's account, then, I may affirm my belief, affirm it as true, and affirm it as the whole truth. Yet I may also concede that this affirmation is not one which reason itself fully underwrites. Reason runs out without running into pluralism, since the explanation of disagreement lies not in any metaphysical claim about the source or sources of value but rather in an analysis of the nature of reason itself.

There are several stories which might be told about how reason can run out without running into value pluralism, not all of which reduce to Cohen's 'affirmation of faith'. For example, Alasdair MacIntyre argues that the power of Sophoclean tragedy lies precisely in its recognition that there is a single, objective moral order, but that our perceptions of it are such that we cannot bring rival moral truths into harmony with one another (MacIntyre 1985: 143). Unlike the value pluralist, who can find consolation in the thought that rival moral truths *cannot* be brought into harmonious order, the Sophoclean tragic hero is condemned by his commitment to moral truth and his simultaneous inability to respond to all its (legitimate) demands. Conflict persists because human understanding is limited, not because the sources of value are many rather than one. The possibility of tragic conflict bears testimony to that fact.

More prosaically, Rawls's discussion of the facts of pluralism emphasises that the ways in which we weigh evidence and assess experience is dependent upon our total outlook, and in the modern world the differences between different outlooks are so great as to make disagreement predictable and largely unavoidable. On Rawls's account, this is not because the values themselves are in principle irreconcilable (again, it is not because the sources of value are many rather than one). Rather, it is because there is no prospect of publicly available evidence and argument yielding uniquely determinate solutions that are rationally compelling upon all. Rawls writes:

> Many conceptions of the world can plausibly be constructed from different standpoints. Diversity naturally arises from our limited powers and different perspectives; it is unrealistic to suppose that all

our differences are rooted solely in ignorance and perversity or else
in the rivalries that result from scarcity.

(Rawls 1980: 542)

So whereas some have argued that differences 'go all the way down' and that
there is no way in principle of reconciling the conflicting claims made by
adherents of rival outlooks, Rawls appears to accept that resolution might be
possible in principle, but simply notes that the diversity characteristic of the
modern world is such as to make it unattainable in practice. This, however,
does not lead to value pluralism, but simply to an acknowledgement of the
facts of pluralism as facts that we cannot reasonably expect to eradicate in
conditions of modernity.

Finally, and at a yet higher level of generality, it has been pointed out that
the persistence of disagreement might be explicable, not by appeal to value
pluralism, but by the scope for indeterminacy in moral argument. John
Skorupski notes that:

Justice may dictate impartiality. And justice is plausibly a fundamental norm. But it may well be underdetermined by those norms what
exactly impartiality requires ... It is not that in these circumstances
there is more than one right theory of justice – there isn't one at all.

(Skorupski 1996: 15)

Underdetermination leads, not to value pluralism, but to indeterminateness;
not to the recognition that there are many right answers, but to the acknowledgement that there is none.

These three accounts all explain disagreement by appeal to the limitations
of reason's powers and although, in each case, the precise nature of those
limitations is differently understood, none of them leads inevitably to a commitment to value pluralism. Some, however, do imply that ultimately the
explanation of disagreement will rest upon scepticism, and certainly Cohen's
claim that in the final analysis we 'affirm' our belief as a matter of sectarian
faith, appears to raise that spectre. For if, in the end, 'irresoluble rivalry'
merely amounts to distinct and conflicting affirmations of faith, affirmations
which are, *ex hypothesi,* recalcitrant to reason, then it seems to follow that liberalism cannot commend itself as true (even though, of course, its adherents
believe it to be true), but only, and at most, as one faith amongst others. And
we might wonder whether that will be enough, for the Rawlsian project was
to explain disagreement in a way which did not involve appeal to metaphysics, but which could nevertheless amount to more than a mere accommodation to power; while the specific challenge posed in this paper is to
show that liberalism can distance itself from the philosophical inconveniences
of disenchantment – value pluralism and scepticism.

Cohen's explanation of persistent disagreement as traceable to the nature
of reason secures the requisite distance from value pluralism, but it seems to

109

do so by turning liberalism into 'just another faith' – one which will be hard-pressed either to assert its superiority as a faith, or to discriminate between faiths on grounds which can rise above the purely pragmatic. It appears, in brief, to purchase freedom from value pluralism only by embroiling itself in moral scepticism. And some commentators have indeed concluded that scepticism is the price liberalism must pay for metaphysical abstinence.

In his recent book, *Justice as Impartiality*, Brian Barry has argued that the proliferation of beliefs characteristic of the modern world must lead us to conclude that liberalism is ultimately grounded in scepticism understood as involving doubt rather than denial. He writes:

> The sheer weight of evidence in favour of scepticism seems over-whelming. It is hard not to be impressed by the fact that so many people have devoted so much effort over so many centuries to a matter of the greatest moment with so little success in the way of securing rational conviction.
>
> (Barry 1995: 171)

The facts of disagreement, then, may avoid implication in value pluralism, but they do imply 'moderate scepticism'. They imply that we must entertain doubt about our moral and political convictions, and this doubt both reflects the existential condition of disenchantment and contributes to the philosophical justification of politics in a disenchanted world.

However, in discussing Rawls's commitment to pluralism, it was noted that there is an important difference between the facts of pluralism and value pluralism. Not only is it the case that the recognition of the former does not entail acceptance of the latter; it is also the case that recognition of the former should lead Rawls to abstain from judging about the latter. Can anything similar be said about philosophical scepticism, or are the facts of disagreement ones which entail that liberalism be grounded in scepticism? Barry clearly thinks that they are. He tells us not only that 'scepticism supplies the premise that is needed to get from the desire for agreement on reasonable terms to the conclusion that no conception of the good should be built into the constitution', but also that *only* this premise will suffice to facilitate that move: 'alternative premises that have been put forward in recent years either presuppose scepticism or can be made coherent only if taken to entail scepticism' (Barry 1995: 172–3).

Amongst the alternative premises which Barry canvasses is that of 'epistemological restraint', which is proposed as a way of justifying liberal neutrality without appeal to scepticism. However, Barry denies that epistemological restraint is a coherent idea, and claims that in order to be made coherent it must be seen as implying scepticism. Therefore, in order to show that liberalism can avoid appeal to scepticism, something must be said in defence of epistemological restraint against Barry's attempt to reduce it to 'moderate scepticism'. What kinds of considerations can be adduced?

In the first place, it is important to be clear what purpose the appeal to epistemological restraint is meant to serve. As employed by Nagel, it aims to provide a justification of liberal neutrality from the basis of an assumption that people are motivated to try to secure agreement. The liberal state recognises that people have different and conflicting conceptions of the good, and it aspires to neutrality between those conceptions. Now one obvious justification of such neutrality is the belief that there is no single correct conception of the good, or at least that we cannot be sufficiently certain about any conception of the good to warrant imposing it on others who do not share it (this is the justification in terms of scepticism). The doctrine of epistemological restraint aims to provide an alternative justification of neutrality, one which does not require that we doubt or deny our own conception of the good (it does not require that we adopt a sceptical attitude towards our conception of the good), but only that we 'abstract from' our commitment to it in deciding what can legitimately be imposed on others. Nagel writes:

> We accept a kind of epistemological division between the private and the public domains: in certain contexts I am constrained to consider my beliefs merely as beliefs rather than as truths, however convinced I may be that they are true, and that I know it. This is not the same thing as scepticism. Of course if I believe something I believe it to be true. I can recognize the possibility that what I believe may be false, but I cannot with respect to any particular present belief of mine think that possibility is realized. Nevertheless, it is possible to separate my attitude toward my belief from my attitude toward the thing believed and refer to my belief alone rather than to its truth in certain contexts of justification.
>
> (Nagel 1987: 230–1)

The question that now arises is whether epistemological restraint, so understood, can provide a coherent foundation for liberal neutrality and whether, in particular, it can justify liberal neutrality without collapsing into scepticism. As we have seen, Barry denies that it can. Taking a conception of scepticism as involving doubt rather than denial, he alleges that epistemological restraint requires that I continue to believe something with conviction even when I am unable to persuade other reasonable people of the truth of it. This, he says, is an implausible demand:

> I question, however, whether certainty from the inside about some view can coherently be combined with the line that it is reasonable for others to reject that same view. The most promising case would seem to be that of a private religious revelation. Suppose that God

were (as it seemed to me) to grant me a vision in which certain truths were revealed. A partisan of epistemological restraint would suggest that I might be absolutely convinced of the veridical nature of this revelation while nevertheless admitting that others could reasonably reject my evidence. But is this really plausible? If I concede that I have no way of convincing others, should that not also lead to a dent in my own certainty?

(Barry 1995: 179)

For Barry, then, everything depends on the extent to which the agent's inner conviction can legitimately withstand his or her failure to persuade others: the philosophical justification of liberal neutrality makes essential reference to the attitude which the agent can legitimately adopt towards his or her beliefs.

For Nagel, by contrast, there is at least the hope that questions of inner conviction might hang free of the success or failure of persuasive strategies, for he claims that:

When we look at certain of our convictions from outside, however justified they may be from within, the appeal to their truth must be seen as merely an appeal to our beliefs, and should be treated as such unless those beliefs can be shown to be justifiable from a more impersonal standpoint.

(Nagel 1987: 230)

And in saying this he implies that it is at least possible to retain conviction 'from the inside' even when it is impossible to persuade those who are 'on the outside'. Crucially, he also claims that we can abstract from our own conviction and differentiate between an appeal to our belief and an appeal to the truth of our belief: my attitude to my belief is separable from my attitude to the thing believed.

Despite (or perhaps because of) Barry's warnings, I want now to suggest that the doctrine of epistemological restraint is one which can illuminate the project of political liberalism. The explanation of how that can be will take us back to the argument adduced by Cohen, and mentioned in the previous section. It will also take us forward to a richer understanding of Taylor's claim that, in a disenchanted world, the world of modernity, we both must be and yet cannot be 'strong evaluators'.

At the beginning of the paper I noted that the analysis of disenchantment offered by Taylor, MacIntyre and others operates at an 'existential' level, and what I meant by that was simply that they concentrate, in large part, on what it may feel like 'from the inside' to inhabit a world which lacks certainty or, in Taylor's terminology, 'unchallengeable frameworks'. By contrast, the preceding discussion of liberalism, pluralism and scepticism has operated at a more justificatory level. Here, we are not concerned with the existential predicament of the individual in modernity, but with the political arrangements that can rationally be defended in a world characterised by disagreement and diversity. Barry's rejection of epistemological restraint as a means of defending liberal neutrality yokes together the justificatory and the existential, for his claim is that there will be (or certainly that there should be) doubt in the mind of the individual who finds himself unable to persuade others of the truth of his own beliefs. Two, rather different, responses may be made to this claim: first, we may wonder whether, in the specific case, doubt is quite as appropriate and straightforward as Barry implies. Second, we may ask what are the wider consequences of yoking together considerations of existential condition and considerations of political justification. I shall take these in turn.

In the example of religious revelation Barry argues that it is not appropriate to remain convinced myself if I am unable to convince others: 'If I concede that I have no way of convincing others, should that not lead to a dent in my own certainty?', he asks. In the specific case, the answer may well be 'Yes, it should'. If, however, we move beyond the case of a specific revelation and consider the religious believer over a longer temporal span, or in a wider conceptual framework, then it may be less clear that he should take the inability to convince others as a reason for entertaining doubt himself. One reason for this is that belief in divine revelation will characteristically occur within a wider framework of religious belief. So when the religious believer fails to persuade in the specific case, his argument will broaden to more general claims about the order of the world, the ways in which it makes manifest the existence of a divinity, and so on. Now it may be said that this simply pushes the argument one stage back: just as my belief in a specific case of divine revelation must be shaken if I fail to convince others, so my religious beliefs generally must be shaken if they fail to convince others. At the very least, I cannot hold them with the same degree of certainty once I recognise that the reasons I adduce in their support are not reasons which others find convincing. But why should we think that the latter case is simply the former case writ large? Barry's own reflections on the intransigence of religious disagreement suggest that the actual case is more difficult than this: religious wars sprang not only from a failure to persuade others by rational argument, but also from a failure to shake the conviction of others, and this fact persists whatever may be said about the appropriateness or legitimacy of retaining conviction in the face of disagreement.

Moreover, the insistence that failure to persuade should generate doubt assumes that standards of evidence are shared by believer and non-believer alike. It supposes, that is to say, that they are in agreement about what count as good or compelling reasons for something. But notoriously, the case of religious belief is a case in which what counts as evidence for the believer may be quite different from what counts as evidence for the non-believer. Or, more accurately, the two may see the same phenomenon as evidence for different kinds of things. This, I take it, is what is implicit in Cohen's suggestion that it may be in the nature of reason itself that it generates diversity rather than unanimity. And it is also a plausible gloss on Rawls's claim that the way we weigh evidence is shaped by our total experience and that in the modern world forms of experience are so diverse as to make disagreement predictable in many cases. It is, then, far from clear that the inability to persuade others either will or should generate doubt in the simple and straightforward way which Barry demands. Indeed, it is precisely the failure to generate doubt that has historically been the cause of the problem, so an insistence that doubt is required is unlikely to contribute in any significant way to the solution.

Additionally (and this introduces the second consideration mentioned earlier), Barry's objection to the doctrine of epistemological restraint is couched almost entirely in terms of the propriety of certainty, but the argument from epistemological restraint is not designed to show that feelings of certainty are legitimate despite one's inability to persuade others. Rather, it is designed to sever the connection between certainty in the mind of the agent and the legitimate use of power on the part of the state. Barry implies that if there were certainty, then the use of political power would be legitimate, and Gerald Dworkin also seems to subscribe to this view when he claims that people in the original position would not (or should not) feel their integrity to be threatened by the suppression of a view known to be false (Dworkin 1974: 492). For these writers, the problem in modernity is quite simply that certainty cannot survive the failure to persuade others and recalcitrant disagreement must therefore generate doubt.

However, Nagel's account of epistemological restraint, while it does claim that certainty may survive the inability to persuade others, is more centrally concerned with the kinds of justifications of political power which can properly be invoked. Thus, echoing Rawls, he urges that there must be restrictions on the sorts of convictions that can be appealed to in political argument, and I take it that his point here is simply that feelings of certainty are irrelevant to the justification of political power. More generally, Barry and Dworkin insist that the existential condition of the agent in modernity must properly be a condition of doubt, and from this existential observation they draw conclusions about the conditions under which political power is justified. The doctrine of epistemological restraint, however, is designed to show that even if we were certain, we would not, simply by virtue of that fact, be entitled to impose our conception of the good. The existential condition of the agent can and must be separated from the legitimation of political power.

The question which liberalism must answer is 'when are we justified in forcing people to do things which they do not wish to do, or which run counter to their convictions?' And the argument from epistemological restraint is designed to show that the answer 'when we are certain ourselves' will not do. If this is right, then Barry's claim that in cases such as the case of divine revelation we are not *entitled* to certainty is largely irrelevant, for the point of the argument is to show that even if we were entitled to certainty, it is not certainty which justifies. In this respect, the appeal to moderate scepticism is analogous to the appeal to pluralism: just as liberal recognition of the facts of pluralism need not lead to an endorsement of value pluralism, so liberal recognition of the persistence of disagreement need not lead to an endorsement of scepticism. Whether there is legitimate doubt about, say, the existence of God or the moral acceptability of abortion is something on which liberals should remain silent, for the certainty with which I hold a view is not the sort of thing which can properly be invoked in justifying the use of political power.

My argument so far has attempted to show that liberalism can explain the facts of disagreement without being implicated in either scepticism or pluralism. Pluralism can be avoided, and the facts of disagreement explained, by appeal to the nature of reason itself as tending towards diversity. There are many reasonable positions, none of which is fully underwritten by reason. This avoidance of pluralism, however, appeared to raise the spectre of scepticism, for if reason cannot fully underwrite our beliefs, then it seems that we must entertain doubt about them – and doubt is all that is needed for moderate scepticism. However, the discussion of epistemological restraint aims to show that this conclusion is too quick: doubt will be more difficult to engender than Barry supposes, and even if it is true that our inability to persuade others should generate doubt, that does not entail that liberalism must be grounded in scepticism – only, and at most, that it is compatible with scepticism. For, *pace* Barry, the argument from epistemological restraint is not intended to show that conviction can withstand the inability to persuade others, but rather that conviction is an inappropriate reason for compelling others. More generally, it is meant to show that the internal state of the agent is an illegitimate consideration in the justification of political power. This, however, takes us back, finally, to the connection between the existential condition of the agent and the justification of liberal neutrality.

Politics in a disenchanted world

The question that must now be answered is 'what is the relationship between the existential condition of the agent in modernity and the justification of liberal neutrality?' In the preceding section I argued that Barry mislocates the aim of the doctrine of epistemological restraint and that, far from insisting that personal conviction can survive the inability to persuade others, it is in fact meant to preserve distance between personal conviction and the ability to persuade others: epistemological restraint aims to sever the connection between the (legitimate) state of mind of the agent and the justification of political coercion. I also gave some, fairly inconclusive, reasons for thinking that distance might be easier to maintain than Barry suggests. However, the crucial question is 'why is it important for liberalism, as the politics of a disenchanted world, to maintain that distance?'

One very pragmatic reason lies in the origins of liberalism itself, which was born out of a recognition of the intractability of conflict, and which begins by noting that certainty in the mind of the individual is a factor which contributes in no small part to conflict. As we have seen, Barry attempts to respond to this by arguing that certainty is rarely warranted, and that it is the appropriateness of doubt which legitimises the move from the agreement motive to neutrality between competing conceptions of the good. The argument from epistemological restraint, on the other hand, takes a different tack and suggests that, even if certainty can withstand the inability to persuade others, it is not itself a sufficient reason for deploying coercive political power. The existential state of the agent, whether it is a state of certainty or of doubt, is not a legitimate consideration in the justification of coercive political power in general, and of liberal neutrality in particular.

And yet, as was pointed out at the beginning of this paper, it is the existential condition of the agent that is central to the characterisation of disenchantment offered by Taylor. He draws connections between the way things are for 'us' moderns and the proper aspirations of moral and political philosophy. In particular, and interestingly, he emphasises the fact that, in conditions of modernity, certainty (especially about frameworks) is difficult to obtain and even more difficult to justify. In this sense, he agrees with Barry, but draws rather different political conclusions. Where Barry argues that lack of certainty should lead us to embrace moderate scepticism as the means of moving from the agreement motive to liberal neutrality between competing conceptions of the good, Taylor argues that liberal neutrality is deeply unsatisfactory if construed as *the* guiding principle of political life. For him, the lack of unquestionable frameworks, and the connected difficulty of being strong evaluators should lead us to eschew dependence on a single principle in favour of an approach to political life which acknowledges the diversity of goods, the impossibility of organising them according to a single principle, and especially of organising them according to the principle of liberal neutrality alone. The details of the argument need not concern us here, for the central point is a simple one. It is that there is no clear and uncontroversial route from the acknowledgement of uncertainty to the endorsement of a single political principle. Far from being the *only* thing which can facilitate a move from the agreement motive to neutrality between competing conceptions of the good, scepticism (understood as doubt rather than denial) may itself be incapable of facilitating that move, for Taylor's claim is that uncertainty and disagreement should lead us to conclude that neutral liberalism is 'a formula for paralysis, or else for hypocrisy' (Taylor 1994: 253).

Reflection on the appropriateness of uncertainty therefore leaves questions about political organisation unresolved, and the reason for this, I suggest, is that scepticism, understood as doubt rather than denial, may be construed either as an epistemological claim or as a claim about our existential condition, or both. Barry is concerned to argue that it must be seen as an epistemological doctrine and for this reason he rejects Larmore's categorisation of it as embodying 'controversial ideals of the good life', retorting that scepticism 'is not a view of human flourishing. It is an epistemological doctrine about the status of conceptions of what constitutes human flourishing' (Barry 1995: 174). However, the description of disenchantment given at the beginning of this paper is a description of a world in which those two questions have become inextricably intertwined. The condition of modernity is one in which our views of human flourishing can only ever have provisional status, never the status of unquestionable truth, and this itself is part of what it is to inhabit a disenchanted world: disenchantment is precisely the existential condition of being unable to hold our beliefs with certainty or to see anything as beyond question.

To put the point rather more directly, Taylor's description of the existential condition of disenchantment reveals that it is not merely *what* we believe which contributes to and constitutes our ability to flourish; it is also the way in which we are entitled to believe it. If this is right, then scepticism, while it might not be 'a view of human flourishing', is nevertheless an epistemological position which contributes to (or detracts from) one's capacity to flourish, and indeed the uncertainty with which we must hold our beliefs in a disenchanted world is itself something which renders those beliefs very different ones from the ones they were in earlier times when frameworks could be accepted unquestioningly. To build scepticism into the political order is therefore to institutionalise exactly the epistemological conditions that militate against our flourishing. And it is for this reason that the doctrine of epistemological restraint, understood as abstracting from certainty rather than denying its legitimacy, promises a more satisfactory justification of neutrality than scepticism. In the final section I shall try to say a little more about why that is.

Conclusion

My main aim in this chapter has been to cast doubt on the claim that liberalism, understood as the politics of a disenchanted world, must rest upon either value pluralism or scepticism. The proliferation of conceptions of the good, and their recalcitrance to rational resolution, appear to lend support to the belief that the sources of value are many and not one (to value pluralism). However, liberalism (especially Rawlsian liberalism) aims to explain and accommodate disagreement without appeal to any metaphysical claim and, for this reason, it is well-advised to take no view on the truth or otherwise of value pluralism. If disagreement is to be explained, therefore, it must be in some other way. Following Joshua Cohen, I have suggested that that

117

other way might be by analysis of the nature of reason itself, which is such that its operation will predictably deliver diversity rather than unanimity. This, however, appears to raise the spectre of scepticism, for if reason cannot fully legitimise our views, then we seem not to be entitled to hold those views with certainty – and this, it was suggested, is sufficient to show that liberalism must be grounded in moderate scepticism.

However, the appeal to scepticism may also be averted by the argument from epistemological restraint, where that is understood as an attempt to separate the existential condition of the agent (as a condition of doubt or uncertainty) from the justification of coercive political power. So understood, liberal neutrality is not based on our own uncertainty about which conception of the good is best, but on the rejection of certainty as an appropriate deciding factor in the deployment of political power. This, however, raises a very general question about the relationship that holds between the existential condition of the agent in circumstances of modernity and the justification of political power. Here, I have suggested that there is an interesting ambivalence in some responses to that question. Where liberalism is grounded in scepticism, it appeals to the appropriateness of doubt as a means of legitimising the move from the agreement motive to the requirement of neutrality (scepticism is the only thing which can fill in the gap between the agreement motive and the exclusion of conceptions of the good from the political constitution). Such an appeal to the existential condition of the agent must not, however, be construed as an appeal to a conception of human flourishing, for liberalism aspires to be neutral between different and conflicting conceptions of human flourishing. Therefore, if the sceptical argument is to work, it must retain a clear distinction between the manner in which we hold our conceptions of the good and those conceptions themselves. This, however, is a controversial requirement, not least because it misses some of the significance of the description of disenchantment given by Taylor. For it is central to Taylor's argument that a conception of the good which is held provisionally or with doubt is in important respects a different conception from one which is held with certainty. More generally, the *manner* in which I hold a view about human flourishing may be inseparable from the *content* of that view. This is why, according to Taylor, we are in a 'fundamentally different existential predicament from that which dominated most previous cultures and still defines the lives of other people today' (Taylor 1989: 18).

It may seem that this point threatens the plausibility of the argument from epistemological restraint, which appeared to be premised on the assumption that we can abstract from the manner in which we hold a view. In fact, however, it tells in favour of epistemological restraint, understood as a means of maintaining distance between the existential condition of the agent and the justification of political power. Because the argument from scepticism yokes together the legitimate frame of mind of the agent and the justification of political power, it must seek to undermine claims to certainty, especially where those claims would issue in non-liberal uses of power. The sceptical justification of liberalism thus destabilises conceptions of human flourishing which are held with conviction, and in doing this it reinforces, at a political level, the existential inconveniences of living in a disenchanted world.

By contrast, the argument from epistemological restraint can concede that a conception of human flourishing is transformed by the manner in which it is held, but nevertheless insist that transformation not be the ground of political justification. By aspiring to retain this distance between existential condition and political justification, the doctrine of epistemological restraint avoids the implication in metaphysical claims which, I have suggested, sceptical arguments cannot avoid. Sceptical arguments can be made to work only by adopting an ambivalent and ultimately contradictory attitude towards the relationship between existential condition and political justification.

Of course, none of this delivers the conclusion that an analysis of reason as tending to disagreement can provide an adequate explanation of the facts of pluralism. Nor does it show that the doctrine of epistemological restraint is sufficient to bridge the gap between the agreement motive and liberal neutrality. What it does suggest, however, is that attempts to ground liberalism in pluralism or scepticism carry more metaphysical baggage than their proponents admit, and that if liberalism really is to avoid commitment to metaphysics or to controversial conceptions of human flourishing, it must distance itself from both pluralism and scepticism, since these are simply, and in the end, new forms of metaphysics invented to replace the ones we lost when God died.

Notes

1   Earlier drafts of this paper were delivered at University College, Dublin, at the Political Thought Conference, Oxford, and at the Political Theory Workshop at the University of York. I am grateful to all the participants on those occasions, to Gordon Finlayson and Keith Spence for their penetrating written comments, and to my colleagues Duncan Ivison and Matt Matravers for their tireless willingness to discuss these topics. I would also like to thank Maria Baghramian and Attracta Ingram for inviting me to participate in this project.

6

CROOKED TIMBER AND LIBERAL CULTURE

Jonathan Riley

Introduction

John Gray (1995, 1998) suggests that Isaiah Berlin's moral and political thought is muddled because it seeks to combine tragic value pluralism, which holds that plural and incommensurable values conflict in ways that cannot be reasonably resolved, and liberal rationalism, which holds that liberal values are reasonably viewed as superior to any competing values. Michael Ignatieff evidently agrees with Gray:

> [T]he real difficulty is that a pluralist logically cannot put liberty first. Liberty is simply one of the values that must be reconciled with others; it is not the trump card. If so, why should a free society be valued above all?
>
> (Ignatieff 1999: 286)

Gray proposes to reconstruct Berlin's doctrine as an 'agonistic' liberalism that lacks any foundations in rational choice: 'Berlin's agonistic liberalism – his liberalism of conflict among inherently rivalrous goods – grounds itself on the radical choices we must make among incommensurables, not upon rational choice' (Gray 1995: 8). 'Radical choice' is 'ungoverned by reason,' 'without criteria, grounds, or principles,' and is at 'the heart of Berlin's liberalism' (Gray 1995: 23, 61). 'His is an unfamiliar and challenging liberalism,' therefore, 'that is subversive of the rationalist foundations of all the traditional varieties of liberal thought' (Gray 1995: 9).

As reconstructed, Berlinian liberalism lacks the resources to mount any decisive objection to a liberal culture being overrun by non-liberal alternatives. Given that liberal and non-liberal values can be incommensurable such that conflicts between them cannot be rationally settled, reason cannot underwrite any moral victory for liberalism. Rather, any commitment to liberalism must be a 'radical choice' in Gray's sense. Non-rational attitudes, including inclinations to blindly imitate or rebel against established social customs, must be what ultimately sways the choice one way or the other.

Even Gray, however, backs away from the agonistic reading to a limited extent. He concedes that, for Berlin, a 'universal framework of categories and norms of moral thought' limits the scope of any agonising choices associated with tragic conflicts of incommensurable values (Gray 1995: 157). That common moral horizon apparently disqualifies certain highly illiberal and barbaric value-systems (such as a slave system or a Nazi system) as irrational and unfit for human beings. '[I]t does not, however, ground or privilege liberalism' (Gray 1995: 158). Rather, any commitment to a liberal value-system 'is a groundless one, which nothing in reason compels us to make' (Gray 1995: 168). Given the force of tragic pluralism, liberal cultures are not rationally comparable with many non-liberal ones that are not barbaric. There are decent cultures that are in no sense liberal, it seems, in that they fail to recognise or give priority to even some minimum of liberal rights (see, for example, Margalit 1997). Thus, the superiority of liberal values over these non-liberal yet non-barbaric alternatives cannot in general be rationally justified: 'Where liberal institutions claim universal authority,' he says, 'liberals and pluralists must part company' (Gray 1998: 34).

Gray's concession that a common moral horizon underlies Berlin's approach and restrains the scope of pluralism may seem innocuous. After all, liberal values can still be incommensurable with non-liberal yet non-barbaric ones. Liberalism remains a 'radical choice' rather than a rationally determinate one in the presence of those decent non-liberal options. Nevertheless, Gray's concession is significant. It arguably amounts to an inconsistency in his unbridled agonistic interpretation. Given the concession, Berlin's liberalism is grounded on 'radical choice' only in so far as that choice is kept within certain *reasonable* boundaries set by the common moral horizon. In other words, there is an implicit claim that it is rational to treat as 'radical' some choices between liberal and certain non-liberal values that are not barbaric. But there are no 'radical choices' between barbaric and other values: barbaric options such as slavery and genocide are vetoed as irrational because they are incompatible with the common moral horizon. Thus, even on Gray's reading, Berlin's liberalism apparently does have a minimal rationalist foundation. It is rooted in a view of reason that restricts the scope of tragic pluralism to choices between liberal and certain non-liberal yet non-barbaric value-systems.

But there is more to be said about this element of rationalism in Berlin's doctrine. The assumption that decent non-liberal cultures exist is open to serious doubt. A more sensible hypothesis may be that any decent or civilised – as opposed to barbaric – system of values is at least minimally liberal in the sense that it (at least implicitly) privileges some minimum set of human rights. To avoid the barbarism of slavery, for example, a culture must give suitable priority to a moral claim tantamount to an equal right not to be enslaved. To veto ethnic and racial cleansing, a culture must recognise the importance of equal rights not to be killed arbitrarily on the basis of ethnic or racial characteristics. If this is right, the common moral horizon must be at least minimally liberal. Moreover, the reach of tragic pluralism is restricted to different value-systems all of which are at least minimally liberal. Any non-liberal value-system is rejected as barbaric and irrational.

I shall not attempt fully to defend this hypothesis that decency is equivalent to at least minimal liberalism.[1] As we shall see, however, Berlin himself seems to view the common moral horizon as at least minimally liberal. He says that every system of values that is intelligible to reasonable human beings as opposed to irrational barbarians privileges basic liberal rights, or at least a minimum of them (Jahanbegloo 1992: 39, 114). He thus implies that his liberalism is rooted in a conception of reason that restricts the scope of pluralism to choices between value-systems that are at least minimally liberal. Myriad distinct liberal cultures may be incommensurable with one another but they are all reasonably ranked as superior to the barbaric and illiberal alternatives.

'Fundamentally, I am a liberal rationalist,' Berlin claims, seeking to 'take account of ... where the cracks' are in 'liberal principles and rational analysis' (Jahanbegloo 1992: 70–1). In what follows, I shall offer an interpretation of his thought that takes him at his word. The theory that emerges is a rationalistic liberalism with 'cracks' or imperfections built into the power of reason to resolve ethical and political conflicts (including conflicts of equal rights). It is a tragically pluralistic version of liberalism with rationalist foundations. Possible labels for it are *agonistic liberal rationalism* and *rationalist agonistic liberalism*. Whatever name is attached to it, however, the key point is that the theory consistently combines the pluralism, liberalism, and rationalism that are at the heart of Berlin's outlook. It shows the logical possibility of a liberalism in which suitable priority for a minimum core of equal rights is rationally justified even though a genuine pluralism reaches into the values attached to different rights themselves.

I should hasten to add that I am not endorsing the appeal of Berlinian liberalism thus interpreted. Rather, my claim is that, contrary to what Gray and Ignatieff suggest, there is no necessary contradiction between pluralism and liberal reason in Berlin's doctrine. Thus, to have any force, a critique of Berlinian liberalism must go beyond the conceptual level to examine deeper methodological and epistemological issues that figure in the justification of his doctrine.[2]

Rationalism: fake versus genuine

It deserves emphasis at the outset that when Berlin refers to himself as 'a liberal rationalist,' and when I attribute to him a species of rationalistic liberalism, no endorsement is implied of the mainstream Western rationalist tradition, which Berlin repeatedly attacks as incoherent and (despite appearances to the contrary) dangerous to liberty. In his view, mainstream rationalism, exemplified by Socrates as represented in Plato's dialogues, by Enlightenment philosophers such as Voltaire, Helvetius, Condorcet, and (to some extent) even Kant, Schiller and Goethe, by utilitarians such as Bentham, James Mill, and even J.S. Mill, by Marx and Marxists, and by Hegel and his Anglo-American followers including Green and Bosanquet, is committed to fake social utopias of various descriptions, the pursuit of which inevitably leads to state oppression (Berlin 1969: xxxvii–lxiii, 167–72; 1991: 1–48; 1999: 21–34, 105 ff, 118 ff). The fundamental mainstream error is the belief that 'virtue is knowledge': more specifically, that reason (variously defined) is sufficiently powerful to discover how to resolve any and all ethical and political conflicts, whether by maximising some single ultimate value, such as happiness, or by adjusting plural ultimate values into an ideal pattern of perfect harmony. Some in the mainstream even go so far as to depict the moral truths revealed by reason as necessary truths of universal applicability. But others are less rigid and see them as warranted inferences contingent on particular social circumstances. Whether seen as necessary and universal or as contingent and possibly varying across different social contexts, however, these truths are assumed to be mutually compatible and to give a complete picture of how people ought to act, everywhere or in the particular social context, as the case may be. As a result, rationalism of this dominant sort, which might be called utopian rationalism or perfectionist rationalism, misses the importance of non-rational forces in nature (including human nature) which cannot be completely subdued by reason and misconceives the good life as 'a jigsaw puzzle' that can be pieced together by suitably educated people (often elites).

Despite his clear rejection of mainstream rationalism as a fake and dangerous doctrine, however, it would be a mistake (or so I shall argue) to read Berlin as hostile to all conceivable forms of rationalism, including those which combine their commitment to reason with a belief that reason is incapable in principle of resolving all ethical and political conflicts. Mainstream rationalism exaggerates the power of reason to classify and arrange the moral universe, he thinks, and thereby distorts and obscures a genuine rationalism, which recognises the true limits of reason and makes room for agonising moral choices that lack rational justification. Indeed, I suggest that Berlin's depiction of himself as 'a liberal rationalist' is far from careless, and may be intended to encourage us to investigate more closely the distance between mainstream utopian rationalism (which he sees as fake and illiberal) and his more moderate and imperfect rationalism (which he sees as genuine and liberal). Thus, he provides ample clues as to the differences between the two kinds of rationalism, by pointing to various 'cracks' in the mainstream picture which, once taken account of, result in a much less grandiose picture of reason's authority. Though its power may be weak, however, reason remains for Berlin the ultimate guide in ethical and political life.

Some of the 'cracks' in the mainstream ideology are 'faint dents' recognised by Enlightenment rationalists themselves, he tells us. To take account of Montesquieu's relativism and Hume's scepticism, the mainstream picture had to be adjusted somewhat to allow rational moral truths to be seen as contingent on particular social circumstances rather than as necessary and eternal (Berlin 1999: 30–4). But that adjustment left the mainstream project essentially intact, as I indicated earlier. True, some contingent truths may well vary across social contexts: what makes a Persian happy may be observed to differ markedly from what gives a Parisian delight. But other contingent truths remain more or less universal since they are reiterated across a very broad range of social circumstances. Persians and Parisians are both inferred to pursue happiness, justice and liberty, for instance. It is simply held to be reasonable for them to choose different means of achieving these common ends as a result of differing social circumstances, including soil, climate, history, customs, political institutions, and so on. In any case, there is no denial of the key mainstream premise that 'virtue is knowledge'. Reason can still in principle resolve any and all ethical and political conflicts, even though the rational means of achieving utopia will generally vary across different social circumstances.

Far more serious 'cracks' in the mainstream picture are apparent once account is taken of the Romantic reaction against it, Berlin argues. He views romanticism as largely a German phenomenon, with roots in pietism, and traces its development through such disparate thinkers as Hamann, Herder, Kant, Schiller, Fichte, Schelling, the Schlegels, Schopenhauer, Tieck, and Goethe (Berlin 1999: 34–147).[3] This tide of anti-rationalism is of great importance, he stresses, because it 'attacked and gravely damaged the old proposition that virtue is knowledge' and thereby dispelled the mainstream illusion that the art of life is 'a jigsaw puzzle' to be fit together by reason (Berlin 1999: 118–19). Although the essence of the romantic alternative is not easy to state with precision, he suggests that it 'may be summarised under two heads.' First, men do not *discover* their values and ideals by the correct use of reason. Rather, men must spontaneously *create* their ideals. Second, and closely related, it makes no sense to speak of a rational social utopia that could serve as a benchmark to assess the different values and ideals created by men. Rather, the moral universe involves 'endless self-creativity' that transcends rational assessment (Berlin 1999: 119).

As Berlin explains, the most ardent romantics see this creative process as 'literally infinite,' an 'inexhaustible' stream of freely chosen ideals and values (Berlin 1999: 101). The creative will, or spirit, or imagination, or passion – whether at the level of the individual or of the group – is not something that can be caged or ordered by reason. Ultimately a mystery, it is the stuff of religion and myth (Berlin 1999: 99–109, 121–2).[4] Thus, since rational standards are lacking, the ideals created by one individual or nation cannot be judged to be more or less reasonable than those chosen by another. Rather, men ought to defend their ideals at all costs, however foolish or irrational their creations may appear. True, when different ideals clash as they inevitably will, the human consequences may be tragic since reason cannot resolve the conflict. But the pure romantic accepts this and assigns 'the highest importance' to 'such values as integrity, sincerity [or authenticity], readiness to sacrifice one's life to some inner light, ... fighting for your beliefs to the last breath, martyrdom as such, ... [and] dedication to [your] ideal ... no matter what it was' (Berlin 1999: 8–14; 139–41).[5]

The upshot of 'unbridled romanticism' is that there is nothing worth salvaging from the mainstream rationalist tradition. Virtue is not knowledge but creative self-expression and a willingness to die for one's ideals no matter what they are. The good life is not 'a jigsaw puzzle' that can eventually be grasped and understood by rational people. It is an endless striving to express one's own true and perfect nature, endless because that creative nature is literally inexpressible and beyond the power of reason to articulate. As such, the good life cannot ever be pinned down by rational methods. Rather, human life is necessarily tragic, replete with romantic 'nostalgia' if not 'paranoia' (Berlin 1999: 104–9).

If he accepted unbridled romanticism, Berlin could not consistently call himself 'a liberal rationalist' because no form of rationalism could survive. The picture of mainstream rationalism would be replaced by a picture of unlimited value pluralism in which there are no rational standards to settle conflicts between ideals created by different people – or even by the same person. But Berlin makes clear that he does not endorse unrestrained romanticism. He points out that some common values must exist for people to understand and communicate with each other at all.

> To the extent to which there are common values it is impossible to say that everything must be created by me; that if I find something given, I must smash it; that if I find something structured, I must destroy it in order to give free play to my unbridled imagination. To this extent romanticism, if it is driven to its logical conclusion, does end in some kind of lunacy.
>
> (Berlin 1999: 145)

In short, romanticism and its focus on creative self-expression must be restrained by some common ethical and political norms that are accepted as given. This common moral horizon properly overrides any competing ideals which may be chosen spontaneously by individuals or groups. It is evidently something which Berlin thinks can be discovered by rational methods. Its structure is the focus of a genuine liberal rationalism.

For Berlin, then, the 'cracks' in the mainstream picture on which romanticism throws light are fatal to that picture but not fatal to rationalism altogether. Mainstream rationalism must be given up in favour of a more complex liberal rationalism that makes room *to a limited extent* for a tragic pluralist conception of moral life. All hope of a rational social utopia must be abandoned since reason cannot always (or perhaps even often) resolve conflicts of values. At the same time, however, the more complex doctrine must include liberal *limits* on the pluralist conception which are rationally justified. In other words, the scope of pluralism must be limited by a common moral horizon such that the elements of the horizon are reasonably held to take precedence when they conflict with any other ideals and values created by men. Thus, a belief in reason – rational choice as opposed to radical choice in Gray's sense – is *at the foundation* of Berlin's liberal doctrine.

I shall next discuss what seem to be the main building blocks of Berlin's doctrine, in light of what he says. The goal is to see how a liberal can consistently maintain his belief in reason while at the same time modifying and enlarging his system of rationalism to make room for the non-rational and mythopoeic aspects of ethical and political life brought to prominence by the Romantics.[6]

Pluralism: tragic and benign

Berlin argues that the Romantics left a lasting legacy:

> The notion that there are many values, and that they are incompatible; the whole notion of plurality, of inexhaustibility, of the imperfection of all human answers and arrangements; the notion that no single answer which claims to be perfect and true, whether in art or in life, can in principle be perfect and true – all this we owe to the romantics.
> (Berlin 1999: 146)

Tragic pluralism, which holds that the plural ideals created by men conflict in ways beyond the power of reason to resolve, is a valid moral outlook, he suggests, at least with respect to some limited domain of choices. As a result, any idea of a rational social utopia, in which reason has reconciled conflicting values to produce complete ethical and political harmony, must be dismissed as false.

These romantic insights into tragic pluralism and the imperfection of reason are confirmed by reason itself, Berlin insists. There is no mystery about what he means by genuine rational methods of ethical and political inquiry: 'Rational methods, roads to the truth, ... are, as Socrates taught, of cardinal importance to the fate of individuals and societies: about that the central traditions of Western philosophy are right' (Jahanbegloo 1992: 39). But he is concerned to show that these rational methods are abused by mainstream rationalist ideologues, who have an unwarranted belief that reason is omnipotent. Mainstream rationalism is truly a species of irrationalism 'enunciated by over-rational and over-scientific analysts' (Berlin 1999: 146).

Thus, he emphasises that the notion of a rational utopia or best option, in which all truly valuable things find their proper place, is genuinely inconceivable, even though people have long been beguiled by some such false vision. 'Since some values may conflict intrinsically,' he says, 'the very notion that a pattern must in principle be discoverable in which they are all rendered harmonious is founded on a false *a priori* view of what the world is like' (Berlin 1969: li). Even great defenders of liberty have been misled by this mainstream rationalistic illusion. J.S. Mill's liberal utilitarianism is said to be a utopian rationalism of this fake a priori sort, for example, 'with a special rider about the need for individual liberty as a necessary condition for the attainment of final harmony' (Berlin 1969: li).

Against the mainstream, Berlin argues that rational methods tied to empirical observation confirm the validity of tragic pluralism and thus the impossibility of finding a best option all-things-considered:

> [I]f we are not armed with an *a priori* guarantee of the proposition that a total harmony of true values is somewhere to be found – perhaps in some ideal realm the characteristics of which we can, in our finite state, not so much as conceive – we must fall back on the ordinary resources of empirical observation and ordinary human knowledge. And these certainly give us no warrant for supposing (or even understanding what would be meant by saying) that all good things, or all bad things for that matter, are reconcilable with each other. The world that we encounter in ordinary experience is one in which we are faced with choices between ends equally ultimate, and claims equally absolute, the realisation of some of which must inevitably involve the sacrifice of others.
>
> (Berlin 1969: 168)

Like the Romantics, he seems convinced that some values naturally belong with others in that they are observed to evolve together in particular clusters or cultures, from which they cannot be extracted without loss of vitality (Gray 1995: 45–9, 70–5, 129–31). As spontaneous creations of particular groups, cultures are living webs of interconnected values. The elements of one web cannot be artificially mixed with those of others to form some artificial utopia. Virtues peculiar to the pagan culture of Periclean Athens cannot be ripped from it and rationally combined with virtues peculiar to Christian culture, for example, as Mill (1859: 266) mistakenly supposed. The values of 'pagan self-assertion' and 'Christian self-denial' are incommensurable and cannot be balanced within the same culture without loss, an insight which Berlin (1981) attributes to Machiavelli. The notion of a cultural utopia, in which these incommensurable virtues are rationally adjusted and arranged into harmony, is a rationalistic pipe-dream.[7]

In short, Gray seems correct to suggest that, for Berlin, genuine pluralism involves plural values which are incommensurable in the sense that their directives cannot be reasonably compared and ranked. As Charles Larmore puts it:

> Berlin seems to believe that, being equally ultimate, not derivable from a single form of good, plural values cannot be weighed together and their directives ranked and ordered hierarchically. This being so, we apparently cannot believe, in Berlin's view, that where our values differ in this way from those of others, our own are legitimately superior.
>
> (Larmore 1996a: 161)

Conflicts implicating incommensurable values are tragic because they cannot be rationally resolved. There is no possibility of finding a best option in which these plural and incommensurable values are brought into rational harmony.

Other, more benign, versions of pluralism are also discussed in the literature. Berlin himself points to the possibility of a benign pluralism which holds that plural and incommensurable values *can* be reasonably adjusted or balanced into a perfect overall pattern or utopia. But he typically dismisses it as a false pluralism, no more plausible than a utopian monism. Such a benign pluralism says that if incommensurable values come into conflict, their respective directives (or rankings of the options) can still be compared and adjusted so as to yield a complete and consistent all-things-considered ranking of the given options which truly reflects the nature of value. It posits a plurality of sources of value which threatens to damage the power of human reason to make fully determinate ethical evaluations. But then it relents. The commensurability typical of monism is ruled out, that is, the directives of one basic value (say, justice) cannot be compared to those of another (say, mercy) by reducing both values to a common scale of, say, happiness such that a best option all-things-considered is one which ranks highest in terms of that common scale of value.[8] Also ruled out perhaps is a single lexical scale that arranges the plural basic values and their respective directives into a fixed hierarchy in terms of which conflicts can invariably be sorted out. But comparability is not ruled out altogether. The claims of one value can still be reasonably judged to carry more weight than the conflicting claims of another when choosing between them. It is just that there is no simple algorithm for doing so. Rather, the demands of justice might reasonably be judged as more important than those of mercy in some situations, for example, whereas the demands of mercy might reasonably be ranked higher in other situations, even though justice and mercy are incommensurable values. Thus, a best option all-things-considered can still be found in any situation.

Larmore defends benign pluralism when he insists that '[v]alue commitments may be … *comparable* without being *commensurable*, the directives they offer in a given situation being rankable without appeal to a common standard providing the reasons for the ranking' (Larmore 1996a: 157, emphasis original). Herder too, he thinks, is properly read as a benign pluralist. Yet he admits that he himself has 'no fully satisfactory answer' to the question of 'how incommensurable values may still be comparable'. Nevertheless, he downplays the problem and urges us to 'follow Herder' rather than Berlin (Larmore 1996a: 162).

Remarkably, even Berlin sounds at times like a benign pluralist, who accepts that the demands of incommensurable values may still be rationally compared and balanced. In an article co-authored with Bernard Williams, for example, he argues that even in conflicts of incommensurable values, it can be reasonable to give more weight to the directives of one value over those of another. There isn't a common currency of value such as happiness, however, or a single lexical priority rule on which reasonable people can rely when making their judgements (Berlin and Williams 1994: 307). Rather, a reasonable person simply makes intuitive judgements of relative weight that can vary from situation to situation. Similarly, Larmore says that 'sometimes we can find a solution to such a conflict [of incommensurable values] not by appealing to a common denominator of value but simply by recognizing that one consideration carries more weight than another' (Larmore 1996a: 157).

If pluralists can proceed in this way, then it is not too much to hope for true complete and consistent overall orderings of options, which could in general be represented by the utility functions of modern decision theory (without thereby bringing back commensurability).[9] Indeed, rational indeterminacy becomes of no more than passing interest since there is no reason for it to persist if the directives of the competing values can be reasonably ranked in any situation. Best options are conceivable in principle. Nevertheless, benign pluralism is contrary to the romantic spirit of Berlin's approach. Like Gray, Larmore, Crowder (1994) and others, I believe that it is more typical of Berlin to claim that conflicts of incommensurable values cannot be rationally resolved, in which case the Berlin-Williams (1994) piece must be regarded as anomalous.

Moreover, as it stands, benign pluralism seems uninteresting. It offers no account of the rational capacity that permits incommensurable values to be genuinely compared in the absence of a common denominator like happiness. This flaw might be remedied in various ways. Benign pluralists might show that Aristotle's conception of *phronesis* involves such a capacity, for example, and clarify how the relevant acts of judgement can be distinguished from arbitrary acts of will.[10] In the meantime, tragic pluralism seems more interesting than its benign cousin.

Tragic pluralism and rational indeterminacy

A rationalism that admits the validity to some extent of tragic pluralism, and insists on the imperfection of reason, may be described as pluralistic and anti-utopian. Such a rationalism is already quite distinct from mainstream rationalisms of the utopian sort which Berlin attacks as fake. As yet, however, it isn't necessarily a liberal doctrine. Pluralism is not logically connected to liberalism, as Berlin himself confirms: 'liberalism and pluralism are not logically connected,' he says, and '[t]here are liberal theories which are not pluralistic' (Jahanbegloo 1992: 44). To produce a recognisably liberal doctrine, rational methods will need to confirm much else, including the 'immense value' of liberal rights across a wide range of social contexts. I shall return to these matters in due course. But the next step is to clarify the implications for rationalism of its limited embrace of tragic pluralism.

Tragic pluralism defines incommensurable values as rationally noncomparable. Conflicts implicating them cannot be resolved by reason. As Amartya Sen points out, however, the term 'incommensurable' is ambiguous in the literature (Sen 1987: 61–3). It is used to rule out either or both of two separate things, namely, value monism (that is, 'descriptive homogeneity' of the given valuable options as, for instance, just so many quantities of happiness) and – something quite different – the possibility of a genuine complete and consistent all-things-considered ethical ordering of the given options. Benign pluralism uses the term to rule out monism alone. Tragic pluralism uses it to rule out both monism and fully determinate overall evaluations.[11] In the latter case, conflicting and incommensurable values, being 'equally ultimate' and giving rise to 'equally absolute' directives, cannot be reasonably compared and adjusted to yield a best option sitting at the head of a complete and consistent overall ranking of options implicating those values. Any true overall ranking of the options must generally be indeterminate over some (possibly large) portion of its range.[12]

Following Sen, two forms of indeterminacy in the ranking of options may be distinguished, namely, *incompleteness* and *overcompleteness*. Incompleteness arises if and only if the demand for a complete overall ranking is abandoned. Suppose that justice and mercy are noncomparable values, for example, and that justice directs us to rank option A higher than option B (because there is more justice at A than at B) whereas mercy directs us to rank B higher than A. No other values are implicated in the choice situation. If both justice and mercy are taken into consideration, the conflict between them cannot be reasonably resolved. According to the 'incompleteness' interpretation, there is no all-things-considered ranking of A and B because agreement between the directives of justice and mercy is necessary and sufficient to determine an overall ranking of A and B. The directives conflict and they cannot be rationally weighed or ranked to resolve the conflict. Of course, if the values did not conflict but called for an identical ranking of A and B, then it is uncontroversial that 'dominance' reasoning would generate that same overall ranking of A and B.

Overcompleteness arises if and only if the demand for a consistent overall ranking is abandoned. As Sen remarks, 'faced with an irreducible conflict of compelling principles, [the overall ranking] may admit both the superiority of one alternative over the other and the converse' (Sen 1987: 66). The ranking may include both the directive of justice to rank A higher than B, for example, and the directive of mercy to rank B higher than A. Agreement between the directives is not necessary for an overall ranking, though it remains necessary for a consistent one. Although the admission of inconsistency may seem 'bizarre,' decision-makers may reasonably accept 'the compelling nature of two [or more] potentially conflicting principles of overall judgement with an overlapping domain' (Sen 1987: 66).[13]

Some will object that justice and mercy *are* comparable values, say, equally weighty ones. In that case, a reasonable all-things-considered ranking of options implicating those values is complete and consistent in principle. The overall ranking of A and B, for example, is one of indifference when the (ordinalist) directive of justice to rank A higher than B is given equal weight to that of mercy to rank B higher than A (so that in effect as much justice and mercy are combined at A as at B). But the tragic pluralist denies that justice and mercy are comparable in this way.

Sen argues that the presence to some extent of indeterminacy in all-things-considered moral rankings of options entails 'no departure from rational choice' (Sen 1987: 67).[14] There is nothing incoherent about an agonistic rationalism that accepts as reasonable such gaps – limited zones of incompleteness or of inconsistency – in its overall moral evaluations. It is rational to make what Gray calls a 'radical' pick of any option from the given subset of options comprising any particular zone. To illustrate this unfamiliar sort of rationalism, consider Berlin's suggestion (which he traces to Machiavelli) that Christian and pagan cultures are incompatible and incommensurable webs of values. Let X represent a purely pagan Florence, and Y a purely Christian one. Since these two conflicting cultures are held to be incompatible and incommensurable, there is no third feasible option Z at which pagan and Christian elements are blended to produce a rational Florentine utopia. Any mixture tends to sap the vitality of the ingredients and cannot be viewed as an ideal culture. Restricting attention to the two feasible options, X is ranked higher than Y from a pagan perspective whereas Y is ranked higher than X from the Christian point of view. But the conflict between these rankings cannot be rationally settled, since pagan and Christian values are by assumption rationally noncomparable. According to the 'overcompleteness' interpretation, both of these pairwise rankings are compelling, so that the conflict between them results in inconsistency in an overall moral evaluation that takes account of both pagan and Christian values: the overall evaluation displays both $X > Y$ (by paganism) and $Y > X$ (by Christianity), where the symbol '>' denotes 'better than' or 'ranked higher than'. According to the 'incompleteness' reading, however, neither ranking is compelling unless they point in the same direction. Conflict between them now results in incompleteness in the overall evaluation: there is no rational overall ordering of X and Y at all in the present case. Under either interpretation, reason is silent about which option is best overall. Picking either X or Y is not unreasonable. It may still turn out that X and Y are both consistently ranked higher than some other feasible option W, however, where pagan and Christian elements are mixed to form some non-utopian culture.

Consider another example in which justice and mercy come into conflict and are viewed as noncomparable values. Suppose that there is a domain of options A, B and C such that justice generates A > C > B whereas mercy yields B > A > C. Justice increases as we move from B to C to A, in other words, whereas mercy increases as we move from C to A to B. These three options might be described as follows. At A, a duly convicted murderer is sentenced to fifty years in a state penitentiary with a chance for parole after twenty years; at B, this criminal receives a pardon for the crime based on extenuating circumstances, in particular, the history of abuse which he has suffered at the hands of the dead man, his drug-addicted father; and at C, the killer receives the death penalty. The 'overcompleteness' reading yields an overall evaluation that displays inconsistency with respect to some pairs of options, to wit, C > B (by justice) and B > C (by mercy), and A > B (by justice) and B > A (by mercy). Reason is silent about how to resolve these binary inconsistencies. But there is no inconsistency with respect to the remaining pair of options: both values rank A > C. Thus, it is unreasonable to select C when A is available, although it is not unreasonable to choose A or B. Similarly, the 'incompleteness' interpretation yields a partial overall ranking, namely, A > C. Since justice and mercy point in the same direction with respect to A and C, dominance reasoning tells us that C ought not to be chosen over A. Where the values conflict, however, as they do over the other two pairs of options, reason is silent about how to complete the relevant pairwise rankings in the overall evaluation. Again, it is not unreasonable to choose either A or B, although C is an inferior option when A is available. Under either interpretation, the overall evaluation displays gaps of incompleteness or inconsistency which cannot be rationally removed, so that there is no best or utopian option.

A third illustration is discussed by Sen, namely, the classic story of Buridan's ass, which starved to death because it could not come up with a complete and consistent ranking between two identical stacks of hay. Rather than starve, a rational beast would surely pick one of the stacks to eat, even though the chosen stack is no better (or worse) than the other. As Sen puts it, 'only an ass will wait' for a best option that sits at the head of a complete and consistent ordering when no possibility exists of finding one (Sen 1997a: 765).[15]

As these examples suggest, the sorts of indeterminacy associated with tragic pluralism seem compatible with rational ethical and political evaluation. Reason is simply viewed as too weak to resolve the underlying moral conflicts. Worthy of emphasis is that, for Berlin, such indeterminacy is *per-*

manent: it can never be genuinely remedied because incommensurable values are genuinely noncomparable. The indeterminacy is not contingent on lack of information or faulty deliberation. It reflects the genuine structure of human morality. Even the most penetrating examination based on perfect information cannot tell us how to rationally compare the conflicting directives of incommensurable values. The conflicts impose limits on rationality which are relentless and inescapable.

The intractability of the indeterminacy is important. Even value monists have no trouble admitting indeterminacy which is contingent on mistakes in judgement or lack of information about the quantities of value (such as happiness) involved at some options. But they insist that any indeterminacy arising from these familiar sources is remediable. Complete and consistent orderings might be discovered since the directives of competing values are always rationally comparable in principle. The possibility of a complete and consistent ethical evaluation is not denied.[16]

Evidently, rationalism cannot admit unlimited tragic pluralism without destroying itself. As Berlin points out in his critical assessment of 'unbridled romanticism,' however, unrestrained pluralism would amount to 'a kind of lunacy' (Berlin 1999: 145). The next step is to clarify how pluralism might be restrained in a political theory like his. This brings us to the 'liberal' part of agonistic liberal rationalism.

Rational grounds for liberal politics

To give rise to a recognisably liberal doctrine, genuine rational methods must affirm that weighty liberal values fix common boundaries within which the field of tragic pluralism is properly restrained. In particular, it must be reasonable to think that some weighty liberal procedure is needed to pick between the directives of incommensurable values when they come into conflict with respect to an overlapping domain of options. After all, it remains necessary to choose: people cannot simply remain paralysed in the face of tragic conflicts of values, even though the conflicts cannot be genuinely resolved by rationally comparing and ranking the values. Liberals like Berlin will understandably opt for some liberal choice procedure rather than an illiberal one.

A rational procedure will impartially consider the directives of all competing values in order to generate a ranking over any given set of options. If the conflicting values are comparable in terms of some common measure over a given pair of options, then the procedure must duly weigh the conflicting directives to yield a pairwise ranking. If conflicting and incommensurable values are implicated, however, then the procedure is not longer required by the nature of value to yield a particular ranking over the relevant pair. Rather, it can freely pick either option and thereby 'reveal' a ranking over the pair. But the revealed ranking is not rationally justified: it

133

simply reflects the radical pick of one option rather than the other. The procedure cannot remove the genuine indeterminacy in the overall moral ranking of the options. Rather, it takes as given the conflicting rankings of options which emanate from the plural sources of value and makes a radical pick within the bounds of the liberal procedural norms. What makes any radical choice within liberal bounds a reasonable one, according to this approach, is that it is the product of a suitable liberal procedure, which is not unduly biased for or against any of the directives being counted. Keeping in mind that genuine moral indeterminacy exists such that no best or utopian option is available, a reasonable choice is any that satisfies the axioms (or norms) that jointly characterise the liberal procedure, whereas an arbitrary decision does not. As Sen points out, axiomatic social choice theory, which analyses and classifies the distinctive procedures available for counting over noncomparable individual rankings of options, can be especially helpful in this context, keeping in mind the obvious analogy between individual persons and individual values (Sen 1987: 64–5). Evidently, the liberal process must be viewed as public and political if the different values to be counted are assumed to be located in different persons. But it can also be viewed as private and ethical if the different values are assumed to be located in a single person.

If liberal rationalism is spelled out in this way, the relevant procedural values (whatever they are) must be given suitable priority over values which conflict with them. Given that a reasonable procedure is in some sense 'liberal,' certain liberal political values, including basic rights and other constitutional essentials, must be seen as generally more weighty than competing values, perhaps even infinitely so.[17] But then the liberal values are taken to be rationally comparable to illiberal ones. The directives of the former are ranked as superior to those of the latter in cases of conflict. Thus, to escape Berlin's charge of lunacy, a pluralistic liberal rationalist maintains that some liberal procedural values are generally superior to any other ideals created by men: the field of noncomparability must be duly circumscribed. In effect, some such weighting arrangement, in addition to the liberal procedural norms themselves, must be built into the meaning of any reasonable process for counting over the directives of incompatible values.

Given that conflicts of incommensurable values cannot really be rationally resolved, however, it is intriguing to ask just what any such liberal counting procedure is doing within the agonistic rationalist framework. If it is not truly resolving conflicts of noncomparable values, what does it accomplish and why is that accomplishment reasonable? Unlike a mainstream rationalist, Berlin cannot say that a liberal political process produces – through open discussion and deliberation – information that can permit citizens to genuinely resolve their basic value conflicts. Like the Romantics, he is committed to the claim that conflicting and incommensurable ideals are inherent in the nature of morality and forever beyond rational resolution.

Berlin must reject, for example, an epistemic view of the political process as a method for generating a complete and consistent ranking that is most likely to represent the true unobservable all-things-considered ranking of the options. Peyton Young (1988, 1995) adopts an epistemic perspective, for example, when arguing on the basis of Condorcet's work that simple majoritarian procedures can be extended to generate a complete and transitive ranking that is a maximum likelihood estimate of the true ranking. But Berlin insists that true rankings are indeterminate with respect to some subsets of options because noncomparable values come into irreconcilable conflict over those subsets. On his view, rather than try to make a best guess at how to remove this indeterminacy, rational people must recognise that it is genuinely irremediable and make radical choices that lack rational justification.

Berlin, it seems, must treat the liberal political process as a reasonable device for making radical picks among options that implicate conflicting and incommensurable values, where any pick is compatible with liberal purposes (as reflected in the liberal procedure) but does not imply that the underlying conflict of values has been truly resolved or that one value is genuinely superior to others.[18] The point is that a decision may be needed for public purposes now, at a given time and place, even though a best option sitting at the head of a complete and consistent ranking cannot be rationally determined. By picking one option over others, liberal rationalists of Berlin's ilk do not imply that it is best or that the underlying value conflicts have been remedied once and for all. Rather, the conflicts can never be genuinely resolved. Thus, the liberal political process itself can be viewed in romantic terms as an inexhaustible creative process, a continuing public decision procedure in which citizens may freely participate in an indefinite series of picks without ever being constrained to provide a complete and consistent ranking of any given set of options.

Against this dynamic romantic view, it might appear that any liberal political procedure must weigh or compare the incommensurable values to count their respective directives. But this is not so. If simple majority rule were thought to be a liberal procedure, for example, then any individual, to resolve internal conflicts of incommensurable values over any pair of options, would pick the pairwise ranking favoured by a majority of his values; and any polity of individuals, to resolve conflicts among their revealed overall personal rankings, would pick the ranking favoured by the majority of individuals. When counting the various pairwise directives, either at the level of the person or the politys there is no need to weigh or compare one underlying value with another.[19]

This is not to say that liberal procedural values are exhausted by majority rule. Arrow's impossibility theorem and related results show that majority rule will generally fail to make pairwise choices which can be combined to reveal a complete and consistent overall ranking of all the options.[20] Given the fact of tragic pluralism, though, the lack of a complete and consistent majority ranking of the options is hardly unreasonable – after all, the nature of value precludes any genuinely rational ordering of this utopian sort. To that extent, the romantic spectacle of majority cycles – whether stretching through time or across different societies at the same time – is quite compatible with Berlinian liberal rationalism. At the same time, however, there is a need for liberal institutional devices (basic rights, for example) to keep majority rule within liberal limits. These devices serve to veto illiberal options even if majority cycles over the liberal options remain.

Perhaps Larmore and other critics of Berlin's tragic pluralism might find it less objectionable when it is restrained by some variant of this liberal procedural approach. They may accept that, although conflicts of incommensurable values cannot rationally be resolved by genuinely comparing the values and weighing their competing directives, reasonable people can agree nonetheless on a suitable liberal procedure to take account of the directives and make radical choices of winning options at any time or place. In this case, the mystery of a rational faculty that somehow directly compares and ranks incommensurables is replaced by a set of liberal procedural conditions, in other words, concepts and axioms which jointly establish the meaning of a reasonable political procedure in this context. These conditions establish an explicit understanding of 'political reasonableness' as a well-defined procedure or instrument, open for all to see, which any and all citizens in the given society must use to pick among options that implicate conflicting and incommensurable values. But political rationality so understood is not concerned with discovering a true resolution of the relevant conflicts of values. Rather, it is concerned with protecting certain liberal values from illiberal encroachments, insisting all the while that such liberal values generally cannot issue in a complete and consistent overall moral ranking of the options open to liberals. Superior liberal procedural values might be viewed as more or less universal norms, part of a common moral inheritance, or, alternatively, as local norms, specific to, say, advanced democratic societies. Berlin apparently takes the former line.

Plural liberty

The next step is to see that the force of tragic pluralism extends even within liberalism's citadel: 'It goes all the way down,' as Gray puts it, 'right down into principles of justice and rights' (Gray 1995: 60). Given that liberal principles themselves cannot be insulated from pluralism, different basic rights may implicate rationally noncomparable values that clash irreconcilably when the rights conflict with one another.

Berlin's basic idea of liberty relates to the number and variety of opportunities open to an individual with normal capacities to make his own choices: 'Freedom is the opportunity to act … [It] entails … the absence of obstacles to possible choices and activities – absence of obstructions on roads along which a man can decide to walk' (Berlin 1969: xxxix, xlii). Freedom in this basic sense is 'the possibility of action,' not action or choice itself, and so is compatible with inaction (Berlin 1969: xxxix–xl). It apparently has at least two distinct aspects – negative and positive – which 'may clash irreconcilably' (Berlin 1969: xlix). The concept of liberty is itself plural. Its conflicting aspects are associated with plural and noncomparable values:

> If the claims of two (or more than two) types of liberty prove incompatible in a particular case, and if this is an instance of the clash of values at once absolute and incommensurable, it is better to face this intellectually uncomfortable fact than to ignore it, or automatically attribute it to some deficiency on our part which could be eliminated by an increase in skill or knowledge; or, what is worse still, suppress one of the competing values altogether by pretending that it is identical with its rival – and so end by distorting both.
>
> (Berlin 1969: l)

Negative liberty (or freedom *from* interference) relates to the area of activities where the individual has opportunities to choose without interference by others: 'The wider the area of non-interference the wider my [negative] freedom' (Berlin 1969: 123). Those who focus on this aspect of liberty are concerned to specify some protected zone where the individual ought to be free from coercion by others:

> Such libertarians as Locke and Mill in England, and Constant and Tocqueville in France [assume] that there ought to exist a certain minimum area of personal freedom which must on no account be violated. It follows that a frontier must be drawn between the area of private life and that of public authority.
>
> (Berlin 1969: 124)

Positive liberty (or freedom *to* choose) relates to the rational and moral agency of the individual; more specifically, his capacities to control and make whatever choices are open to him. It 'derives from the wish on the part of the individual to be his own master' (Berlin 1969: 131). This aspect of liberty apparently makes reference to certain capacities (including a capacity for reasoning) that, for Berlin, are inseparable from what it means to be a normal human being. Anybody who lacks the relevant capacities lacks the opportunity to act. He faces obstacles which are incompatible with the freedom of a normal human agent. Those who defend positive liberty are concerned to specify and protect what is meant by self-government, including democratic extensions of the idea, without necessarily being concerned about the proper 'area of private life'.

Positive liberty may be 'at no great logical distance' from negative liberty, Berlin admits, and the two aspects of freedom 'cannot be kept wholly distinct'

(Berlin 1969: 131, xliii). But they are not the same thing. Democracy, for example, is 'logically uncommitted' to negative liberty (Berlin 1969: 165). Moreover, rights to participate in self-government might clash with property rights or rights to privacy, and the values attached to the respective rights may be noncomparable.

Berlin does not doubt that positive liberty is 'a valid universal goal' and 'something valuable in itself' (Berlin 1969: xlvii). Yet he emphasises that it (unlike negative liberty) was twisted historically into some fake ideal of rational self-perfection, the alleged desirability of which was used to justify forms of authoritarianism. He is careful to point out that a similar history of perversion 'could equally have been the fate of the doctrine of negative liberty.' Still, that did not happen, he says: 'Hence, the greater need, it seems to me, to expose the aberrations of positive liberty than those of its negative brother' (Berlin 1969: xlvii). In his opinion, negative liberty does not possess the confusing historical connotations associated with positive liberty, and is thus less likely to obscure the basic idea of freedom as opportunity (Berlin 1969: lxi–lxii). As a result, he tends to identify the basic idea with its negative aspect. But that shouldn't blind us to the value of positive liberty, or to the possibility that values attaching to conflicting rights may be noncomparable.

Given that the idea of liberty itself is not immune from the force of pluralism, it follows that there are plural and noncomparable liberal cultures or constellations of values *per se*. Each liberal culture may be built on a distinctive conception of freedom or set of rights and liberties. More generally, each culture may be associated with a distinctive liberal political procedure. If conflicts arise between the directives of these noncomparable liberal cultures with respect to some overlapping domain of options, then it is reasonable to expect some indeterminacy in any all-things-considered universal liberal ranking of the options. There is no best or utopian liberalism which could remove this indeterminacy.

The 'immense value' of equal rights

Even though he says that liberalism itself is not immune from the force of pluralism, Berlin does not hesitate to claim that equal liberty is of 'immense importance' relative to competing values. He argues that a capacity to recognise this is inseparable from 'what we mean by being a normal human being':

> [T]here must be some frontiers of freedom which nobody should be permitted to cross. Different names or natures may be given to the rules that determine these frontiers: they may be called natural rights, or the word of God, or Natural Law, or the demands of utility or of the 'permanent interests of men' ... What these rules or commandments will have in common is that they are accepted so

widely, and are grounded so deeply in the actual nature of men as they have developed through history, as to be, by now, an essential part of what we mean by being a normal human being. Genuine belief in the inviolability of a minimum extent of individual liberty entails some such absolute stand.

(Berlin 1969: 164–5)

Since 'nobody' should be allowed to violate the relevant frontiers of freedom, equal rights for all must be established. Moral rules must distribute equal rights even if these equal claims do not actually receive equal protection under prevailing laws and customs, as a result of prejudice or ignorance in particular social contexts. Also, the system of equal rights must be viewed as being of paramount moral value. The values attached to basic rights must generally override other values in cases of conflict, so that 'a minimum extent of individual liberty' may remain 'inviolable'. Thus, Berlin's pluralism apparently does not foreclose for him the possibility that some minimum extent of equal liberty has universal and paramount value.

Indeed, he says it is a 'general truth' that human rights are essential to any 'decent, even tolerable way human beings can live with each other' (Jahangebloo 1992: 114). This is not an isolated statement. He also suggests that every decent or civilised society – as opposed to barbarian populations, which are 'unintelligible' to 'normal' or civilised humans – privileges human rights:

The idea of human rights rests on the true belief that there are certain goods – freedom, justice, pursuit of happiness, honesty, love – that are in the interest of all human beings, as such, not as members of this or that nationality, religion, profession, character; and that it is right to meet these claims and to protect people against those who ignore or deny them. I think that every [intelligible] culture which has ever existed assumed that there exist such rights – or at least a minimum of them.

(Jahanbegloo 1992: 39)

By implication, any intelligible culture is at least minimally liberal in the sense that it suitably privileges at least some minimum core of equal rights for all.[21] A value-system which does not do this is illiberal and barbarian.

Admittedly, Berlin does not say much about the nature of the rights which he considers essential for any minimally liberal culture. As a result, it may seem difficult to draw a clear line between liberal culture and illiberal alternatives. He does reject Mill's view that every civil society should recognise an equal right to do as one pleases with respect to purely self-regarding acts, because 'everything that I do may have results which will harm other human beings' (Berlin 1969: 155). But otherwise he suggests merely that the inviolable sphere of equal liberty is 'a matter of argument, indeed of haggling' (1969: 124). No explicit content is assigned to 'natural rights,' for example, or to 'the demands of utility,' other than what is 'widely accepted'.

Berlin apparently thinks that common sense reveals a minimum extent of equal liberty definitive of a minimally liberal culture. But more needs to be said to clarify this, otherwise the reach of his tragic pluralism cannot be suitably restricted. If there is no reasonable basis for distinguishing between liberal and illiberal rights when clashes of rights can implicate rationally noncomparable values, an unbridled pluralism emerges such that, for example, a clash between one person's right not to be enslaved and another's right to enslave him can implicate noncomparable values. If the values attaching to these two conflicting rights are noncomparable, however, it cannot be unreasonable for either right to prevail over the other. Such unbridled pluralism is incompatible with liberal rationalism. Slavery can't be ruled out as unreasonable.

To keep tragic pluralism within liberal limits, it must be possible to distinguish liberal rights and values from their illiberal counterparts. Conflicts of *liberal* rights can implicate rationally noncomparable values, as can conflicts of *illiberal* rights. But conflicts between a liberal right and an illiberal one cannot implicate noncomparable values. Rather, liberal rights (and, more generally, liberal political procedures) are far more valuable than illiberal ones.

Despite his failure to clarify the basis of a distinction between liberal and illiberal rights, something can be learned from Berlin's insistence that every liberal culture must privilege at least some minimum core of *human* rights due equally to all humans. To escape from barbarism, he says, society cannot deny equal liberty altogether. But this means that some putative rights are not eligible to be liberal rights. A right to enslave others is an illiberal right, for example, as is a right to sell oneself into slavery: these rights are incompatible with the preservation of any extent of equal liberty for all.[22] It makes no sense to say that liberal culture can involve equal rights to enslave each other. There is no equal liberty in a slave society. Rather, an equal right not to be enslaved is essential to minimal liberalism.

Again, a right to arbitrarily kill innocent members of particular ethnic or racial groups is an illiberal right. It denies that a minimum core of equal rights attaches permanently to each person by virtue of his humanity. An equal right to be free of such ethnic and racial violence must be an element of any liberal minimum core.

For a Berlinian liberal, illiberal rights reflect illiberal values which are trumped by liberal values embodied in liberal rights. Any conflict between liberal rights and their illiberal counterparts doesn't implicate rationally noncomparable values. Rather, the superiority of the liberal side is deemed reasonable. The liberal value of freedom from slavery is far more important than any illiberal value of slavery, for example, just as the liberal value of freedom

140

from arbitrary attack by others is far more important than any illiberal value of ethnic or racial purity. As a result, any havoc wreaked by tragic pluralism is contained, for committed liberals like Berlin, within the boundaries of minimal liberalism. Liberal reason may be weak but it still has some bite.

I have called attention to a couple of equal rights which seem to be elements of a liberal minimum core. No doubt there are others. Even with just the two mentioned, however, the requirement of suitable priority for a minimum core of equal liberty has remarkably powerful implications for liberal culture. For example, given that an equal right not to be killed arbitrarily by others is essential, any minimally liberal culture may entail an equal right to be free of starvation caused (however indirectly) by social and economic institutions. In that case, liberal property rights would have to be tailored accordingly to permit redistribution of wealth when required to prevent starvation. The idea that private owners have an absolute right to retain their surplus wealth when others are starving would become an illiberal perversion of the idea of negative liberty. Myriad examples of this sort are conceivable. Thus, the requirement of at least a minimum extent of equal liberty may place many constraints on what claims can count as liberal rights in any given social context.

I shall not attempt to delineate with any precision the contours of a liberal minimum core of equal rights. Whatever minimum marks the boundary between liberal culture and barbarism, however, rights that conflict with those in the minimum core must be illiberal rights. Adding illiberal rights to the liberal minimum doesn't expand the extent of equal liberty but instead compromises the minimum. On the other hand, many liberal rights can be added to those in the minimum core, recognising that liberal rights outside the minimum are by definition equal rights that don't conflict with the minimum rights. Liberal property rights or political rights can be added, for example, without violating the right not to be enslaved or the right not to be starved arbitrarily. Adding liberal rights to the liberal minimum does expand the extent of equal liberty, even though clashes of liberal rights outside the minimum may implicate rationally noncomparable values.

Agonistic liberal rationalists can certainly argue that civil societies should expand their liberal systems of equal rights well beyond any liberal minimum. Even if a rational liberal utopia remains inconceivable, a greater extent of equal freedom for all can be reasonably viewed as superior to a lesser extent, at least under certain conditions. A kind of liberal progress remains conceivable, in other words, as the members of any particular society become more capable of appreciating and exercising a greater number of equal rights. But it must be emphasised that this progress is nothing like the mainstream Enlightenment model. There is no advance towards a liberal social utopia in which justice, happiness and other goods are simultaneously maximised. There is no progress towards a utopian liberal system of rights in which rights are rationally adjusted and balanced into perfect harmony. Rather, clashes of liberal rights continue to implicate noncomparable values and thus give rise to agonising dilemmas. If liberal property rights or rights of privacy or rights to free expression conflict with liberal rights of political participation, for example, there may be no rational resolution to the conflicts. It may not be unreasonable to pick any of these liberal rights over the others in cases of conflict, recognising that slavery, death to the innocent, and the like are not liberal moral options. Keeping in mind that tragic pluralism continues to exert its force, the idea of progress is limited to an expansion of equal liberty accompanied by a corresponding expansion in the numbers of agonising dilemmas associated with clashing rights. Different liberal societies will generally progress in various noncomparable directions, as different choices are made as to which of any two liberal rights to pick in cases of conflict that implicate noncomparable values.

To advance beyond minimal liberalism, any particular civil society must expand its system of equal rights beyond the minimum core by removing more and more inequalities and special privileges. Tragic pluralism does not have to alter the familiar liberal aim of establishing like liberties for all far beyond the minimum, even if a greater extent of freedom does not imply increases of happiness or justice. As a liberal society advances in this sense, its members may decide through their political process to add certain liberal property rights and equal political rights to the minimum rights, for example, and to pick the political rights whenever they conflict with property rights. In this case, bans on 'second-class citizenship' and other unequal degrees of political status become accepted as reasonable customs, even though conflicts between political rights and property rights may implicate noncomparable values. But a different liberal culture may advance along a different path by picking the liberal property rights rather than the political ones. A minimally liberal culture does not necessarily rule out an unequal franchise or special political privileges for some groups, so long as these are not associated with the denial of the minimum core of equal rights to some people, as under slavery, genocide, 'ethnic cleansing,' and other forms of barbarism.[23]

At the same time, I do not mean to suggest that the minimum core of equal liberty whose moral priority is essential to liberal culture is entirely free of ambiguity. Consider the case of abortion. Is a foetus a person with rights? If so, then a case exists that a quite rigid 'pro-life' position is essential to minimum liberalism: a person's right not to be aborted is subsumed under his right not to be killed without reasonable cause. In this case, abortion of the innocent foetus appears to be reasonable only if there is no other way to save the life of the mother or to prevent the birth of a severely defective child who is incapable of enjoying any rights. If these conditions are not met, then protection might extend even to a foetus conceived by rape or incest. If an unborn child is not a person with rights, however, no case exists that the minimum core of equal rights includes a right not to be aborted. Rather, a strong 'pro-choice' position may become associated with liberal cultures as they advance beyond the minimum core to recognise an equal right to personal autonomy. The difficulty of providing a reasonable answer to the question of when personhood begins does create some ambiguity at the foundation of any rationalist liberalism.[24]

Nevertheless, with these caveats, Berlin's claim that every civil society presupposes suitable priority for a least a minimum core of liberal rights is tolerably clear.

Rationalist agonistic liberalism

It is time to draw together the threads of my reconstruction of Berlin's agonistic liberal rationalism. He certainly rejects the possibility of a rational liberal utopia, an implication of his tragic brand of pluralism. He is palpably averse to any suggestion that a full and coherent liberal system of equal rights can be rationally justified in terms of some grand moral ideal of autonomy or happiness. It is inconceivable to him that conflicting rights might be perfectly adjusted and balanced such that nothing of liberal value is lost. Thus, he warns against the vain pursuit of any ideal or best option (even a liberal one), sitting at the head of an all-things-considered complete and consistent ranking of distinct feasible cultures. Like Buridan's ass, liberals may lose everything if they persist in searching for the non-existent ideal.

But it is compatible with this to claim that a common moral horizon confines reasonable humans to more or less imperfect liberal cultures, which assign 'immense value' to at least some minimum core of equal rights, including rights not to be murdered, enslaved and the like. Even if all ideas of progress are rejected so that one liberal culture cannot be said to be any more advanced than another, each and every liberal culture can still be rationally justified as what Sen (1997a: 763) calls a *maximal* option that is not beaten by any other option. No particular liberal culture can be rationally justified as a *utopian* or *best* culture that beats or at least ties every other option. But any liberal culture (however imperfect, however few or many equal rights it recognises beyond the essential minimum) can be justified as a maximal option that beats every non-liberal alternative (since all non-liberal options are non-maximal) yet does not beat or tie any of the other maximal options. Any liberal culture is reasonably ranked above any non-liberal one because the latter fails to meet the common moral standards – it does not protect even a minimum core of equal rights. Yet no liberal culture can be reasonably ranked above another liberal one because noncomparable values attach to the different rights in their distinctive liberal systems of equal liberty when conflicts arise between the systems (keeping in mind that conflicts between them cannot arise with respect to the common minimum core of equal rights). It is not that any two liberal cultures are equally good. Rather, any two maximal options are rationally noncomparable. Complete indeterminacy exists in the ranking of distinct liberal cultures.

The upshot is that, despite tragic pluralism reaching into liberal values themselves, a reasonable all-things-considered partial ranking of feasible cultures exists which, though completely indeterminate over a top set of at least minimally liberal cultures, does veto every illiberal option from the top set.

In contrast, under an unbridled agonistic approach, every culture (liberal and illiberal alike) must be seen as a maximal option. No all-things-considered ranking of different cultures is possible. Highly illiberal options (including slave systems and Nazi ones) cannot be ruled out as inferior to liberal options because liberal values are not rationally comparable to illiberal ones. Even Gray and Ignatieff back away from such an unbridled agonistic reading of Berlin's doctrine. They rely on the common moral horizon to veto the highly illiberal options. But then it seems they should embrace the liberal rationalist interpretation instead of claiming that there is a 'radical choice' between liberal cultures and decent non-liberal ones that do not recognise any human rights. The latter cultures simply do not exist, given that a system of values must be barbaric if it does not privilege at least some minimum of liberal rights.

As suggested earlier, however, an agonistic liberal rationalist can defend an idea of progress in the sense of movement toward a greater extent of equal freedom to choose (though not necessarily a greater level of general happiness or justice). A particular liberal culture advances by adding to its stock of equal rights. There is simply more freedom of choice in the more advanced culture, even though in general an increasing number of agonising dilemmas must also be faced because more conflicts between liberal rights outside the minimum core implicate noncomparable liberal values. At the same time, each particular society advances along its own peculiar path. There is no single rational path of progress toward a greater extent of equal liberty. Rather, different liberal cultures advance along incompatible and noncomparable paths by picking different liberal rights and values when clashes occur outside the minimum core. Any pick is not unreasonable from a liberal perspective because none of the added rights and values violates the liberal minimum.

This idea of progress is relative to each particular liberal society. Each society pursues its own distinctive path of development towards a greater extent of equal freedom. In effect, each society exhibits its own more or less advanced cultural phases as it moves along a trajectory from its minimally liberal phase toward a maximal one. Any two cultures are on the same path of development if and only if, when the set of rights recognised by the less advanced of the two is considered, they give the same priority to the same rights when conflicts arise that implicate noncomparable values. The more advanced culture recognises all the basic rights recognised by the less advanced one and then some. Moreover, accompanying the larger set of rights recognised by the more advanced culture will generally be a greater number of agonising dilemmas and radical choices associated with conflicts of rights outside the minimum core.

Given such a notion of progress, the top set of maximal options is narrowed to include only the more advanced liberal cultures. But myriad advanced liberal cultures can be maximal options, which cannot be reasonably compared or ranked *vis-à-vis* one another. Any maximal liberalism must give suitable priority to an extensive system of equal rights for all, far beyond the minimum core. But different maximal liberalisms will give priority to different equal rights beyond the minimum. It is not unreasonable for different cultures to pick different rights when rights conflict, provided the minimum core is not compromised, because the conflicts implicate plural and incommensurable liberal values. Any maximal liberalism must also generally refuse to recognise as legitimate any special privileges or immunities which conflict with its extensive system of equal liberty for all. This requirement makes maximal liberalism far more demanding than minimal liberalism, which merely protects the minimum core of equal rights by refusing to recognise the legitimacy of any claim to annihilate it through slavery, arbitrary killing, and so on.

In addition to being ranked above non-liberal alternatives, any particular maximal liberal culture is now ranked above less advanced liberal cultures along the same path of development (less advanced versions of itself, so to speak). A maximal liberal culture protects a greater extent of equal liberty, and a smaller (perhaps zero) extent of unequal privileges and immunities, as compared to a less advanced liberal culture that is moving along the same path. Any agent has a greater number of equal opportunities to make his own choices in the more advanced culture, which recognises all the same rights as the less advanced society and then some. True, maximal options are path-dependent: a liberal culture that is maximal with respect to one path is not maximal with respect to other paths and, indeed, cannot even be rationally compared to liberal cultures which have made their own peculiar picks in cases of conflict between liberal rights that implicate noncomparable liberal values. But this does not alter the fact that every less advanced liberal culture is vetoed from the top set because it is reasonably ranked as inferior to *some* more advanced culture on its same path.

The upshot now is that a genuine all-things-considered partial ranking of feasible cultures exists which, though still completely indeterminate over a top set of more advanced liberal cultures, does veto every other culture – less advanced liberal ones and illiberal ones alike – from the top set. Moreover, the partial ranking is indeterminate over much more than the top set. In particular, there is no determinate ranking of any pair of liberal cultures which are following different paths of development. If they pick different rights when conflicts arise that implicate noncomparable values, then the two cultures are noncomparable and it is not unreasonable to defend either. Nevertheless, it remains reasonable to choose a more advanced culture over a less advanced one travelling down the same path.

It should be stressed that a maximal liberal culture is unlikely to stir much excitement in a mainstream utopian liberal rationalist. The various equal rights which can be included in its extensive system of rights are not mutually harmonious and their clashes may implicate noncomparable values. Because one right rather than another must be picked in cases of conflict, tragic sacrifices of liberal values cannot be avoided. Within the same culture, one right might be picked over another in some situations whereas the reverse pick is made in other situations. Different cultures can make different picks in like situations and still remain maximal. Moreover, unless equal liberty is given something like lexical priority over all competing values, a maximal liberal culture might occasionally recognise unequal privileges and immunities as more important than equal rights, with the caveat that such unequal claims cannot go to the length of authorising their holders to annihilate the equal rights of others. In short, the liberal cultures justified as maximal in terms of our common moral horizon may be a far cry from rational liberal utopias. At the same time, they are surely distinguishable from, say, a feudal culture, whether the latter is viewed as a less advanced variant of liberalism or as an illiberal option.[25]

Philosophical issues

Before Berlinian liberalism as interpreted can be accepted as an appealing doctrine, however, more explanation is required of the common moral horizon in which the fundamental concepts and categories of the doctrine are supposedly embedded. For example, by what philosophical methods can we acquire knowledge of this common morality? How do we come to know that reason is, on the one hand, strong enough to give more weight to liberal directives when they conflict with those of illiberal values and yet, on the other, too weak to assess the relative importance of at least some mutually incompatible liberal directives? Berlin's own methodological and epistemological views are difficult to pin down, as Gray points out (1995: 61–75). It is unclear, for example, whether he subscribes to a kind of rational intuitionism reminiscent of W.D. Ross (1930), in which the universal minimum morality is discovered as an independent order of fundamental concepts and categories whose reality does not depend on human activities, or to a type of neo-Kantian constructivism, in which the common moral horizon is constructed as an expression and amplification of rational activity itself.[26]

Berlin suggests at times that the universal moral minimum is comprised of truths which 'are presupposed (if that is the correct logical relation) by the very notions of morality and humanity as such' (Berlin 1969: liii). Tragic pluralism and the relative priority of liberal rights and values over illiberal alternatives are necessary moral truths, it seems, which are apparently confirmed by sufficiently careful interpretation of the experience of ordinary human beings over a very broad range of history. For example, pluralism is depicted as an 'objective' truth distinct from moral relativism and subjectivism (Berlin 1969: lii–liii; 1991: 10–14). As Gray remarks: 'The vital difference is in Berlin's claim that we *know* that the conflicts between ultimate values are genuine: that they are conflicts among goods that are irreducible and incommensurable' (Gray 1995: 162, emphasis original). Similarly, Berlin is not content to argue that any notion of a rational utopia is a product of imagination, unconfirmed as yet by empirical observation. Rather, he insists that 'the belief that some single formula can in principle be found whereby all the diverse ends of man can be harmoniously realized is demonstrably false' (Berlin 1969: 169). It is inconceivable that man could ever develop an ideal liberal character of the sort which Mill associated with the maximisation of general welfare:

> That we cannot have everything is a necessary, not a contingent, truth … [T]he very concept of an ideal life, a life in which nothing of value need ever be lost or sacrificed, in which all rational (or virtuous, or otherwise legitimate) wishes must be capable of being truly satisfied – this classical vision is not merely utopian, but incoherent.
> (Berlin 1969: li, 170)

This charge of incoherence 'may madden' mainstream utopian rationalists. 'Nevertheless,' he insists, 'it is a conclusion that cannot be escaped by those who, with Kant, have learnt the truth that out of the crooked timber of humanity no straight thing was ever made' (Berlin 1969: 170).

Berlin goes on to say that the question of identifying the elements of the common moral minimum is:

> Of a quasi-empirical kind. I describe this as quasi-empirical because concepts and categories that dominate life and thought over a very large portion (even if not the whole) of the globe, and for very long stretches (even if not the whole) of recorded history, are difficult, and in practice impossible to think away; and in this way differ from the more flexible and changing constructions and hypotheses of the natural sciences.
> (Berlin 1969: liii)

The relevant moral knowledge is more than merely empirical knowledge, it seems, because of the inconceivability in practice of thinking otherwise. But it remains unclear why he feels compelled to make this move, or why he thinks it is justified. For surely the relevant claim of inconceivability demands a kind of knowledge which cannot in principle be recovered from ordinary experience of human beings. Something that seems inconceivable on the basis of experience to date, for example, may well become conceivable on the basis of subsequent experience.

Berlin's reference to quasi-empirical necessary truths of morality and humanity raises a suspicion that some elements of transcendental idealism may linger within his approach. Indeed, his test of necessary moral truth, namely, the inconceivability of thinking otherwise, is a stock test of transcendental idealists.[27] He does explicitly deny the suggestion that he is committed to anything like Kant's hypothesis that the basic concepts and categories of rational morality are fixed a priori (Gray 1995: 67–8). Nevertheless, doubts creep back in when he suggests that tragic pluralism and the immense value of some minimum of human rights are permanent principles of the common moral minimum rather than contestable moral generalisations which may prove to be transitory. As it stands, his claim that tragic pluralism is a necessary truth comes dangerously close to sanctifying certain conflicts among conventional concepts and categories as inescapable features of morality, forever beyond reasonable resolution. Similarly, his claim that the paramount importance of some minimum extent of equal liberty is a necessary truth seems to ensconce liberal culture in a privileged position, forever beyond reasonable dispute.

Gray struggles to resolve this particular ambiguity in Berlin's epistemology. He suggests that 'the common human framework of moral categories is neither *a priori* in the full Kantian sense nor an empirical generalisation of supposedly universal substantive moral norms, but something in between' (Gray 1995: 69). But coherence seems to demand that Berlin should go one way or the other. He could repudiate the suggestion that the common moral horizon is comprised of essential a priori concepts and norms, for example, in which case tragic pluralism and the immense value attached to equal liberty would cease to be viewed as necessary moral truths and become contingent on certain institutions and states of education. At times, he appears to endorse this option.[28] If it is taken seriously, however, then he must admit the possibility that tragic pluralism and even liberalism might be dropped from the common moral horizon. He cannot insist, for example, that, despite any additional education and deliberation on the part of humans, a liberal utopia must always remain inconceivable for liberal rationalists.

Fortunately, there is no need to settle such methodological and epistemological issues for present purposes. Berlinian liberalism can be viewed as a form either of rational intuitionism or of quasi-Kantian constructivism without doing violence to my argument. After all, I am making a conceptual claim, to wit, the concepts and categories of minimal liberalism, tragic pluralism and rationalism can be combined into a coherent agonistic liberal rationalism, contrary to Gray's view. In effect, my argument is that the common moral horizon itself, which is made up of these basic concepts and categories, is a coherent array of rational and moral principles (whether these are viewed as intuitions or empirical generalisations). The principle of tragic pluralism is merely one of these various principles. It should not be conflated with the fact that the moral horizon – and thus agonistic liberal rationalism – consists of plural principles. Rather, it is duly restricted by liberal reason to be compatible with a distinct principle of the priority of some minimum core of liberal rights and values.

Berlin himself speaks of our need to maintain a 'precarious equilibrium' among the principles of the common moral minimum so that we can prevent ourselves from making 'intolerable choices' and keep within the bounds of 'a decent society' (Berlin 1991: 17–18). At the same time, we have the power to empathise with other rational humans and thus appreciate the 'precarious equilibria' which they may have achieved in different cultural settings, he insists, provided we can interpret and make sense of their conduct and feelings in terms of the common moral horizon.

The common moral horizon may well include various other principles in addition to the principles of pluralism and minimum liberalism. Berlin suggests that a suitably restricted principle of utility might also be included, for example.

> Utilitarian solutions are sometimes wrong but, I suspect, more often beneficent. The best that can be done, as a general rule, is to maintain a precarious equilibrium that will prevent the occurrence of desperate situations, of intolerable choices – that is the first requirement for a decent society.
>
> (Berlin 1991: 17–18)[29]

The priority given to liberal rights and values over illiberal ones might ultimately be explained in terms of general welfare, for example.[30] And perhaps clashes of liberal rights don't always implicate noncomparable values. Some liberal values might well be more important than others in terms of general welfare. In that case, some paths of liberal progress might be viewed as more expedient than others. Some liberal rights beyond the minimum might be less costly than others for any society to establish and enforce. Indeed, some equal rights might be too costly to pick at all.

Although some such restricted principle of utility may well be reasonable and seems to have been endorsed by Berlin himself, agonistic liberal rationalists are not required to subscribe to any suitably restricted form of utilitarianism. Their doctrine is coherent even if no further moral principles are added to its mixture of liberal rationalism and tragic pluralism. As intuitionists or constructivists, they can maintain that reasonable humans who carefully reflect on these matters will not only give priority to liberal rights and values in conflicts with illiberal counterparts, but also seek the greatest possible extent of equal freedom for all while appreciating that clashes of liberal rights outside the minimum will generally implicate noncomparable liberal values. The key point is that the various principles making up the common moral horizon are mutually compatible. There is no contradiction between liberal rationalism and tragic pluralism in Berlin's doctrine as interpreted, and thus no agonising conceptual dilemma which cannot be reasonably resolved.

Conclusion

I have argued that Berlin's liberalism is grounded in rational choice as opposed to 'radical' choice undetermined by reason. The Berlinian doctrine is more plausibly conceived as an agonistic liberalism within rational limits, rather than an unbridled agonistic liberalism that lacks any rational basis for barring the door against illiberal and barbarian intruders. Even Gray agrees that Berlin does not subscribe to an unbridled agonistic liberalism – the common moral horizon vetoes barbaric options as irrational. Indeed, a central lesson of my argument is that much (if not all) of what Gray says about agonising choices within the limits of a common moral horizon can be said consistently with Berlin's depiction of himself as a 'liberal rationalist'.

I have also suggested that one of Berlin's main concerns is to unveil what he considers a genuine liberal rationalism in stark contrast to mainstream utopian rationalisms, which he repeatedly attacks as false and dangerous to liberty. He emphasises that reason is too weak to ever resolve certain tragic conflicts of values. A genuine rationalism must make room to a limited extent for a tragic pluralist moral outlook of the sort implicit in romanticism. Such a rationalism is necessarily anti-utopian: it must recognise that some conflicts of rationally noncomparable values will inevitably frustrate any rational vision of ethical and political perfection. Yet reason, though weaker than its mainstream promoters would have us believe, remains for Berlin the ultimate guide in ethical and political life. It apparently justifies a common moral horizon that is minimally liberal in content. In particular, liberal political procedures, including at least some minimum core of equal rights, should be given suitable priority over illiberal values. The freedom to create and pick plural and incommensurable ideals, so prized by the Romantics, is thus kept within reasonable liberal limits.

Berlin's integration of romantic insights with a commitment to liberal reason yields a doctrine with both Enlightenment and Romantic aspects, to wit, a liberal rationalism with significant 'cracks' or 'gaps,' that is, zones of indeterminacy within which conflicts of values cannot be rationally settled. Within such zones, individuals and groups are free to choose as they wish: it is reasonable to choose any of a variety of distinct options. But the boundaries of the zones are defined such that the freedom to choose does not extend to illiberal options: a minimum core of basic liberal rights must not be violated, even though liberal rights outside that minimum may conflict with each other in ways that implicate plural and incommensurable values. As a result, the Berlinian amalgam may have considerable attraction for liberals, especially if we keep in mind that further principles (including a restricted principle of utility) might be consistently added to the amalgam.

On the one hand, it exhibits a romantic aspect to the degree that it imagines reason as struggling in vain to completely cage or order the 'literally infinite' process of ethical and political creation. Some conflicts of values cannot be rationally resolved. On the other hand, it exhibits a rationalist aspect to the degree that it relies on reason to confirm the overwhelming importance of certain liberal values in that ethical and political process. Conflicts between those liberal values and illiberal ones *can* be rationally resolved in favour of the former. Thus, the tension between romanticism and enlightenment within Berlin's pluralistic liberal rationalism is such that neither element achieves a full victory over the other.

Despite its interest, however, Berlin's distinctive liberalism is open to objection. Even if reason is weaker than mainstream rationalist ideologues contend, for example, why should the line between the sphere of rationally noncomparable values and the sphere of comparable ones be drawn where Berlin apparently draws it? Without further argument, it seems *ad hoc* to claim that conflicts between liberal and illiberal values can generally be reasonably resolved to the former's advantage whereas conflicts between liberal values or between illiberal ones *per se* cannot always (or perhaps even often) be rationally settled. If the superiority of liberalism over its competitors can be rationally justified in terms of, say, general happiness, then why can we not invariably turn to general welfare to rationally dispose of conflicts involving different liberal rights? Why should we believe that some conflicts of values are forever beyond the power of reason to settle? Why is it impossible to imagine a rational liberal utopia sitting at the head of a complete and consistent ordering of all feasible cultures?

These objections, which are of a sort likely to be pressed by mainstream utopian liberal rationalists, go to the truth of tragic pluralism and deserve further study. Even Berlin himself has admitted that there are liberalisms which are not pluralistic, in which case mainstream rationalist liberalisms might be conceivable after all. As he recognises, for example, Mill makes room in his rationalist utilitarian liberalism for the romantic creative spirit, without accepting the validity of tragic pluralism (Berlin 1969: l–lii, 173–206). This is not the place to critically assess Mill's peculiar way of blending Enlightenment and Romantic elements. As is well known, however, he holds out the possibility of an ideal utilitarian liberal culture and defends – both as an ingredient of that rational utopia and as a means to its achievement – an equal right for individuals and groups to act spontaneously in accord with their own values and ideals, provided no harm is directly caused to other people (for further discussion, see Riley 1998, 2000). Moreover, it is clearly open to a mainstream rationalist like Mill to admit that there may be some indeterminacy in utilitarian ethical and political judgements because of lack of information and insufficient deliberation. Such an admission does not require any sacrifice of utopian aspirations. This contingent sort of indeterminacy can in principle be remedied through additional information and more careful deliberation.

What makes Berlinian liberalism so distinctive within the liberal pantheon is its assertion that some indeterminacy is *irremediable* by virtue of the inherently pluralistic nature of morality. But it is by no means clear how the assertion could ever be proven, at least until reason has attained its highest power under conditions of full information – only then could we know whether it is incapable of resolving some conflicts of values.[31]

Notes

1   Obviously, I am using the term 'liberal' broadly since it extends to all decent cultures that suitably privilege some minimum of human rights or, equivalently, some minimum of vital human interests that ought to be regarded as rights. Some may prefer to confine the term 'liberal' to advanced societies that give priority to sets of liberal rights far beyond any such minimum. But this is merely a semantic difference as long as any non-liberal culture is viewed as decent if and only if it privileges some minimum of human rights.

2   Galipeau (1994) also emphasises Berlin's coherence. Yet he agrees with Gray that any notions of reason and decency which may be implicit in Berlin's common moral framework do not privilege liberal cultures over non-liberal ones.

3   As Berlin admits, some of these figures did not view themselves as counter-enlightenment thinkers. Kant 'hated romanticism', for example, and both Schiller and Goethe are essentially mainstream rationalists (Berlin 1999: 68, 86–7, 112). For further discussion of romanticism, see Riasanovsky (1992), Larmore (1996b) and Malia (1999).

4   Riasanovsky (1992) argues that the romantic cult of the creative poet and artist was grounded on 'the pantheistic or panentheistic belief of sharing in divine power … It was at this point that German idealistic philosophy in general and Fichte's philosophy of the ego in particular was [sic] most closely connected with the emergence of romanticism. The poet or artist was, thus, a demiurge creating the world' (Riasanovsky 1992: 89).

5   Berlin suggests that 'the romantic hero genuinely emerges … in Germany' by 1780 (1999: 84). Riasanovsky (1992) dates the emergence of romanticism in Germany and England a bit later, to the 1790s.

6   It has been suggested to me that confusion may be caused by labelling Berlin's doctrine as a form of rationalism. Nevertheless, I have resisted dropping the label since it seems to me that much would be lost by doing so. In this regard, I certainly agree that mainstream rationalism must be distinguished from a belief in reason, and that Berlin firmly rejected the former while affirming the latter. But Berlin does refer to himself as 'a liberal rationalist,' which suggests that his use of the term 'rationalism' is sufficiently flexible to accommodate more than the mainstream ideology. Moreover, since he thinks his liberal form of rationalism is genuine whereas the mainstream ideology is fake, it seems important to speak of two forms of rationalism in order to clarify the differences between them. Why should the term 'rationalism' be forever exclusively associated with an exploded mainstream ideology? Finally, if the rationalistic label is dropped, we are in danger of losing sight that a belief in reason is at the foundation of Berlin's liberalism. That belief is one which Berlin does share with the mainstream ideologues, even though he rejects the mainstream view of reason as an unlimited power in favour of a less grandiose view. Gray's failure to see that Berlin's pluralistic liberalism is grounded on an unconventional conception of reason is less likely to be repeated, perhaps, if the label of rationalism is retained.

7   By implication, Mill's vision of an ideal utilitarian liberal culture, in which Pagan spontaneity in self-regarding conduct is integrated with Christian obedience to general rules of other-regarding conduct, is incoherent. For a defence of Mill's vision, see Riley (1988, 1998, 2000).

8   'In general, values are commensurable', as Larmore puts it, 'if they can be compared in terms of the extent to which they promote or express some common value' (1996a: 159). He goes on to distinguish among 'cardinal', 'ordinal,' and 'imprecisely cardinal' forms of commensurability.

9   The modern idea of utility, which boils down to the value of a function representing any consistent choice of behaviour, has nothing to do with ethical evaluation. Unlike the classical utilitarian ideas of pleasure or desire-satisfaction (with which it is still conflated), it may be employed without making any commitment to descriptive homogeneity in objects of value.

10 But Larmore argues that Aristotle is not properly viewed as a pluralist (1996a: 163–7). Gray also seems unsympathetic to this line (1995: 36). For discussion of the traditional view of Greek ethics in which *phronesis* roughly corresponds to prudence broadly conceived, see T. H. Irwin (1995).

11 Some usages of the term 'incommensurability' rule out complete and consistent rankings of options but do not rule out value monism. John Broome suggests that the term should be confined to mean indeterminacy in overall rankings of options, for example, because he apparently thinks that 'all values are commensurable to some extent' and what we are interested in is ranking options which 'realize values to different degrees' (Broome 1997: 2). In his view, which essentially ignores the issue of pluralism versus monism relating to sources of value, full commensurability amounts to fully determinate rankings of options. Although his approach has considerable merit, I do not adopt it for present purposes since it does not tie incommensurability to pluralism. Moreover, it allows plural sources of value to coexist in principle with fully determinate ethical evaluations, something which Berlin rejects as 'incoherent'.

12 It is not that 'equally ultimate' values are equally valuable, in which case we could compare their conflicting rankings of options and select one that gives us a best option in terms of value overall. Rather, the values are equally basic, having no common source, and their directives cannot be reasonably compared at all when conflicts arise. Even Gray at times seems not to appreciate that indeterminacy *must* arise in an overall ranking of any two options if the directives of noncomparable values come into conflict with respect to that pair. See e.g. Gray (1998: 27).

13 Sen points to the example of Agamemnon's dilemma. It should be noted that intransitivity can be associated with overcompleteness. Gray at one time followed Raz in claiming that 'incommensurability among values discloses itself as a breakdown or failure in transitivity' (Gray 1995: 50). But he now backs away from that claim (Gray, 1998: 35, n. 6). In any case, as Raz admits, intransitivity is not a sure-fire mark of incommensurability. Intransitivity can arise even if all values are roughly commensurable. Overcompleteness and incompleteness may both signal noncomparable values. But neither is a sure-fire mark.

14 For the state of the art, see also Sen (1997a: 763–9). Interesting discussions of related interpretive issues can be found in Chang (1998).

15 As Sen remarks, however, not everyone accepts that the donkey's dilemma is a case of indeterminacy. Commensurabilists argue that indifference between the two equally valuable haystacks leads to the beast's demise. Moreover, given that eating either haystack is more valuable than starving to death, the beast is clearly irrational on either interpretation.

16 A similar *distinction* between 'tentative' and 'assertive' indeterminacy is drawn by Sen (1997: 763–4). See also Sen (1996).

17 In the latter case, the procedural values are assumed to take lexical priority over the others. Strictly speaking, if one value takes lexical priority over another, the directives of the first are incommensurable with (though infinitely more valuable than) the directives of the second.

18 Rawls's (1993) *Political Liberalism* relies on a similar distinction between criteria of truth and standards of public reasonableness. I do not mean to suggest that Rawls's doctrine is similar to Berlin's liberal rationalism in other respects.

19 Majority rule does not necessarily presuppose that the individual rankings being counted must be given *equal weights*. Rather, the rankings may be noncomparable one to another: But they must be counted in an unbiased manner, where 'unbiased' has a precise meaning in terms of procedural conditions of anonymity, neutrality, and so on. See Sen (1970: chapter 5). I do not mean to imply that majority rule cannot be suitably redefined to make equal weighting part of the definition. But, among other things, I am trying to take seriously the tragic pluralist thesis.

20 See Arrow (1963), Sen (1970) and Riker (1982).

21 Following Nozick, liberal culture might be described as a form of life in which respect for the equal liberty of others is prescribed as a side-constraint on the individual's actions. Liberty might then seem to be a necessary condition of pursuing whatever is valuable in life, rather than a pre-eminent good in itself. If the agent must respect others' rights as a near-absolute constraint on his actions, however, then he must in effect assign immense value to equal liberty. In short, the language used by deontologists to describe liberal culture can be suitably translated into the language used by consequentialists, or so I shall suppose.

22 For a similar statement, see Mill (1859: 299–300).

23 Recall that Mill, for example, advocated 'plural voting' even in advanced liberal contexts. See Mill (1861: 47–79).

24 For further discussion of the abortion issue and its resolution in the context of Mill's utilitarian liberalism, see Riley (1998: 202–6).

25 A feudal order would be included among non-maximal liberal cultures if it recognises the immense value of at least some minimal core of equal rights. It is not necessary that lords and peasants enjoy equal liberty in all respects. But a feudal order in which some are in effect enslaved would be an illiberal option, unintelligible in terms of the common moral horizon (or 'natural law') of civilised human beings. For related discussion, see Galipeau (1994: 117–19).

26 For further discussion of the contrast between 'rational intuitionism' and 'constructivism,' see Rawls (1993: 91–107).

27 On inconceivability as a test of truth, see Mill (1865: 66–88, 125–48).

28 To illustrate, Berlin says there is a 'universal human belief' that human rights are essential to any 'decent, even tolerable way human beings can live with each other' (Jahanbegloo 1992: 114). For now, it seems inconceivable that a decent human life could dispense with such rights. '[B]ut this does not assume something unalterable,' he admits. Humans might cease to believe what they have universally believed to date. A 'general truth' does not reflect 'direct non-empirical knowledge, intuition, inspection of eternal principles' (Jahanbegloo 1992: 114). Rather, it is merely an induction by simple enumeration of human beliefs across a broad range of social contexts.

29 For other discussions of the possibility of some mixture of utilitarian-type balancing and indeterminacy precipitated by noncomparable values, see Griffin (1998) and Hampshire (1983).

30 The requisite moral structure might even take the form of a lexical priority rule, whereby liberal values are given indefinitely more weight than illiberal ones in any civilised social context. I do not mean to suggest that Berlin himself argues for the inclusion of such a priority rule within his agonistic liberal rationalism. But perhaps it is not inconceivable that a justification for it could be found in a less familiar version of utilitarianism, again, of suitably restricted reach.

31 An earlier version of this paper was delivered at a conference on pluralism at the Royal Irish Academy, Dublin.

7

DEALING WITH DIFFERENCE:
The Republican public-private distinction

Iseult Honohan

Introduction

Participants in current debates about pluralism and the best way to accommodate moral and cultural difference politically tend towards one of two positions – either that profoundly different moral and cultural values, though tolerated, must be restricted to the private realm, or (in the case of those who consider identity central to politics) that they should be recognised or somehow established in the public realm.

This issue of the neutrality of the public realm sets most liberals (and French republicans) on one side of a dividing line and many communitarians as well as cultural pluralists on the other. For the former the public realm must be thin and procedural, for the latter it must embody a substantive good or goods. Both responses present difficulties. Public neutrality is unsatisfactory because it takes issues that are too significant off the agenda. Publics which reflect substantive difference are problematic, because it is not clear if you can fully recognise more than one way of life in a single political community.

Many of the arguments that this issue has provoked rely on lingering assumptions from a conception of the relationship between public and private as radically opposed spheres. In order to understand more clearly what is at stake, in this article I draw attention to three dimensions of the complex-structured concepts of 'public' and 'private' and to varying emphases underlying different political uses. I focus in particular on two political traditions for which strikingly different versions of a public-private distinction are central – liberalism and republicanism.[1]

I look first at the liberal use of the distinction. Taking control as the central dimension of the public, liberals tend to elide the public and the state and advance the principle of public neutrality as an alternative to oppression or radical conflict. I then assess arguments that the liberal private-public distinction is oppressive and exclusive, peripheralises values, and is inapplicable to modern states.

Even if we accept some of these criticisms, the alternative is not to dismiss the distinction entirely. I show that the public-private distinction as employed by civic republicans does not merely draw the line in a different place from liberals, or reverse the priority of the spheres, but is *paradigmatically different*, constructing the meaning of the distinction on a significantly different basis. Republicans see interest, which is more diffuse than control, as the central dimension. A form of deliberative politics acts as a filter between the private and the public. Two senses of the public are distinguished – spaces of open expression and discussion, on the one hand, and authoritative law-making or the state, on the other. These are two kinds of public realms, related but not immediately mutually entailed. These publics can accommodate difference and allow expression and potential recognition of people's deepest convictions without permanently entrenching particular values. I conclude that this may imply a public realm with commitments more substantial than most liberals recommend but less than communitarians, nationalists or cultural pluralists assume.

The republican conception of the relations between public and private offers a potentially better basis for thinking about how to deal with difference than either the liberal model, which relegates it to the private, or the communitarian and radical cultural pluralist models, which establish one or a rainbow of ways of life in the public world.

The three dimensions of public and private

To understand the dimensions of publicness and privateness I adopt a schema that combines elements of analyses outlined by Benn and Gaus (1983) and Pitkin (1981). Benn and Gaus note that 'public' and 'private' are complex-structured concepts contrasted pervasively in modern discussions of social life. Three fundamental dimensions can be distinguished (all of which tend to have descriptive, normative and prescriptive elements).

First, that of *accessibility or visibility* – what is public is open to all, any or many, what is private is hidden or accessible only to one, few or specified individuals. Instances of 'public' are a theatre or public house, of 'private' a bank account or private function. It is primarily (or least contentiously) on this dimension that public and private are equated with the activities of civil society and the family respectively.

Second, that of *control or agency* – what is public is controlled by all, many, or their agents, what is private is controlled or owned by one, few, or specified individuals. In a 'private house' this is usually the primary sense conveyed. The public here often implies actions of, or ownership by, the state as agent of all – the 'public sector'. On this dimension the public and the private tend to be equated with the state and individuals in civil society – hence 'privatisation'.

Third and finally, there is the dimension of *interest or relevance* – what is of public interest concerns or affects all, any or many (though it may not be visible to, or controlled by, them); what is of private interest concerns one, few or specified individuals. We speak of the public health implications of industrial pollution; and a private joke is one only I and (at most) a few friends can appreciate.

In any instance of use one dimension is usually in mind – contrast the different dimensions conveyed in 'public house' (access) and 'private house' (control). But it is not always certain into which category, public or private, an action, practice or institution falls – what is private in one sense may be public in another and vice-versa; theatres are often privately controlled – cabinet debates are carried on by the agents of the people and are doubtless relevant to them, but not accessible. There are many intermediate or hybrid entities such as churches, universities, banks. How we classify something will often be a function of which dimension we regard as most salient either in this particular case or more generally. Privacy rights invoked in legalising contraception have been justified variously in terms of *access* – arguing that the state should not inquire into private – that is, properly hidden – relations, and in terms of *control* – arguing that the state should not control what is properly a matter of individual agency.

It should already be clear that while the three are separate dimensions, political arguments often assume that they are systematically linked and that one dimension is determinant of the others. In a political ideology which dimension you emphasise affects your view whether something is normatively public or private. For libertarians, for example, the most salient dimension is *control*, and this determines the normative domain of interest: what is privately owned is, it is argued, a private concern – often minimising its wider impact – and need not be publicly accessible.

For many radicals, socialists and feminists, however, *interest or relevance* is the primary dimension; what affects many should be in some sense accessible to and controlled by many, or by the state on their behalf. Interest has been the pressure point in the extension of the public by feminists and has often closely entailed control and regulation.[2] Debates about the control of basic industry and, more recently, about the environment and the distribution of pornography revolve around the relations between the three dimensions.

The analysis that follows tends to deconstruct the clear-cut opposition of private and public. We can also see how a sharper boundary may tend to be drawn by those who prioritise the dimension of agency or control, which lends itself to being more clearly defined, than by those who prioritise interest or access, which can be wider and more diffuse in scope. 'Who controls?' expects a more specific answer than 'Who is affected?' or 'Who can see?' So in considering accounts of public and private there are two issues that arise: which dimension is most salient? and how closely entailed are the other two dimensions?

The liberal conception of the public-private distinction

My account of liberal ideas necessarily involves some generalisation. This is, I believe, justified in the context of the specific topic in question: the application by major contemporary liberal thinkers of the public-private distinction to the problem of difference, with particular reference to what can be admitted to the public.

Liberals, up to and including the later Rawls, rely on a clear distinction between public and private. Benn and Gaus note a particular tendency in liberalism to assume a dichotomous distinction. The most salient dimension is *control* – what is or may be regulated. Adopting the tendency to see this in sharply defined terms, public and private are routinely identified with the *state* and *civil society* respectively, envisaged as distinct realms. Thus in political terms something public is, quintessentially, controlled by the state; what is private is not – it is or ought to be controlled only by individuals or groups in civil society. As Moon, a sympathetic critic, has put it, 'the liberal distinction between public and private does not depend on whether an activity is conducted in the presence of unrelated others, but on whether it is the kind of activity the civic authority may regulate' (Moon 1993: 151).

Liberalism is arguably a defence of a certain conception of *individual* autonomy in reaction to the threat of excessive state authority, or, in contemporary terms, an attempt to treat all with equal respect. One of the central ways it meets this challenge is by establishing a private realm, a boundary beyond which the power of the state may not invade – often, but not always, defined in terms of rights. This was for much of the history of liberalism modelled precisely in terms of ownership, though it is now more often defended in terms of individual *autonomy*. The principle of public neutrality is advanced as an alternative to conflict and oppression.

While focusing on the dimension of control, mainstream liberals tend to see a looser connection between this and the other dimensions of privateness and publicness than libertarians. However, they tend to link control to access, and to interest (understood also in a highly individualised sense). What the state does should be visible and accessible to all; people should have a voice in matters that directly and specifically affect them, whoever owns or controls these affairs. To deem something political implies that it is open to public discussion *as* potentially controllable by the state.

Liberals have also tended to subsume a distinction with older roots – that between the wider (or in modern terms, *civil*) society and domestic or family life, which has complicated matters; a distinction that looks clear-cut on the surface contains more complex undertones, as feminists have insisted (Pateman 1983).

It is often assumed that liberalism privileges the private whereas republicanism privileges the public aspects of social life, (and this underlies much of the deepest suspicion of republican ideas), but things are not quite so clear-cut.

The relative status of the public and private realms in liberalism requires some clarification. The private is logically prior, as the individual is to the state, and it is privileged by rights; it is seen as the locus of freedom often defined negatively as the absence of interference. Relations in the private realm are seen as based on freely undertaken commitments, whether of contract, love or trust. For some liberals at least, a life lived entirely in private could be a satisfactory life, even if it is not *the* privileged locus of the good life.

The public, by contrast, is a fairly thin edifice constructed to allow individuals to live in peace; though often based on contract, it is the scene also of conflict and exercises of power. Public political participation is regarded as just one option among many ways of living.[3]

How does the liberal public-private distinction deal with difference?

Although the relation of public and private is not wholly clear-cut, nonetheless public and private are still seen in dichotomous terms when it comes to liberal treatments of the problem of difference, and the distinction has a lot of weight to bear – the public should adopt principles derived from an overlapping consensus and exclude differing substantive visions of the good (Rawls 1993). Arguments derived from differing comprehensive doctrines may not be used in public affairs.

Critique of the liberal public-private distinction

The liberal public-private distinction itself has been the focus of much criticism. The main charges briefly are as follows.

First, the distinction is intrinsically *oppressive*; it reinforces inequalities and exercises of power, while masking this with the formal equality of the public sphere; matters defined as private are taken off the agenda of public scrutiny, debate and regulation, even if they affect the interests of many. Defining the public-private boundary itself is seen as an exercise of power – calling something private short-circuits arguments about its normative status. Feminists in particular have targeted the public-private distinction as an instrument of the oppression of women, in deeming family and women's issues on the wrong side of the barrier for debate or regulation. (Some of this criticism relates more immediately to equality rather than difference issues, but it is not always possible to draw a clear line between them).

> The discourse of privacy in areas such as sexuality and private life has in political fact become a mechanism whereby women's oppression is not only constituted and maintained, but also and more damagingly rendered apolitical.
>
> (Frazer and Lacey 1993: 73)

There are well-substantiated claims that the distinction is inconsistently and ideologically used in practice to protect property rights rather than individuals, pornography rather than free speech.[4] However, the inconsistent or ideological *use* of the distinction should not be grounds for rejecting the distinction itself if it can be defined in terms of individual autonomy or personal inviolability for both men and women and is not identified in terms of rigidly defined realms (Cohen 1996). Thus no area of life would be defined as in principle non-political, beyond public discussion and scrutiny.

I now turn to criticisms, which focus more specifically on the private-public distinction as a part of a solution to the problem of difference.

Second, even if the aforementioned inequalities are removed, and the private is revised to protect the individual autonomy of all, it is alleged that the liberal private-public distinction operates to *exclude* or *marginalise* from the public those who do not conform to a particular male, rational model – to suppress difference. The requirements of liberal public life and its public culture demand modes of reason, impartiality, and a commitment to autonomy, which exclude women or those who are culturally different (Young 1990). This too may not be sufficient warrant to reject the distinction, but constitutes the basis of an argument that we should, for example, expand the notion of the individual and of rationality, reassess the characterisation of women and other cultures as irrational, and reconsider the relation of reason and emotion. We might diversify modes of public action, and provide for modes of minority expression. Therefore the exclusions involved may not be of such serious and wide-ranging scope as has been suggested. It may still be that, however modified, a liberal public culture will still favour some and exclude others by virtue of its priority of autonomy or an equivalent, and that liberals should admit that liberalism is 'a fighting creed' (Taylor 1992: 62).

Third, the public-private distinction *privatises values*. It both limits recognition of people's values to the private sphere and diminishes the significance of the public in their lives, giving up 'the hope of the kind of richer public life which human interdependence suggests may be possible' (Frazer and Lacey 1993: 205). If comprehensive doctrines are restricted to the private, the most deeply held convictions of its members are (for some at least) excluded from public recognition. If values and practices are more than purely subjective, critics argue, they involve a claim to be realised or recognised as having a wider validity. The distinction *peripheralises* an important aspect of human existence – the aspect of values: religious, cultural, and moral beliefs based in comprehensive doctrines (Cooke 1997: 4).

Furthermore this use of the distinction tends to make public activity formal and universalistic, concerned with constitutional and legislative issues of state intervention, and marginalises public political action as optional. It undervalues the self-realisation or sense of self-worth derived from contributing to or expressing one's values in public, political terms, from being able to influence the character of society and collective life.

This criticism suggests that relegating deep convictions to the private realm at least has serious costs; and unnecessarily alienates from the public realm needs that might somehow better be met. Since deep convictions (or expressions of cultural identity) will not easily go away, and are an important dimension of people's lives, excluding them from the public will not pre-empt conflict. It is not the most adequate way of dealing with difference in order either to avoid conflict or to meet needs.

Finally, the liberal public-private distinction between what is controlled by the state and what is not cannot be sustained; the distinction and the possibility of public neutrality breaks down. The family and intimate personal relations themselves are shaped by public political decisions, the state and civil society cannot be systematically separated; and more fundamentally, public agreement on principles of justice cannot clearly be separated from agreement on more substantial visions of the good.

I will consider aspects of this in turn. First, *states define the terms of private life*, what constitutes a marriage, a spouse, a parent or a family. Moreover, states that have extensive education, health and welfare functions (undertaken in line with liberal concerns for more-than-formal equality), cannot easily avoid embodying substantive views of the good in their activities. Tolerating in private different ways of treating, for example, fertility or terminal illness is no longer the main issue, but what services the state delivers and how.

> A state committed to providing a wide range of services, in a way that is consistent with the self-respect of their recipients, cannot possibly be 'neutral' among different conceptions of the human good, and different ideals of human excellence.
>
> (Moon 1993: 70 ff.)

Moreover, it is no longer appropriate to think of a single central sovereign authority distinct from civil society – the *public power operates at many levels* – in constitutional, legislative, political activities, through local and administrative agencies, and interconnected with businesses, semi-independent agencies and so on. In addition, regional and supra-national government are developing more importance. All these features are reflected in the increasing resonance of the more diffuse concept of governance.

Rather than being an *absolute barrier* the public-private distinction outlined so far is not even particularly effective in defending individual autonomy; as Nedelsky puts it:

> The characteristic problem of autonomy in the modern state is not … to shield individuals from the collective, to set up legal barriers around the individual which the state cannot cross, but to ensure the autonomy of individuals when they are *within* the legitimate sphere of collective power.
>
> (Nedelsky 1989: 13)

162

As a means of reconciling different moral views, this absolute distinction cannot be successfully applied. People with different ideas on the value of life and the importance of religion will have difficulty agreeing on public principles of justice to deal with euthanasia, abortion, religious and sex education in schools, to name just a few examples. Comprehensive moral views and public shared principles of justice are hard to separate:

> People who have different beliefs about the place of marriage among the ends of life will hold different beliefs about the conditions under which divorce is acceptable. Even if everyone accepts the public conception of justice, it is by no means clear that this conception will be adequate to settle such disputes, since in these areas there is no clear way of separating the public, shared conception of justice, and the private, diverse conceptions of our ends and ideals.
>
> (Moon 1993: 59)

The likely implied result is that either people will not agree on procedures of justice or that they will be unreconcilable on crucial issues which require decisions, and in which comprehensive views are embodied.

Thus the liberal public-private distinction, when relied upon as a resolution of the problem of difference, may exclude some people while attempting to be neutral, requires people to set aside in public some of their most central convictions, and implies that both the state and civil society, on the one hand, and principles of justice and comprehensive doctrines, on the other, can readily be distinguished, and that these distinctions can be systematically applied.

The civic republican conception of the public-private distinction

Like liberalism, classical civic republican theory has many interpreters. In addition, it has also been less clearly elaborated in contemporary terms, due to its relatively recent revival as a distinct position. Thus the republican public-private distinction will require more detailed elaboration, and my account will be more exploratory and tentative than presenting a fully articulated theory.[5]

A public-private distinction is fundamental to republican thought: the term itself derives from the *res publica* – matters of public concern. But is it paradigmatically different from that of liberalism, and does not merely redraw the boundaries or reverse the priorities. Applying my schema, we may say that for republicans the most salient dimension of the public is *interest* or relevance; what is quintessentially public is in the interest of all; what is private is in the interest of or relevant to one, few or specific individuals, or section of society.

Civic republicanism is based on recognising the interdependence of members of a political society, who are subject to a common authority. It relates the freedom of citizens to their participating in self-government and realising the common goods they share in an historically evolving political community. While the public interest is frequently identified as the aggregate of private interests, republicans focus particularly on shared interests, more often referred to as common goods.[6]

For some communitarians who assume unitary religious or cultural accounts of the common good or public interest, control may be closely entailed by interest: the common good, it is argued, should be enforced by the public or its agents. For republicans, however, the dimension of access follows more closely than that of control. Shared goods tend not to be as easily identifiable or immediately valued as individual interests. Recognising and defining the public interest requires the input of many in expression, discussion and action. To make the public interest publicly accessible there must be a public sphere of action and debate. Since it is defined in terms of interest, the public may be seen as rather diffuse, extending throughout the citizenry rather than necessarily being concentrated in a single agency or institution such as the state.[7] Since the dimension of control is not immediately entailed, characterising something as in the public interest does not directly imply its enforcement by the state.

There is a recurrent criticism of republican thought along the following lines: the public is what is controlled by the state, the private is what is not controlled by the state; what is private and what is public are mutually exclusive; in republican thought this is expressed as the opposition of individual and general interests; republicans put general before individual interest; this means imposing general interest through state control and dismissing the private; therefore republican thought is fundamentally authoritarian. But this criticism is misapplied to this account; it derives from simply reversing liberal categories of public and private. However, republicanism is not simply antithetical to liberalism. While communitarians and some republicans have expressed matters differently, it is possible to present a coherent, non-authoritarian account of the republican public-private distinction.

The republican distinction between the public and private is initially between two different orientations within individuals. It highlights a tension *within* each person between the immediately perceived particular advantage of each and the general interest of the citizen as an interdependent member of the polity, and requires each to be active in pursuit of the common good, to have *public spirit*, and to participate in public service. 'The better the state is constituted, the more does public business take precedence over private in the minds of the citizens' (Rousseau 1968: 140).

Purely private preferences are somehow *heteronomous*, and do not take account of interdependence (Sunstein 1993). These are seen as problematic, as arbitrary, limited or unreflective. They are not whatever is culturally or morally *different per se* but the purely particular. So we may try to minimise our tax payments even when we agree on values and principles such as, for example, that there should be public health care and education provision. It is this focus on particular interests which is here identified with the private. The public by contrast is what is in our long-term considered interest as interdependent citizens. Immediate particular preferences are subject to transformation: 'Individual identity, desire and value all become objects of political critique, challenge and social transformation' (Frazer and Lacey 1993: 125). But they *are* malleable and capable of transformation, not fixed or just a matter of bargaining, as preferences are often taken to be.[8]

The priority of the public is not a matter of the good of an entity *over and above* any of the citizens but the good of the citizens themselves as members of a political community, as distinct from their good as singular individuals. Machiavelli's notorious pronouncement, 'I love my country more than my soul' may be understood not as an expression of *self*-abnegation before the whole, but as a different view of what is central to the self – more like: 'I see myself more as a citizen of Florence than as an individual Christian soul'. In this perspective the considered good of the citizen takes priority over desires, preferences and values that are separable from his character as a member of this political society.

The primacy of the public over the private is not that of the good of the *majority* over the minority, but a division within each citizen. For everyone has both a public and a private interest – even the industrialist *qua* citizen has an interest in breathing clean air. Heteronomous private preferences are self destructive – they put immediate purely individual advantage ahead of the advantages enjoyed as a citizen. Those who put private before public interest are not just short sighted; they suffer from serious blind spots, and fail to see where their real advantage lies, and the importance of questions of who they are as well as what they want.

But things that we often think of as private in the sense of personal or individual – intimate relations, family life, personal success and economic security – are not utterly dismissed as valueless; in republican thinking these are variously seen as either the necessary basis or the ultimate purpose of public life. For a modern republican such as Arendt, these aspects of private life are seen as the sheltered basis from which actors can emerge into the public.[9] In another interpretation, enjoyment of such things is the ultimate point of the republic, but must be secondary, because it can only be achieved through first contributing to the joint endeavour – private benefits are logically secondary (Skinner 1990).

From this we may see that the public is in some sense prior in republican thought. Concern for the public interest is at least the precondition for enjoying private benefit. Though interpreters differ as to whether this should be seen as positive or negative, freedom is strongly identified with public activity in something like the classical sense of participating in self-rule.

Public action is an intrinsically valuable (for some the most valuable) part of life. This may take various forms of public service; while historically the emphasis was on military action, in contemporary republicanism it is on participation in political deliberation, or collective self-determination, self-development and recognition in public. The public is an area of self-development and self-expression, if not *the* privileged locus of the good life.

The primacy of the public means that duties come before rights. This is not to say that there are no rights, but that these are secured politically rather than seen as natural attributes of individuals. Matters that are guaranteed on private grounds in liberalism are justified as the basis of equal citizenship here – in particular property, and its relatively equal distribution. Rights to privacy may exist, but these are grounded in the common life and public discussion (Miller 1995: 449). The public life of the republic constitutes rights and guarantees liberties.

However, this limited priority of the public does not mean that in principle everything is to be regulated by the *state*, but that individuals should give priority to shared over purely individual goods, and act to realise these common goods. Not all public activity is governmental; the state does not simply determine and implement the public interest.[10]

The republican public-private distinction operates differently from the liberal version. Rather than reversing the priorities still within the focus of control, it takes interest as the central dimension of public and private, which allows a more diffuse sense of the public than that of the state or specific individuals. Public and private are not radically opposed as two separate spheres, but as different orientations within individuals. Individuals can modify and transform their preferences.

Moreover, what is in the public interest is not immediately self-evident. In contemporary republican thought, interactive deliberation by individuals in a public sphere of action and debate is the key process through which transformation occurs, and the public interest is defined.

Pluralising the public – deliberation as the filter between private and public

We note that the republican focus on the public is less preponderantly on control, on the central state and its coercive powers and more on the activity of citizens, and their resolution of the tensions between particular and general interests. There is an increasing emphasis among republicans (to a greater extent than liberals) on the need for an expanded public realm of *deliberation*. This is entailed precisely because citizens have different perspectives on questions of common concern, since pre-political shared understandings, or ethnic identity as the basis for loyalty are not assumed or guaranteed in states. In most states we find ourselves, rather than starting *ab initio:* 'a polity consists of people who must live together, who are stuck with one another' (Young 1996: 126). There is no immediately obvious common good or shared goals. It follows then that the political determination and contestation of what may be considered common concerns or goods is central.[11]

This approach allows us to see the public as *pluralised*, disengaged from total identification with the legislative and coercive state. There are two crucial kinds of 'realms' of the public – first, multiple spaces of discourse, which are not necessarily sharply bounded, many of which are rather informal (as we speak, for example, of the reading public) and in which opinions are exchanged in comparatively open-ended ways. Secondly, there are spaces of deliberation oriented directly to policy-making and the authoritative state (Fraser 1992: 134). These are informed by and subject to critique by the deliberation of the wider publics. Such spaces already exist to some extent, but this approach argues that they should be greatly extended.[12]

This approach calls on the wider field of discourse theory and specifically on ideas advanced by Habermas, without entailing all the claims made therein. What is envisaged here involves discourse that is real, participatory, and informal as well as formal, and does not necessarily assume that full consensus must or will be reached.[13] (In particular it should be noted that the conception of republican politics advanced here is rather different from that which Habermas contrasts to discourse politics [Habermas 1994]).

In deliberation all individuals and groups are entitled to make proposals, advance views in their best light, and offer their reasons for these – there are no barriers to the claims and demands that they can make. Any voice may be heard, any claim expressed. These are not taken as sealed bids, so to speak – deliberation is often contrasted with bargaining between preferences. Every claim can be dismantled and subjected to further scrutiny by others. Here people are expected to give an account of 'where they are coming from'. All positions are to be respected, (a kind of recognition) but full recognition (or acceptance) depends on the process of deliberation. The aim is to develop considered judgements, and define collective aspirations.

This process may be fairly loosely structured without narrow institutional procedures or formal requirements for participants – other than a willingness to expose a point of view or practice to the light of discussion, to respect others right to contribute and to accept that no position is guaranteed acceptance by the mere fact of its being expressed or the strength of conviction with which it is held. This requires reciprocity; people may have to moderate their position if they are to influence others. In itself this encourages people to take more account of the public interest; so this process acts as a *filter*. As Benhabib puts it:

> [T]he very procedure of articulating a view in public imposes a certain reflexivity on individual preferences and opinions ... The process of *articulating good reasons in public* forces the individual to think of what would count as a good reason for all others involved.
> (Benhabib 1996: 71–2)

But this involves reflecting on, not bracketing, beliefs based on deep-seated moral convictions.

> At the very least this may lead to *better understanding* of different positions. For those moral conflicts for which there is no deliberative agreement at present, ongoing deliberation can help citizens better understand the moral seriousness of the views they continue to oppose, and better cooperate with their fellow citizens who hold these views.
>
> (Gutmann and Thompson 1996: 43)

But it may also lead to *transformation* or reconciliation: 'the moral promise of deliberative democracy depends on the political learning that reiterated deliberation makes possible' (Gutmann and Thompson 1996: 356). People may change their views without thereby betraying their identities. It is in expression that identity is defined and developed, rather than coming to it ready formed. In this approach to politics transcending one's initial position is always possible and often essential.

This form of deliberation does not presuppose *consensus* on questions of the good life. In this understanding of republican theory, what is involved is more than discovering or articulating already existing understandings (which cannot be assumed). It is not a matter of what Habermas has described as 'hermeneutical self-explication of a shared form of life' but collectively recognising and building on the basis of often unsought interdependence (Habermas 1994: 4).

It may help to *establish* or construct common understandings of the common good or public, shared interest. Deliberation may take place diffusely through society in multiple opinion-making forums of all kinds at many levels and may sometimes, without any appeal to legislative institutions, influence people to act in the public good on their own initiative; in Dryzek's account of discursive democracy, he argues persuasively that complex social problems may often be best addressed through discourse that inspires voluntary compliance, consciousness raising and decentralised problem solving (Benhabib 1996: 86).

So, this approach does not assume that full consensus is the final *target*. Consensus, as critics have pointed out, is not always an index of resolution. Briefly, what is more feasible are provisional formulations of the common concerns, tentative embodiments of the common goods of those who deliberate, and more reflective judgements of how to deal with continuing differences, as well as expanded self-understandings. Not all deliberation will issue in legislation or coercive state action. But the actions of the state public must be informed and subject to critique by the wider public realm. All outcomes are open to change through further consideration.

Dealing with difference: how well does the republican approach succeed?

We have seen that the public-private distinction does not operate to exclude, but to transform convictions, and may be potentially better fitted to accommodate modern moral and cultural difference. I next review the objections raised against the liberal public-private distinction and see if the republican distinction escapes them.

Oppression

Since the public-private distinction is not understood in terms of a barrier between spheres, which excludes certain areas in principle from public discussion and regulation, charges of *oppression* based on such a distinction are not appropriate here. No area of life is deemed in principle private and beyond discussion and possible regulation. Since a single state policy is not the immediate aim of all public discourse, there is more room for different perspectives to appear. Thus the oppression and inequality which a radical public-private distinction may reinforce is not the issue here. What is required by privacy, and how the filter of deliberation operates is itself subject to critical consideration. (The obverse may be thought to be the problem – that this perspective oppresses by not making a sufficiently clear distinction, by *not* excluding any area of life – this will be discussed below).

Exclusion

However, everyone presenting a claim is required to enter discussion, to engage in presenting their viewpoint. It has been argued that like the liberal distinction this may *exclude* or *marginalise* those who do not conform, may impose masculine, western norms of reason or impartiality and privilege particular cultural styles (Young 1996: 126). In effect this public culture too requires people to be more homogeneous than it appears. In practice it excludes the inarticulate, the absent, the silent.[14]

In response, it would appear that this is not a very serious a problem if discussion and deliberation are less formal and occur at multiple levels – not all of which are modelled on law courts or parliament; forms of discourse can be expanded (as Young recommends) to include narrative and other styles. The fact that everything is subject to discussion means primarily that nothing is excluded by definition. It does not impose particular standards of reason, just a willingness to give an account to the other and being prepared to moderate one's claims (Miller 1995). Where there are multiple and graduated public realms, a hearing can be progressively attained for diverse expressions and viewpoints, which to be publicly expressed do not have to conform at once to a single standard of publicity.[15]

But is the requirement of self-disclosure in deliberation itself coercive of those who are different? 'Models of unconstrained discourse rest upon a demand for self-disclosure which can threaten the privacy and personal integrity of participants in a way that can make discourse coercive' (Moon 1993: 96). Again, this seems less of a danger when there are multiple levels of the public:

> [W]hen conceived as an anonymous, plural and multiple medium of communication and deliberation, the public sphere need not homogenize and repress difference. Heterogeneity, otherness and difference can find expression in the multiple associations, networks and citizens' forums, all of which constitute public life under late capitalism.
> (Benhabib 1996: 84)

Moreover the requirement for self-disclosure may not mean that everyone must always disclose themselves, but that they must at least give some kind of an explanation for not doing so (Gutmann and Thompson 1996: 350).

There are, nonetheless, remaining problems of who talks? who is heard? and who has time to talk? which need to be addressed (Fraser 1992: 119–21). There are many necessary prerequisites for giving people a real voice. Some would say that these are precisely the hard parts of politics itself, but this draws attention not so much to a flaw in deliberation as to the importance of its foundations.

Deliberation will exclude some voices if the conditions for equal participation in deliberation are not present. These conditions for just deliberative outcomes are not trivial and cannot be taken for granted. It must be said that there are serious deficiencies in current public realms. Inclusive deliberation requires not only freedom of speech, but also guaranteed public forums, education in deliberation and in respect for other viewpoints, and the counterbalancing of dominant speakers, and of the inequalities which people bring to their participation in public life. This would require substantial material support and some regulation in the service of deliberation. What is involved is not so much a marketplace as a welfare state of ideas.[16]

It remains true that a public culture is a public culture, and it may exclude those who do not value deliberation or who refuse to have truck with politics at all, and instead expect that their beliefs will be implemented without question. They may feel excluded, but deliberative politics (unlike neutralist politics) does not purport to include them. Republicans can recognise that, in this respect, they hold a 'fighting creed' and be robust in reply. Furthermore, for someone with this perspective to be required to explain the basis of their deeply-held beliefs is arguably less counter-intuitive than to be required to bracket them entirely in the public realm.

At any time this public culture will recognise some expressions more fully than others; but, based on deliberation in which all voices can be heard, it is less exclusive than accounts which accord the existing public culture a privileged position. For example, the perspective of liberal nationalism, even if nationality is taken to evolve over time in response to newcomers, entails a sharp boundary between those who share a nationality and those who do not. Thus its extensibility is necessarily limited. Though republican politics is conventionally criticised as exclusive, the model described here is in principle less sharply bounded and more extensible, since interdependence is a matter of degree, of expanding circles, and public realms are multiple and overlapping.

Privatising values

This approach does not peripheralise people's deepest *convictions,* or reduce the value of the public. All claims to a wider validity may be advanced whatever their basis; all seriously held views of the good may be discussed, whether they spring from comprehensive doctrines or not. This is not a common good in which all are supposed to leave behind their particular experience, as criticised by Young (1996: 126).

All are allowed to express their deepest commitments in public; these are respected, in the sense that they are admitted to the public realm and given a hearing. They gain some kind of recognition through greater understanding even if they are not accepted and embodied in law or the constitution. The possibility of such expression may better realise the recognition of values which people seek than certain kinds of reified expression in constitutional or coercive provisions. Additionally this approach gives more substance and significance to political participation itself than that of bargaining between preferences, and recognises the sense of self-worth gained therein.

Unsustainability

This approach recognises the interpenetration of state and civil society, and the difficulty of distinguishing public and private radically and systematically in terms of control or ideas of the good. Rather than ruling out state intervention, or seeking to base it on neutral principles, what can be endorsed and how the state should act is determined through deliberation, the filter between private and public.

Since deliberation acts as a filter rather than a barrier, it emerges that republican politics may endorse commitments more substantial than liberals recommend, though less substantial than communitarians deem appropriate. Liberals now see the public as based on agreement on procedures, principles of justice, or legal or constitutional minima. For Habermas, people agree on rules of discourse and argumentation (though convergence on substance is possible in principle). Communitarians, on the other hand, see the state as expressing the substantive common good, or replicating the pre-political in public. Nationalists in particular take ethnicity or a common background culture to be necessary for a successful politics.

In republican politics it is not possible to dictate in advance what may emerge through deliberation. States that originate in the interdependence of citizens require an acknowledgement of that interdependence, and respect for deliberation itself. But this is not all. Further communal commitments may emerge. It is not the aim of republican politics to be neutral with respect to beliefs, but to develop collective self-understandings.[17] The substance of the public will evolve differently in every case. So, for example, whether education may be run on denominational, multi-denominational or secular lines is not something we can argue on a priori grounds. It will depend positively on what the forms of interdependence are and negatively on what the forms and causes of conflict or marginalisation in a society are, and should be the outcome of deliberation. What can be agreed in some contexts will be oppressive in others. There may be many different practices appropriate in different societies and at different levels.[18] But in this account of republicanism, what is endorsed comes from an equal opportunities process; what justifies the provisional embodiment of any is subject to the public deliberative process, not justified as simply replicating the cultural dominance of one particular group.

Still this model entails more substance than most proponents of civic nationalism or 'constitutional patriotism' allow. Members here are tied not only to agreement on procedures, constitutional arrangements or institutions. Recognising interdependence and sharing in the deliberative outcomes of a public realm itself leads to deeper commitments. So a question remains: if republican politics is more substantial than liberal – admitting matters of deep belief to public expression and discussion and potential embodiment in public recognition – how can it be other than repressive of difference? Here we return to the obverse of the first critique of the liberal private-public distinction. If liberalism oppresses by excluding areas of life from public scrutiny and control, does republicanism by contrast threaten to oppress by *not* separating public and private, by potentially including any aspect of life, especially in the context of radical difference?

The first point here is to emphasise the distance already suggested between public discussion and state regulation. All differences may be expressed in public. Not all matters of public discussion lead to state action, but may generate voluntary action. Even where the state takes action, this does not always take the form of directly coercive legislation, but may be through symbolic endorsement or economic incentives. Different treatments may seem appropriate for issues that can be characterised as personal preference and moral belief or cultural identity.

We should note also that this is a specific objection, related but not identical to the wider question whether certain kinds of coercion are justified. In the republican perspective certain kinds of coercion are understood to be justified, where citizens are bound to their considered judgements, as Ulysses was tied to the mast while he listened to the song of the Sirens. And some degree of coercion may be necessary to provide the basic framework of deliberation – equal access, public spaces, education in deliberation, and so on. Republicans also argue that the state needs to educate its citizens into the public culture, to inculcate a sense of responsibility, if they are not to rely entirely on repeated exhortations to public spirit on the part of individuals. This is education in recognising interdependence and its implications and in deliberating, rather than education as instilling a catechism of particular beliefs. Such coercion could be seen as facilitating the expression of the widest range of perspectives, not as repressing difference. What is particularly at issue here is the position of those whose beliefs, after deliberation, are not endorsed by the public, and who cannot themselves fully accept particular deliberative outcomes. And there will always be people in such positions – those who are shocked by the toleration, recognition or non-recognition of gay marriage, Sunday trading, public blasphemy, the Angelus broadcast, etc. The modern state has to act, and often acts coercively, embodying some moral and cultural perspective. Governments sanction and do not sanction marriages, allow and do not allow euthanasia, provide education which is denominational or secular, monolingual or bilingual and which reflects moral and cultural perspectives.

What can be said here is that in the republican state, these actions are not justified in terms of a single fixed account of the common good based on nature or a single culture. They must be defended, not taken to be self-evidently right, either universally or for *us*. These are interpretations of common goods established, constructed, filtered in deliberation in multiple publics – not pre-politically established or based on already existing overlapping consensus or commonalities.

Secondly we can say that if vigorous public realms of discussion parallel the state public realm, its decisions and actions will be better informed and more reflective of citizens' serious convictions. Those coerced will have had an input in the decisions. Legislation and decision making take account of wider public deliberation. The problem is not the existence of a public that is not neutral, but states that fail to take account of voices or potential voices (Cooke 1997: 15). What is required is to accommodate the deep concerns of all citizens equally by giving all an opportunity to influence the public culture. For example, some Jews and Muslims in Ireland, when asked about the Catholic nature of the public culture, reply that they prefer living in a state that acknowledges the significance of religion to living in a secular or neutral state. But secularists too must be allowed to express their position and receive serious consideration.[19]

Finally, since the view embodied is based on deliberation, it must be open to further evolution; any understanding reached has provisional status and is subject to challenge. It must always be possible also to challenge and contest what has been provisionally established as the public culture and its deliberative outcomes.

Thus, the republican private-public distinction does not suppress difference, but allows its expression and potential recognition. The substance of republican politics is based on interdependence (rather than commonality), is created in deliberation (not pre-politically), and emerges in multiple publics, to which all can contribute, and is not definitive but open to change.

Conclusion: a better solution to dealing with difference?

Moral argument in politics can be socially elusive, politically extremist, and morally inconclusive, but avoiding it for these reasons would be self-defeating. The divisions, the extremism and the inconclusiveness would persist while the prospects for finding better terms of social co-operation would deteriorate.

(Gutmann and Thompson 1996: 347)

The answer to dealing with difference is not a liberal state with a neutral public, nor a nationalist or communitarian one which redraws boundaries so they contain more like-minded people; nor a cultural pluralist one which aims to celebrate difference but remains unclear about how the multiple celebrated differences relate to one another.

Plural societies will best survive and meet the needs of their citizens neither by excluding arguments based on deeply held moral convictions or cultural distinctions from the public realm nor by 'entrenching' or 'celebrating' them. They need to support public spaces of expression and deliberation that do not exclude such arguments in principle from debate, but which are somewhat detached from, yet inform the public of constitutional and legislative authority. Neither can be wholly neutral, but their substance is constituted on the basis of interdependence rather than original difference, and is open to change and development. Such an approach may not pre-empt radical conflict between different groups, but it offers more of an incentive to participate than a neutral public, which requires people who do not automatically identify with the liberal view to put aside their beliefs.

Cultural difference is neither contained nor satisfied by its relegation to the private, and its public replication is fundamentally problematic. This approach acknowledges the significance of moral and cultural difference and claims to recognition, without overlooking the problems that the coexistence of different beliefs and cultures presents. While not fully resolving the problem of dealing with difference, this offers a potentially better way to go about it than the alternatives currently most favoured. By reconsidering the ordering and interrelationships of the complex dimensions of public and private, we may be able to discern ways of meeting demands for recognition that tend to be obscured when all these dimensions are subsumed under state control and its absence.[20]

Notes

1   I will set communitarianism more generally understood to one side; it has been plausibly argued that on this front philosophical communitarians either adopt a liberal position or downplay the significance of the distinction entirely, seeing community as more or less continuous and public as modelled on the private.

2   Some feminists and others have tended to argue that we should abandon the use of the public-private distinction, and assume that the extension of public scrutiny automatically entails greater control by the state. But it may be argued that this is too quick an extrapolation from the exclusion to the inclusion of all matters under state control: 'The crucial part of the argument is the reconstruction of "private" matters as political, of central importance to political theory, rather than any general prescription about remedies in terms of state regulation of the private sphere' (Frazer and Lacey 1993: 75).

3   However, the public has also been seen as an area that lends itself to more reason, equality and universality and the private sometimes characterised as irrational. This is often related to the subsumed public/domestic distinction. It is ultimately hard to disentangle; in much liberal thought the realms of public and private are overdetermined by two levels of distinction.

4   'The dichotomy between the public and the private obscures the subjection of women to men within an apparently universal, egalitarian and individualist order... The profound ambiguity of the liberal conception of the private and the public obscures and mystifies the social reality it helps constitute' (Pateman 1983: 120). 'The analysis which defines pornography as a matter of private preference in one breath constructs it as a matter of public rights to free expression in the next' (Frazer and Lacey 1993: 126).

5   Though the republican version of the distinction has some parallels with what Benn and Gaus describe as the 'organic' side of liberalism (Rousseau/Hegel/Bradley) there are significant differences. Benn and Gaus do not discuss the possibility of a distinct republican model.

6   What is at issue here is shared goods – those that can be enjoyed only as members of a community, including what are often referred to as 'public goods'; shared cultural values are one specific kind of shared goods.

7   For Hannah Arendt, one of the main inspiring forces of the republican revival, the primary dimension of publicity is visibility or access, making her republican theory systematically idiosyncratic in a number of respects. Interestingly, visibility or accessibility is also identified at one point as the primary dimension of publicity by I.M. Young in her radical cultural pluralist approach (Young 1990: 119).

8   The absence of public spirit – corruption – in individuals and culture is the central problem of republican politics rather than excessive state power. This is not to say that such power might not be a problem, but if interest is salient rather than control, misplaced interest is more central than misplaced control.

9   Consistent with Arendt's focus on appearance or visibility, the private is understood as an area that remains outside widespread attention. The point is not entirely that it should not appear because unworthy of the public, but needs to be sheltered to exist at all (Arendt 1958).

10   Indeed republican thought has tended to perceive a need for a strong central figure in setting up states – the founder or lawmaker. Yet the republican lack of emphasis on the state in the account of politics has also often been remarked on critically.

11 Rather than always emphasising the need for total unity, republican thinkers from Machiavelli to Arendt have emphasised the contested nature of political power.

12 For the purposes of this paper I assume that deliberation is in principle both possible and necessary. I also assume that people tend to have not one, but multiple identities, that identities are at least to some extent revisable, and that values are not radically incommensurable, so that communication and some level of understanding is possible between people who are different.

13 Popular communitarians assume a consensus over the common good, and accordingly underestimate the importance of deliberation, and overlook the real danger that the community and the common good are defined by the powerful.

14 Young (1996) has also recently advocated what she calls 'communicative democracy' that has a good deal in common with what is described here. In this account she recognises that the remedy to the deficiencies of deliberation is more talk, not less.

15 The emphasis here on plural though graduated publics follows from the implications of distinguishing access and control. It thus goes further than Miller's account of the potential of republican politics for dealing with difference, which refers to a 'general political ethos' and assumes a common sense of nationality (Miller 1995).

16 This analogy was suggested to me by Philip Cole.

17 But republican politics, rather than aiming not to be neutral, does not aim to be neutral with respect to difference in the sense of being difference-blind.

18 Chris Patten, when Governor of Hong Kong, had a crucifix hanging in his office. In other contexts such a symbol could be construed as oppressive and exclusive; in Hong Kong in 1996 there were more divisive issues. What is more important, when different levels of the public are distinguished, cultural and religious symbols may be admitted to the public without being officially endorsed by the state. There is a difference between officially hanging crucifixes in classrooms, and allowing pupils, and even teachers, to wear religious symbols in school.

19 It should be noted, however, that in Ireland the Catholic nature of the public culture was not arrived at through deliberation of the kind outlined here, but was derived from and long defended in terms of pre-political identity.

20 An earlier version of this paper was delivered at a conference on pluralism at the Royal Irish Academy, Dublin.

Part III

ACCOMMODATING PLURALISM

8

POLITICAL OBLIGATION:
a pluralistic approach[1]

Jonathan Wolff

Any pluralistic position in philosophy presupposes an answer to two questions. First, what is plural? and second, where is it plural? The first question needs little explanation: do we assert that there are plural values, or plural conceptual schemes, or plural something else again? The second question, on the other hand, may seem rather obscure, but it can be stated more clearly once we have an answer to the first. Suppose we are concerned with the question of plural values. Now we must ask: who is supposed to hold these plural values? Does each individual hold just one value, so pluralism arises only on a social level, or is a single individual – or every individual – presumed to hold more than one value? If we use the term 'moral pluralism' this seems to suggest a position in which there are many irreducibly distinct values, and any morally aware agent should hold them all, in so far as that is possible. The term 'cultural pluralism' seems to suggest a picture where pluralism arises only within a larger group. Each individual or smaller group has a singular set of values: the trouble starts only when you put them together.

Pluralism is often represented as trouble, at least initially. Cultural pluralism generates a problem of how people of differing values can live together, and this needs an answer. Moral pluralism generates a different problem: values can conflict, so how, at bottom, can a rational individual hold more than one? Such considerations are sometimes taken to show that pluralism, in some forms, is absurd.

In this paper I want to apply a form of moral pluralism to a problem in political philosophy: the problem of political obligation. My main reason for doing so is that I want to solve the problem, and I believe that a pluralistic perspective is essential in doing this. Now it may be said that even if I succeed I have replaced one problem with a more difficult one: how to make sense of moral pluralism. Some of the difficulties are discussed along the way, but others surely remain. A secondary reason for pursuing this project is to be able to draw a general lesson about moral pluralism. It may be that we will make more progress on resolving moral and political problems if we allow

179

ourselves the room to take pluralistic perspectives seriously. Pluralism need not always be a problem: indeed I hope to show that it can provide a solution to a particular problem. Now I do not wish to suggest that a little bit of pluralism will make all our problems go away. Each case must be set out and established in detail, and perhaps in many cases we do better to reject a pluralistic perspective. Here I simply set out the details in the case of the problem of political obligation, showing the conceptual possibilities that arise once pluralism is accepted.

But what, then, is the problem of political obligation? And what would count as a solution? In this paper I hope to show that a number of often unstated assumptions lay behind much recent work on this topic. All of these assumptions are controversial, and, in my view, all should be rejected. Indeed, some of them are implicitly or explicitly rejected by many writers in the field, but the possibilities that open up by rejecting these assumptions have rarely been explored in any depth. The way is open for various pluralistic models of political obligation.

In the first section of this paper I will provide a general classification of theories of political obligation, while in the second section I shall present the assumptions which, I claim, are an obstacle to progress. I shall give my reasons for questioning these assumptions, and explore the new models of political obligation which become possible once the assumptions are rejected. Finally I shall consider the vexed question of which of the various models we should favour.

Theories of political obligation

How should we classify different approaches to political obligation? It has become customary to think of theories as falling under a small number of general heads: perhaps theories of contract, consent, gratitude, fairness, reciprocity, utilitarianism and now communitarianism, with philosophical anarchism and the 'no-problem' theory as limit cases. Each of these theories appears in several importantly different versions, each version with further variants. The justification for such a classification is largely historical: these are the theories that have been influential throughout the history of the subject, and are still discussed (unlike, say, Divine Right theory).

There have, of course, been various attempts to impose a more systematic form of classification, and it will suit my purposes in this essay to propose my own: a three-way scheme. The scheme takes as its central concepts what we can, for short, refer to as ideas of rationality, reciprocity and reasonableness.[2] The general idea is that rational solutions appeal to ideas of self-interest to ground political obligations, reciprocity solutions appeal to ideas of fair exchange, while reasonable solutions appeal to ideas of justice. By definition I want to say that a theory is rational (in this sense) only if it is a necessary condition of legitimacy or acceptableness of a scheme that it furthers each individual's self-interest; it is reciprocal only if it is a necessary condition of legitimacy or acceptableness of a scheme that it appeals to the idea of an individual making some sort of due or proportional payment for the benefits received (or receiving payment for burdens undertaken); and it is reasonable only if it appeals to ideas of justice which cannot be reduced to the former two categories of self-interest or fair exchange.[3]

Some forms of contract theory most obviously fall under the heading of rational theories, as do theories that appeal to the idea of mutual advantage. Reciprocity theories include gratitude theories, and, most importantly, fairness theories, whereas reasonableness theories include those which incorporate ideas of distributive justice, as well as utilitarian theory, together with certain forms of hypothetical contract theories. Reasonableness theories are characterised by the thought that it can sometimes be legitimate to require people to engage in behaviour which delivers them a net loss: something that would not be so on a rational or reciprocal theory.

As defined, reciprocal theories are a special case of rational theories. Although individuals in a reciprocal scheme are required to pay for benefits received, there would be no point to the scheme unless the total benefits exceed the total costs, and it is to be assumed that there is a failure of reciprocity unless all share in the surplus. Thus all reciprocal principles are rational. But the converse implication does not hold. Rational theories have no place for the idea of proportionality, and so cannot be guaranteed to yield reciprocal solutions. We can see this most clearly in the way rational advantage works in a bargaining situation. Rational bargainers are rewarded according to such things as their threat advantage and power. Reward according to contribution is – coincidentally – one possible outcome, but outcomes that are in no way correlated with contribution are equally possible.

Still clearer is the point that rational theories and reciprocal theories cannot normally be expected to yield reasonable (just) outcomes, even though sometimes accidentally they might. The point is that on rational and reciprocal theories there is no place for an individual to make a net loss, although this is sometimes required by justice: utilitarianism is an obvious example, egalitarianism another.

The distinction between rational, reciprocal and reasonable theories is a way of classifying theories into types, rather than a distinction between particular theories. What I have said is that a theory falls into a certain category if it lays down a certain necessary condition for the legitimacy of a particular arrangement. But actual theories are bound to build in further conditions. For the purposes of this paper, though, I will say very little about how these theories are to be further elaborated, except where necessary for the argument.

The assumptions

Broadly, then, we have noted three types of theories of political obligation: being compelled to obey the law is to our mutual advantage; or it is required by some notion of reciprocity; or required by a concern for justice. Which of these arguments should we prefer?

Must we choose between them? I claimed above that no single principle can be guaranteed to exemplify more than one of these notions (with the exception that reciprocal principles are also rational, on the definition given). But it does not follow that we cannot combine more than one principle in a more complex account. As a methodological hunch (one I cannot defend here, or, perhaps, anywhere) it seems to me that it is unlikely that many richly articulated theories in philosophy – or at least in political philosophy – are wholly in error. Most mistaken theories contain valuable insights, even if those insights are exaggerated, distorted, or mistake partial truth for entire.

This hunch suggests a synthetic project: putting together the insights from different approaches to generate an account of political obligation combining the best of each. Yet what we could call the standard methodology for political obligation stands in our way. A number of assumptions – some more widely recognised than others – have tended to structure much recent writing on political obligation, and if correct would rule out the type of project just outlined. Four such assumptions are as follows:

1　*The burden of proof:* the task of the theorist of political obligation is to refute the anarchist, who, by contrast, has no similar burden to make out in order to establish the anarchist case.

2　*Singularity in ground*: to refute the anarchist, one appeals to a single argument or principle of justification. Thus each one of every citizen's political obligations is justified in the same way.

3　*Universality*: to refute the anarchist it is necessary to show that there are universal political obligations, in the sense that all who reside within the state's borders must be shown to have political obligations.

4　*Uniformity*: all citizens have the same type or level of political obligations.

The relation between singularity in ground and uniformity bears some comment. The two are distinct. Singularity is a doctrine about the source of our political obligations; uniformity about their content. Singularity does not entail uniformity: on some utilitarian views, for example, there is only one ground of political obligation, but obligations can vary from person to person. Uniformity does not presuppose singularity: different individuals can have matching obligations but for different reasons, both intra-personally and inter-personally. (That is, A and B could have exactly matching obligations – and hence obey uniformity – but A's are justified by two different arguments x and y, while all of B's obligations are justified by a third, z, thus violating singularity two different ways.)

Perhaps all four assumptions seem innocuous, although, of course, as soon as any assumption is stated it becomes a proper object of suspicion. In my view, though, together these assumptions have the effect of forcing the theorist of political obligation to adopt a greatly over-simplified, and implausible, view. In the next section I will take these assumptions in turn, and explore the consequences of their rejection.

Rejecting the assumptions

The burden of proof

Considering the first assumption – that the task of the theorist of political obligation is to refute the anarchist – takes us deep into the methodology of political philosophy. Something like this assumption receives classic statement in *Anarchy, State, and Utopia*: 'The fundamental question of political philosophy, one that precedes questions about how the state should be organized, is whether there should be any state at all. Why not have anarchy?' (Nozick 1974: 4).

This assumption underlies the methodology of those who have been termed 'critical philosophical anarchists' (Gans 1992). The strategy of such writers is to show the weakness of particular arguments in defence of political obligations, and then conclude that, as no such argument succeeds, we should accept philosophical anarchism. Typically philosophical anarchism is thought not to be in need of further support – it is the defender of political obligations who has to meet the burden of proof.

My claim is that the philosophical anarchist has no right to make this move: or, more modestly, it should not be taken on trust that the philosophical anarchist has this right. The defender of political obligations is being set a task that the philosophical anarchist refuses – the task of providing conclusive positive arguments for the view, perhaps even a 'knock-down' deductive argument from unquestioned premises. But it is unrealistic to suppose that any position in moral or political philosophy could meet such a burden.

It might be said in reply that this accusation is unfair. The philosophical anarchist does provide a positive argument, based on the presumption of natural liberty. Human beings are naturally free, equal and independent, not naturally under the subordination of any other person. Thus there is a presumption against the state and it is up to the defender of the state to show how this is to be overcome. But how should we understand this presumption of liberty? Virtually no serious thinker has been prepared to allow that human beings have no moral obligations. Now does the existence of such obligations conflict with the presumption of liberty? Here we face a dilemma. If there is a conflict, and morality is preferred to liberty, then it appears that the presumption of liberty is not as strong as the argument pretends. If there is no conflict – if liberty is merely freedom to act within the moral law – then how can we be so sure that liberty conflicts with the existence of the state? In either case we need first to establish whether the state is morally justifiable, and some argument other than one based on the presumption of liberty is necessary to settle that question. This is not to say that we should reject the presumption of liberty. The point is that the presumption of liberty is a far weaker ground for anarchism than is often assumed.

Instead, then, of granting the philosophical anarchist the benefit of the burden of proof, I suggest that we should seek a neutral standpoint – a standpoint from which neither the state, nor anarchism, receives a privileged position. I have argued elsewhere that Rawls's hypothetical contract can be understood as providing such a standpoint, but I will not repeat the arguments here (Wolff 1996a). Here the point is that the theorist of political obligation should accept that there are various possible answers to the question of the extent, type and level of political obligations individuals have, and one possible answer is that no individual has any. At the outset, however, there is no more reason for adopting that view than any other. The task is to show which of the various known options is the best. It is unreasonable to think that any answer must be defended to the standard, say, of mathematical rigour.

Rejecting this assumption changes our approach to the problem of political obligation, but it need have no implications for the main topic of the essay: the possibility of a pluralistic theory. Hence I will say no more about it here.[4]

Singularity in ground

'Singularity in ground' is the name A. J. Simmons gives to the second assumption mentioned above, which, as a prelude to rejecting it, he states as 'the requirement that there be one and only one ground of political obligation' (Simmons 1979: 35).

What could be the motivation for such a view? If there is only one valid ground of moral obligation then singularity would trivially follow. But for those who deny such moral monism, why else adopt singularity? One appealing motivation would be some aspiration to theoretical simplicity. Another is not so much simplicity but economy of effort: the thought that the theorist of political obligation needs seek only a sufficient condition for universal political obligations – it may be that there is more than one such condition, but one alone is enough. Singularity in ground is sometimes implicitly rejected when it is realised that no single argument can meet this task.

Most seriously, perhaps, the idea that there could be more than one ground of political obligation creates the possibility that different grounds could generate conflicts of obligation. If one theory instructs us that we have a certain obligation, while another entails that we do not (or worse, that we have an obligation to do something which conflicts) which do we follow? It will be said that to avoid the possibility of such conflicts – or perhaps to resolve them – we need to assume singularity at some level.

This is a serious issue for a non-singular theory. Yet it remains to be seen whether the different grounds to which we appeal in any given pluralistic theory do generate conflicts, and if so, whether there is any difficulty in resolving them. We will return to this later.

In the meantime we should note that singularity is explicitly rejected by George Klosko (1992: 4), who believes that, as no single argument can ground all of our political obligations, several different arguments are required. Implicit rejections for 'patchwork' reasons possibly go back as far as Hobbes, but certainly to Locke, who offers at least two grounds for political obligation: express consent and tacit consent (Locke 1988). This is also the implication of Nozick's two-stage justification of the state, in which one argument provides the justification for the ultra-minimal state, and a second moves us to the minimal state (Nozick 1974, for discussion see Wolff 1991: Chapter 3).

Singularity is also rejected by clear implication by Chaim Gans, who offers four separate lines of defence of political obligations (1992: 43). Gans is interesting in apparently providing two separate rationales for rejecting singularity in ground. One is that he seems to accept overdetermination: there are several different forms of valid moral argument, he believes, and political obligations can be defended in various different ways. The other thought is that arguments can be used in a mutually supportive fashion: an argument that is weak on its own can be supported by appealing to other considerations.

The clearer of the two examples Gans gives of mutual support combines a Rawlsian natural duty argument with a communitarian argument. Rawls suggests that we have a natural duty to comply with those just institutions which 'apply to us'. Sceptics have questioned what makes an institution apply to us, and Gans appeals to communitarian arguments to provide an answer. I offer no comment here on the substance of this view; the point of introducing it is to show how pluralistic views become possible.

Rejecting singularity of ground, then, already gives us four different models of pluralistic approaches of political obligations.

Model 1: complementary arguments

Different traditional arguments are used in mutual support, as if they are premises in a more complex single argument, as in the example of Gans' use of Rawls and communitarianism. This is pluralistic only in a narrow or conventional sense. Given the way arguments have been used in the past, it is true that more than one argument is being used. But there is no necessity that the arguments should be considered as two separate arguments brought together, rather than one more complex argument.

Model 2: overdetermination

There is more than one valid form of moral argumentation, and at least some political obligations can be justified in more than one way.

Model 3: patchwork of citizens

This is perhaps the most obvious pluralistic model, involving the rejection of singularity of ground. The basic idea is that for some citizens one argument serves to ground their political obligations, and for others a different argument serves this purpose. For example, in Locke's theory some people's obligations are justified by express consent, others by tacit consent.

Model 4: patchwork of laws

Here some of each individual's obligations to obey are justified by one pattern of argument, others of that individual's obligations by other arguments.

Universality

Simmons states this assumption in the following terms, 'if we cannot give an account of political obligation which shows that everyone e.g. in a particular state is bound, then we cannot give an account of political obligation which applies to anyone in this state'. Again Simmons explicitly rejects this assumption (Simmons 1979: 35). An importantly different variant of this assumption is the claim that, although it is possible to show that only part of the population has political obligations, one's project has collapsed unless it can be shown that all are obligated. By implication both assumptions are rejected by Klosko, who writes 'an acceptable theory must be able to establish the political obligations of *all or most* members of society' (my emphasis) (Klosko 1992: 3). Elsewhere I have argued that it may be an advantage of certain theories that they leave certain individuals without political obligations (Wolff 1995a). But in any case it seems we should reject the assumption, certainly in the form rejected by Simmons, and arguably in the weaker form too. At least, we might accept Klosko's position here – we have succeeded in the project if we can show that most people (or, more ambitiously, almost all) have political obligations – although we should be clear that in doing so, we are rejecting the problem of political obligation as it has traditionally been conceived.

This does not, in itself, generate any new models of pluralism, but it allows us to introduce one further modification to the patchwork of citizens model.

It may be that, even with a division of labour, we cannot show that everyone has political obligations. In fact, each of the models so far can be modified in a similar way.

Uniformity

Strictly, all of the pluralistic models so far considered are consistent with uniformity: that the content of each citizen's political obligations is the same. But uniformity most clearly comes into question with reciprocity theories: if burdens follow from benefits, differential benefits should yield differential burdens. Hence there is no reason, on such a theory, to expect uniform obligations. Yet although it is not obvious that uniformity has any fundamental philosophical justification, its political advantages seem undeniable. How can a government expect to cope with the possibility that its citizens have different levels of political obligations? We might even think of this as some sort of second level philosophical justification. Even non-utilitarians ought to be sensitive to the consequences of trying to apply their theories. Pragmatism might be a sufficient justification for the simplifications consistent application requires.

This need not be decisive, however, for two reasons. First the difficulties of non-uniformity can be exaggerated. Political obligations might match over a wide range of cases, and differ in circumstances only where governments can make the relevant discriminations. Thus on one interpretation Locke thought that only express consent can make one a full member of one's political society, and tacit consent generates a lower level of duties. Most notably, those who tacitly consent can escape the government's jurisdiction by emigration, but full members cannot. But this example of non-uniformity will give rise to few political problems. This is not to say that we cannot also think of more troublesome possibilities, but the point is that non-uniformity is not always a practical nightmare.

Second, it is open to certain theorists to eschew consequentialist reasoning of this nature. This could – though it need not – be because they assume singularity of ground, or because they want to insist on a sharp distinction between moral and pragmatic reasons.

The point to make, I think, is that uniformity should not be assumed for its own sake. It may turn out – although I think not – that the best theory will respect uniformity, but I see no good reason to set out in advance that uniformity is a condition of adequacy on any account of political obligation. Denying uniformity, of course, generates another pluralistic model.

Model 5: diversity

Different individuals can have political obligations with different content. We will briefly take up the issue of how governments might respond to this towards the end of this paper.

187

Singularity revisited

Clearly, if we are to consider the possibility of advancing a pluralistic model of some kind, a great deal will turn on the question of singularity. But singularity might seem easy to reject. The assumption that all our political obligations should be justified by the same argument might seem obviously false. After all, why should the argument which generates an obligation to obey the law also generate an obligation to be a good citizen? The nature of these obligations is so distinct as to suggest that their justifications might also be distinct.

However, this reply does not exclude the possibility that if we restrict our enquiry to what might be called 'narrow' political obligation – the obligation to obey the law – singularity reigns. Just one argument explains why we have a duty to obey all the laws that we ought to obey. Should we accept this?

One possible reason for questioning it comes from the difficulty of accounting for the obligation to obey all laws on any single argument. To see this, first we should remember the earlier classification of theories of political obligation; those that appeal to mutual self-interest; those that appeal to reciprocity; and those that appeal to justice. It seems implausible that all laws can be justified by any one of these approaches. Consider the diversity of roles undertaken by governments. Even though contemporary politics encourages us to view our government as an undifferentiated whole, this is a mistake. Perhaps the most useful insight of libertarianism is that different branches of government have different fundamental justifications – for the libertarian, of course, some branches of government have no justification whatsoever, although I do not propose that we take this further step. We can, I think, isolate at least four types of activities typically undertaken by governments:

1 To protect citizens from each other, and from external threat

2 To supply public goods for the benefit of all

3 To supply public goods for the benefit of some only (e.g. sponsoring higher education)

4 To redistribute income and wealth.

These distinctions are not hard and fast: (1) might be a sub-category of (2), and it may be difficult, in some cases, to decide which category to place a certain governmental measure in. But the point is that we should not assume that one argument will explain why the state is justified in carrying out all these activities. Indeed, once these branches are distinguished, it seems highly unlikely that any single argument will succeed in doing this. Consequently – so the argument runs – the grounds of any individual's obligations in respect of different parts of the law may differ. Therefore we should reject the assumption of singularity. It has been implicitly rejected by others (cf. Klosko 1992), but not as self-consciously as it should have been.

In response it might be said that the argument just given runs together two distinct issues:

1 The justification of certain forms of state activity

2 Our obligation to obey particular laws

The argument goes through only if the plurality of justifications for different branches of the state's activity entails a plurality of reasons to obey the state. And, it will be added, there is no reason to think that such an entailment holds. Even though different laws have different justifications, it could be said that nevertheless the moral reason to obey remains the same in every case.

How can we adjudicate this dispute? Before going further we should recognise that while denying singularity on this basis gives further reasons to accept the patchwork of laws model, retaining singularity nevertheless generates yet another pluralistic model.

Model 6: law and its content

One argument tells us why we should obey the law; another, or several others, tell us which laws we should have. On this view there is only one reason why we should obey the law, but there are perhaps many different reasons for having the laws we do.

We should also note that several of the earlier models generated by rejecting singularity, universality and uniformity can be combined.

Model 7: multiple plurality

1 An obligation to obey a particular law may have more than one ground or justification

2 The obligation to obey different laws may have different grounds

3 Certain grounds of obligation may apply only to a subset of citizens.

A picture of great complexity now becomes a conceptual possibility. Imagine there are three political obligations (corresponding to different branches of government) A, B, and C. Imagine that A can only be justified by ground a, and B by ground b, but two further grounds each separately justify C, c1 and c2. Suppose that these grounds are atomistic, in the sense that it is possible for an individual to fall under any possible combination of these grounds. It then becomes possible now to conceive of many logically possible different classes of individuals. Full citizens have all three obligations, on all four grounds. Non-citizens have no obligations, obviously on no grounds. In between the two cases there are another 14 logically possible classes of citizen, each who lack one, two or three grounds of obligation, but two of these classes nevertheless have a full set of political obligations. The pressing question is whether real life is more complex or more simple than this abstract model. Is this model too pluralistic? Or pluralistic in the wrong way?[5]

I do not know how to argue that it is the correct model, but it does seem to me worth taking very seriously. I will end simply by sketching how the model can combine with the three types of theory of justification (rational, reciprocal, and reasonable) to generate an account which, while complex, nevertheless seems reasonably plausible.

The multiple plurality model

Given what I have said about the various possible types of theory of political obligation, and the different roles and justifications of state action, there is an obvious and elegant way of fitting the pieces together. The suggestion will require substantial modification, but I will give it first in its rough, unqualified form.

First we said, there are branches of government that supply means of protection for citizens, from each other and from external threat: the police, the law courts and the army. These, it appears, can be justified on grounds of mutual self-interest (rational justification) and this justification also grounds our obligation to obey such laws.

Second, there are branches of government supplying public goods (clean water, safe environment) for universal consumption. These – and the corresponding obligations to obey – are justified by a principle of fairness (a form of reciprocal justification). Obedience here is generally a matter of paying taxes, although other action, such as complying with water-saving regulations, is sometimes required.

Third, there are branches of government supplying public goods for the use of part only of the population (higher education, sponsorship of the arts). These are difficult cases. If those who benefit are generally the disadvantaged, this can be subsumed under the fourth category: redistributive justice. If – indirectly – there is a benefit for all, as is often claimed in the case of higher education, then there is a case for subsumption under the second category. If in a particular case neither argument works – and public subsidy of the most expensive opera tickets is an obvious example – then either the framework set out so far is incomplete or the measure has no fundamental justification and there is in principle no obligation to obey. The practical consequences of this remain to be explored.

Finally, certain measures are justified by justice (reasonable justification) and justice also grounds the obligation to obey measures reasonably deemed appropriate to bring us closer to a just world.

Now for the qualifications. Obviously all of these remarks need detailed elaboration. Naturally a theory which helps itself to elements from many different theories must be able to show how it responds to the standard lines of objection to the theories it uses. Here, though, I can only be brief.

Returning to the first stage of argument, it was said that the obligation to obey certain laws can be based on self-interest. Now I have said that a rational theory of justification includes as a necessary condition that each person's self-interest is advanced by the arrangement under consideration. There are various ways in which this can be further elaborated, yielding different theories, for there are many different ways in which everyone's self-interest can be advanced: it could be equally advanced; the position of the worst off maximised; left to a bargaining process, and so on. But all of these possibilities appear to suffer from a weakness. That a measure is in my interest might give me some reason not to object to it, but it does not generate a moral obligation to obey. This observation gives us a choice. Either we can accept that not all political obligations are moral obligations, but that some correspond to what we might call indirect prudence[6] (perhaps Hume's view) or that the argument given so far is incomplete.

In fact, until we bring in fairness and justice arguments I do not see how we can go much further than prudential considerations. Even if we take the further step of arguing that because a measure is in someone's interests we can infer that in some unexpressed way they consent, the sense of such consent is surely so weak as to carry very little, if any, justificatory force. Consequently a prudential justification may be all we can muster at this stage.[7]

This, however, opens up a second line of criticism. If my reasons for obeying are merely prudential, and there are cases where my interests would be bettered by disobedience (and I know this) then I have no reason to obey. In other words, it would be better for me to free-ride.

This objection surely depends on how any given individual's interest is going to be taken into account by the particular rational theory under consideration. However, if we think of this argument as providing only a prudential reason, then we seem to have little choice but to allow each individual to pursue their self-interest by whatever means can be expected best to achieve it. For many people free-riding will be the answer, and so that is what is recommended and permitted by the theory.

One obvious response to this would be to appeal to fairness considerations, but I want to remain within rational self-interest theory for this part of the argument. Is this prudential argument vulnerable to a defeating level of free-riding?

This, of course, is a common complaint. But I feel it is exaggerated. If it is mutually advantageous to have certain laws, but these laws are vulnerable to free-riding, then it is surely even more to our advantage to have laws that are as resistant to free-riding as we can sensibly afford. Few, if any, laws could be made proof against free-riding. But many can be made resistant to run-of-the-mill (as distinct from expert) free-riding, and so this is what the rational argument requires.

Here, then, a third objection is appropriate. The last argument tacitly concedes that expert free-riders have no prudential reason to obey those laws which are mutually advantageous to the rest of us. Thus we cannot guarantee universal political obligations on the basis of any argument from self-interest.

In response, all I can do is agree with this objection, but note that it has force only if we assume universality: that the theorist of political obligation must demonstrate that every last individual has political obligations. But I have denied universality, and so this objection is not devastating. I admit, though, that it is rather unsettling to derive the result that expert free-riders avoid political obligations. Fortunately we are not finished yet.

The second branch of government action concerns the supply of public goods. This calls out for some form of reciprocal justification, of which, I think, fairness theory is by far the most promising. I accept, broadly, the following view of fairness: if you benefit from other people's efforts to provide genuinely public goods, then you owe a duty of fairness to do your part; a duty to those who have undertaken costs (provided the scheme as a whole is reasonably just). You benefit, in the relevant sense, if all things considered, you would prefer the scheme and the costs to no scheme and no costs. It is not assumed that we should take people's reports of their preferences as a reliable guide. Rather, at least in the case of the most widely accepted goods, given the difficulties of proof the onus is on the rejecter of the benefits to make out the case, difficult though this may be in many cases (see Wolff 1995a).

The logic of the fairness argument demands that net receipt of benefits is a necessary condition of acquiring burdens. From this alone it does not follow that burdens should be proportioned to benefits, although as we noted above such a view would seem to be in the spirit of fairness theory, where those that benefit most are required to pay most. But whatever we think of that, those who do not benefit at all will escape burdens.[8]

Those who escape political obligations according to the fairness argument are those who do not derive a net benefit from the public goods provided by the state. These are people living on the margins: gypsies, travellers, and those trying to preserve traditional ways of life, who do their best to avoid receiving the benefits that the state has to offer (thus attempting to meet the burden of proof of showing that they would rather have no benefits and no costs).

Note that such people will also avoid the pragmatic obligation of the first argument, for that also depends on the idea of people deriving a benefit from the state. At this point it might be said that the only practical difference between the rational and reciprocal argument is that the second is more inclusive than the former, in that it generates political obligations in every case that the former does, and in others too. As it also provides a moral, rather than prudential, reason to obey, it might be thought that the first argument is wholly redundant.

Now it may be that the rational argument has some advantages over the reciprocal. But even if it does not, this is not a sufficient reason to reject it. For allowing the possibility of overdetermination means that there is no reason to object to the possibility that the same obligations can be justified by more than one argument.

This brings me to the third category of government action: the provision of public goods for the use of part only of society. Here I claimed that, if such activity is justified, it can be assimilated to either the second category (fairness) or the fourth (justice). So we need now to turn to the justice argument.

Here I can only be brief and dogmatic. I assume that all individuals have certain duties of justice to provide assistance to other individuals who meet certain conditions. There can, of course, be enormous disagreement about the nature of those duties, and the conditions others have to meet to be entitled to our help, but for present purposes I need not say any more about this. All I need is the bare assumption that we do have duties of justice to assist others. A second assumption is that such duties cannot reliably be exercised without the state to gather information and co-ordinate responses to it. A third is that these duties can rightfully be enforced by others. The state then appears to be the appropriate enforcement agency, from which it follows that the state has the right to enforce all of us to obey our duties of justice. In essence, again, this is a matter for redistributive taxation.

Note that one is, in principle, subject to such a duty whether or not one benefits from the existence of such arrangements: it can be reasonable to demand sacrifices from one person for the sake of another. Those, for example, who are very well off purely as a result of good fortune can reasonably be required to give something for the sake of those starving through no fault of their own. Thus no one escapes liability to redistributive taxation. In fact, though, many people will not be taxed for redistributive purposes: if they are very poor, they will be net gainers from the scheme, or, for those in the middle, they will neither gain nor lose. Nevertheless even those who have no political obligations under the first two arguments will have them under this. Thus independence is a relative matter.

At this point the problem of conflict of obligations can be addressed. The potential difficulty was that, if we allow several grounds of obligation, we may yield conflicting duties. So, for example, how can we think of the state as both subject to rational justification and to reasonable justification? After all, the former says that it is a necessary condition of the legitimacy of an arrangement that it furthers everyone's self-interest, but the latter denies this. Redistributive policies conflict with rational justification.

However, I think we can avoid this difficulty in the present case if we think of the accounts of justification as each providing a sufficient condition for the legitimacy of government action, not a necessary condition.[9] It is true that rational justification does not license redistribution. But this, on the present view, does not make it illegitimate, for the reasonable argument can provide a sufficient justification. Thus the most stringent obligation overrules any less stringent obligation which conflicts. There will be a difficulty only where, of two conflicting obligations, we cannot say that one is more stringent than the other. In such a case the problem can only be resolved on pragmatic or conventional grounds. But much more detailed treatment is necessary to see if any such case occurs.

Finally, let me sum up the consequences of this account. The largest group of citizens will have political obligations generated in three different ways: from self-interest, from fairness and from justice. Self-interest and fairness may often determine the same duties; justice will typically determine a different set, although there is some possibility of overlap. Other citizens lack some grounds of obligation. For some, self-interest does not give a prudential reason to obey, and some of these people, those who do not derive a net benefit from the arrangements, will also have no duties of fairness. But all, even the semi-independents, have duties of justice. For some (rich gypsies, perhaps) these are the only duties they have. For other semi-independents – the relatively poor among them – although they have such duties in principle, in practice they will not be called on to act, or pay taxes.

How should governments respond to this variability in political obligations? This is a very good question. Clearly governments have to make cruder distinctions than political philosophers. Often they can be excused for acting as if certain individuals or groups have political obligations, when, strictly speaking, they lack them. Furthermore, the arguments given here do not entail that it is right for an individual to break a law when there is no obligation to obey it. For there may be an argument operating at another level suggesting that as breaking a law is likely to have negative consequences, there is always a prima facie obligation to obey even when there is no independent moral ground. Does admitting such a thing undercut the rest of the argument of this paper? Not at all. The negative consequences of disobedience could hardly give us a reason for having laws in the first place. We must also assume that the law is in place, and broadly justified, before we can make such appeal.

Finally, to conclude. In this paper I have tried to do two things. First I wanted to explain how pluralistic models of political obligation are possible, and to give some sense of the options we have. Second, I wanted to give an outline of my favoured sketch. I am aware that other people may think that in addressing the problem of political obligation we need have no recourse to such models. But even if this is so, it is surely worth examining the assumptions underlying much of our theorising, and exploring the conceptual possibilities that open up if we deny them.[10]

Notes

1 This is an extended and developed version of Wolff (1995b).
2 My use of these terms has obvious affinities with their use in Rawls (1993), Gibbard (1991), and Barry (1989, 1995). For further discussion see Wolff (1996b).
3 I do not claim that these categories are exhaustive, or, even, that it is easy to tell to which category a particular theory belongs. Communitarian theories, for example, might be particularly awkward to place in these terms.
4 Attracta Ingram has pointed out that if we reject the assumption of the burden of proof it becomes more difficult to characterise the distinction between reasonable and reciprocal theories. The reason for this is that the difference, as stated here, turns on comparing the post-distribution arrangement with the pre-distribution arrangement, to see if anyone has made a net loss. But what is the pre-distribution point in the case of the state? The anarchic state-of-nature! Hence drawing the distinction between reciprocal and reasonable gives a privileged status to the state-of-nature, but the rejection of the burden of proof is the denial of such a privilege. However, whether this amounts to a formal inconsistency depends on one's reasons for rejecting the assumption on the burden of proof. If one's reason for rejecting it is that state-of-nature theory makes no sense, then, at the very least, a reformulation of the distinction between reasonable and reciprocal theories is called for. My reason, though, is that the assumption is theoretically poorly motivated; hence, all I need to say in reply is that the state-of-nature is given privileged status for one purpose, but not for another.
5 It is also possible that it is not pluralistic enough! Consider *Model 8: radical plurality,* which combines *Multiple plurality* with *Law and its content*. This adds the further point that although there may be multiple justifications for our laws, and multiple justifications for our reasons to obey, there is no neat mapping between the reasons to obey and the justification of the laws.
6 By 'indirect prudence' I mean that I recognise that the existence of certain laws is in my interest. This is distinct from the shallow direct prudential argument that if I do not obey I am likely to be punished.
7 Here I modify some remarks made in Wolff (1990/91).
8 Note that expert free-riders, left out of the scope of the last argument, do not escape this one. For I assume that free-riders do benefit in the sense I explained, they simply manage to figure out a way of avoiding the costs.
9 This is not in tension with the point just repeated that it is a necessary condition of a scheme being rationally justified that it advances everyone's self-interest. The logic of the position is that while A (advancing self-interest) is a necessary condition for B (rational justification), B is a sufficient, but not necessary, condition for C (legitimacy).

10 I would like to thank George Klosko and Veronique Muñoz Dardé for valuable correspondence and discussion which has helped me to formulate some of the ideas in this paper. I would also like to thank members of the Philosophy and Politics Departments, at University College Dublin, for illuminating discussion of a draft of this paper, delivered to the Research Project on Pluralism, organised by Maria Baghramian and Attracta Ingram.

9

WOMEN AND CULTURAL UNIVERSALS

Martha Nussbaum

We shall only solve our problems if we see them as human problems arising out of a special situation; and we shall not solve them if we see them as African problems, generated by our being somehow unlike others.

Kwame Anthony Appiah, *Africa in the Philosophy of Cultures*

Being a woman is not yet a way of being a human being.

Catharine MacKinnon

A matter of survival

I begin with three examples in which cultural traditions pose obstacles to women's quality of life.[1] All three concern the right to employment, which, as we shall see, is both one of the central human capabilities on my list and also a source of many others.

In Beijing in the spring of 1995, the Chinese government announced a new policy to deal with fluctuations in the labour market, giving employers guidance about which workers to lay off first, as employment shifts from place to place. It is called the 'women go home' policy and it is supported by an appeal to Confucian traditions. Confucius, government spokesmen point out, held that women's natural place was in the home. Returning women to their natural functions is thus in accordance with Chinese traditions.[2]

In Indiana in 1994, a Federal District Court heard the case of Mary Carr, first female employee of the tinsmith shop in the gas turbine division in the Indiana General Motors' plant. Men in the tinsmith shop were threatened by the presence of a female worker; they suspected that this would lead to fewer jobs for males. So they decided to drive Carr out. Over a five-year period they carried on an intense and threatening campaign of sexual harassment against her. They wrote obscene words on her toolbox; they cut out the seat of her workman's overalls; they urinated on her from a catwalk; they sent her a Valentine card with an obscene and threatening message. Her complaints to her supervisor brought no action. Eventually she quit and sued GM for damages under the sexual harassment provisions of Title VII. At trial, GM introduced evidence that during that period Carr herself had on several occasions used a swear word. The judge, finding for GM, noted that women should behave in a 'ladylike' manner, and that Carr herself was therefore responsible for 'any hostile sexual environment that consequently arose'. Her untraditional deportment showed that the men's harassing actions were 'not unwelcome' to her (*Carr* v. *Allison* 1994).

In Rajasthan, India, in 1993, a young Hindu widow named Metha Bai, with two young children, described her situation as member of a caste whose women are traditionally prohibited from working outside the home – even when, as here, survival itself is at issue. If she stays at home, she and her children may shortly die. If she attempts to go out, her in-laws will beat her and abuse her children. 'I may die', she told interviewer Martha Chen, 'but still I cannot go out. If there's something in the house, we eat. Otherwise, we go to sleep'. For now, Metha Bai's father travels from 100 miles away to plough her small plot of land. But he is ageing, and Metha Bai fears that she and her children will shortly die with him.[3]

In these cases, as in many others throughout the world, cultural traditions pose obstacles to women's health and flourishing. Depressingly, many traditions have portrayed women as less important than men; less deserving of basic life support, or of fundamental rights that are strongly correlated with quality of life, such as the right to work and the right to political participation. Sometimes, as in the case of Metha Bai, these traditions are resisted by the women themselves. Sometimes, on the other hand, they have become so deeply internalised that they seem to record what is 'right' and 'natural', and women themselves endorse their own second-class status.

Such cases are hardly confined to non-western or developing countries. As recently as 1873, the US Supreme Court upheld a law that forbade women to practice law in the state of Illinois, on the grounds that 'the constitution of the family organisation, which is founded in the divine ordinance, as well as in the nature of things, indicates the domestic sphere as that which properly belongs to the domain and functions of womanhood (*Bradwell* v. *Illinois* 1873). As Mary Carr's case shows, such judgements are still to be found in the federal judiciary. Clearly our own society still appeals to tradition in its own way, to justify women's unequal treatment.

What should people concerned with justice say about this? And should they say anything at all? On the one hand, it seems impossible to deny that traditions, both Western and non-Western, perpetuate injustice against women in many fundamental ways, touching on some of the most central elements of a human being's quality of life, health, education, political liberty and participation, employment, self-respect, and life itself. On the other hand, hasty judgements that a tradition in some distant part of the world is morally retrograde are familiar legacies of colonialism and imperialism, and are correctly regarded with suspicion by sensitive thinkers in the contemporary world. To say that a practice endorsed by tradition is bad is to risk erring by imposing one's own way on others, who surely have their own ideas of what is right and good. To say that a practice is all right wherever local tradition endorses it as right and good is to risk erring by withholding critical judgement where real evil and oppression are surely present. To avoid the whole issue because the matter of proper judgement is so fiendishly difficult is tempting, but perhaps the worst option of all. It suggests the sort of moral collapse depicted by Dante when he describes the crowd of souls who mill around in the vestibule of hell, dragging their banner now one way now another, never willing to set it down and take a definite stand on any moral or political question. Such people, he implies, are the most despicable of all. They can't even get into hell because they have not been willing to stand for anything in life, one way or another.

To express the spirit of this chapter very succinctly, it is better to risk being consigned by critics to the 'hell' reserved for alleged Westerners and imperialists – however unjustified such criticism would in fact be – than to stand around in the vestibule waiting for a time when everyone will like what we are going to say. And this is: that there are universal obligations to protect human functioning and its dignity, and that the dignity of women is equal to that of men. If that involves assault on many local traditions, both Western and Non-Western, so much the better, because any tradition that denies these things is unjust. Or, as a young Bangladeshi wife said when local religious leaders threatened to break the legs of women who went to the literacy classes conducted by a local NGO, 'We do not listen to the mullahs any more. They did not give us even a quarter kilo of rice' (quoted in Chen 1983: 176). The situation of women in the contemporary world calls urgently for moral stand-taking. Women, a majority of the world's population, receive only a small proportion of its opportunities and benefits. According to the 1996 UN Human Development Report, there is no country in the world in which women's quality of life is equal to that of men, according to a complex measure that includes life expectancy, educational attainment, and GDP per capita.[4] Some countries have much larger gender disparities than others. (Among prosperous industrial countries, for example, Spain and Japan perform relatively poorly in this area, Sweden, Denmark, and New Zealand relatively well).[5] If we now examine the Gender Empowerment Measure, which uses variables chosen explicitly to measure the relative empowerment of men and women in political and economic activity,[6] we find even more striking signs of gender disparity. Once again, the Scandinavian nations do well, Japan and Spain relatively poorly.[7]

If we turn our attention to the developing countries we find uneven achievements but, in the aggregate, a distressing situation. On average, employment participation rates of women are only 50 per cent those of men (in South Asia 29 per cent, in the Arab states only 16 per cent).[8] Even when women are employed, their situation is undercut by pervasive wage discrimination and by long hours of unpaid household labour, (if women's unpaid housework were counted as productive output in national income accounts, global output would increase by 20–30 per cent). Outside the home, women are generally employed in a restricted range of jobs offering low pay and low respect. The percentage of earned income that goes to women is rarely higher than 35 per cent. In many nations it is far lower: in Iran 16 per cent, in Belize 17 per cent, Algeria 16 per cent, Iraq 17 per cent, Pakistan 19 per cent. (China at 38 per cent is higher than Japan at 33 per cent; highest in the world are Sweden at 45 per cent, Denmark at 42 per cent and the extremely impoverished Rwanda at 41 per cent, Burundi 42 per cent, and Mozambique at 42 per cent). The situation of women in the workplace is frequently undermined by sex discrimination and sexual harassment.

Women are much less likely than men to be literate. In South Asia, female literacy rates average around 50 per cent those of males. In some countries the rate is still lower: in Nepal 35 per cent, Sierra Leone 37 per cent, Sudan 27 per cent, Afghanistan 32 per cent.[9] Two thirds of the world's illiterate people are women. In higher education, women lag even further behind men, in both developing and industrial nations.[10]

Although some countries allowed women the vote early in this century, some still have not done so. And there are many informal obstacles to women's effective participation in political life. Almost everywhere, they are underrepresented in government. In 1980, they made up only around 10 per cent of the world's parliamentary representatives and less than 4 per cent of its cabinet officials.[11]

As Metha Bai's story indicates, employment outside the home has a close relationship to health and nutrition. So too, frequently, does political voice. And if we now turn to the very basic issue of health and survival, we find compelling evidence of discrimination against females in many nations of the world. It appears that when equal nutrition and health care are present, women live, on average, slightly longer than men – even allowing for a modest level of maternal mortality. Thus in Europe the female/male ratio in 1986 was 105/100, in North America 104.7/100.[12] But it may be objected that for several reasons it is inappropriate to compare these developed countries with countries in the developing world, so let us, with Jean Drèze and Amartya Sen, take as our baseline the ratio in Sub-Saharan Africa, where there is great poverty but little evidence of gender discrimination in basic nutrition and health.[13] The female/male ratio in 1986 was 102.2/100. If we examine the sex ratio in various other countries and ask the question, 'How many more women than are now in country C than would be there if its sex ratio were the same as that of Sub-Saharan Africa?', we get a number that Sen has graphically called the number of 'missing women'. The number of missing women in Southeast Asia is 2.4 millions, in Latin America 4.4, in North Africa 2.4, in Iran 1.4, in China 44.0, in Bangladesh 3.7, in India 36.7, in Pakistan 5.2, in West Asia 4.3. If we now consider the ratio of the number of missing women to the number of actual women in a country, we get, for Pakistan 12.9 per cent, for India 9.5 per cent, for Bangladesh 8.7 per cent, for China 8.6 per cent, for Iran 8.5 per cent, for West Asia 7.8 per cent, for North Africa 3.9 per cent, for Latin America 2.2 per cent, for Southeast Asia 1.2 per cent. In India, not only is the mortality differential especially sharp among children (girls dying in far greater numbers than boys), the higher mortality rate of women compared to men applies to all age groups until the late thirties (Drèze and Sen 1989).

Poverty alone does not cause women to die in greater numbers than men. This is abundantly clear from comparative regional studies in India, where some of the poorest regions, for example Kerala, have the most equal sex ratios, and some far richer regions perform very poorly (Drèze and Sen 1996). When there is scarcity, custom and political arrangement frequently decree who gets to eat the little there is, and who gets taken to the doctor. And custom and political arrangement are always crucial in deciding who gets to perform wage labour outside the home, an important determinant of general status in the family and the community. As Sen has argued, a woman's perceived contribution to the well-being of the family unit is often determined by her ability to work outside, and this determines, in turn, her bargaining position within the family unit (Sen 1990). Custom and politics decree who gets access to the education that would open job opportunities and make political rights meaningful. Custom and politics decree who can go where in what clothing in what company. Custom and politics decree who gets to make what sorts of protests against ill-treatment both inside and outside the family, and whose voice of protest is likely to be heard.

Customs and political arrangements, in short, are important causes of women's misery and death. It seems incumbent on people interested in justice, and aware of the information about women's status that studies such as the Human Development Reports present, to ask about the relationship between culture and justice, and between both of these and legal-political arrangements. It then seems incumbent on them to try to work out an account of the critical assessment of traditions and political arrangements that is neither do-gooder colonialism nor an uncritical validation of the status quo.

One might suppose that any approach to the question of quality of life-assessment in development economics would offer an account of the relationship between tradition and women's equality that would help us answer these questions. But in fact such an account is sorely lacking in the major theoretical approaches that, until recently, dominated the development scene. (Here I do not even include what has been the most common practical approach, which has been simply to ask about GNP per capita. This crude approach does not even look at the distribution of wealth and income; far less does it ask about other constituents of life-quality, for example life expectancy, infant mortality, education, health, the presence or absence of political liberties, that are not always well correlated with GNP per capita.[14] The failure to ask these questions is a particularly grave problem when it is women's quality of life we want to consider. For women have especially often been unable to enjoy or control the fruits of a nation's general prosperity.)

The leading economic approach to the family is the model proposed by Nobel Prize winning economist Gary Becker. Becker assumes that the family's goal is the maximisation of utility, construed as the satisfaction of preference or desire, and that the head of the household is a beneficent altruist who will adequately take thought for the interests of all family members (Becker 1981). In real life, however, the economy of the family is characterised by pervasive 'co-operative conflicts' that is, situations in which the interests of members of a co-operative body split apart, and some individuals fare well at the expense of others.[15] Becker deserves great credit for putting these issues on the agenda of the profession in the first place. But his picture of male motivation does not fit the evidence in a substantial enough way to affect the model's predictive value – especially if one looks not only at women's stated satisfactions and preferences, which may be deformed by intimidation, lack of information, and habit[16] – but at their actual functioning.[17] Furthermore, the model prevents those who use it from getting the information about individual family members on which a more adequate account might be based.[18]

Suppose we were to retain a utilitarian approach and yet to look at the satisfactions of all family members – assuming, as is standardly done in economics, that preferences and tastes are exogenous and independent of laws, traditions, and institutions, rather than endogenously shaped by them. Such an approach – frequently used by governments polling citizens about well being – has the advantage of assessing all individuals one by one. But the evidence of preference endogeneity is great, and especially great when we are dealing with people whose status has been persistently defined as second-class in laws and institutions of various sorts. There are many reasons to think that women's perception even of their health status is shaped by traditional views, such as the view that female life is worth less than male life, that women are weaker than men, that women don't have equal rights, and so forth. In general, people frequently adjust their expectations to the low level of well-being they think they can actually attain (Sen 1990 and Elster 1993). This approach, then, cannot offer a useful account of the role of tradition in well-being, since it is bound by its very commitments to an uncritical validation of the status quo.

More promising than either Becker's model or the standard utilitarian approach is one suggested by John Rawls's liberalism, with its account of the just distribution of a small list of basic goods and resources (Rawls 1970,

1993). This approach does enable us to criticise persistent inequalities, and it strongly criticises the view that preferences are simply given, rather than shaped by society's basic structure. But in one way the Rawlsian approach stops short. Rawls's list of 'primary goods', although it includes some capacity-like items, such as liberty and opportunity, also includes thing-like items, particularly income and wealth, and it measures who is least well off simply in terms of the amount of these thing-like resources an individual can command. But people have varying needs for resources: a pregnant woman, for example, needs more calories than a non-pregnant woman, a child more protein than an adult. They also have different abilities to convert resources into functioning. A person in a wheelchair will need more resources in order to become mobile than a person with unimpaired limbs; a woman in a society that has defined employment outside the home as off-limits to women needs more resources in order to become a productive worker than one who does not face such struggles. In short, the Rawlsian approach does not probe deeply enough to show us how resources do or do not go to work in making people able to function. Again, at least some of our questions about the relationship between tradition and quality of life cannot be productively addressed.

Workers on such issues have therefore increasingly converged on an approach that is now widely known as 'the capabilities approach'. This approach to quality of life measurement and the goals of public policy[19] holds that we should focus on the question: What are the people of the group or country in question actually able to do and to be? Unlike a focus on opulence (say, GNP per capita), this approach asks about the distribution of resources and opportunities. In principle, it asks how each and every individual is doing with respect to all the functions deemed important. Unlike Becker's approach, the capability approach considers people one by one, not as parts of an organic unit; it is interested in seeing how a supposed organic unit such as the family has constructed unequal capabilities for various types of functioning. Unlike a standard utilitarian approach, the capability approach maintains that preferences are not always reliable indicators of life quality, since they may be deformed in various ways by oppression and deprivation. Unlike the type of liberal approach that focuses only on the distribution of resources, the capability approach maintains that resources have no value in themselves, apart from their role in promoting human functioning. It therefore directs the planner to inquire into the varying ideas individuals have for resources, and their varying abilities to convert resources into functioning. In this way, it strongly invites a scrutiny of tradition, as one of the primary sources of such unequal abilities (Sen 1982: 353–72, Nussbaum 1990).

But the capabilities approach raises the question of cultural universalism, or, as it is often pejoratively called, 'essentialism'. Once we begin asking how people are actually functioning, we cannot avoid focusing on some components of lives and not others, some abilities to act and not others, seeing some capabilities and functions as more central, more at the core of human life, than others. We cannot avoid having an account, even if a partial and highly general account, of what functions of the human being are most worth the care and attention of public planning the world over. Such an account is bound to be controversial.

Anti-universalist conversations

The primary opponents of such an account of capability and functioning will be 'anti-essentialists' of various types, thinkers who urge us to begin not with sameness but with difference – both between women and men and across groups of women – and to seek norms defined relatively to a local context and locally held beliefs. This opposition takes many forms, and I shall be responding to several distinct objections. But I can begin to motivate the enterprise by telling several true stories of conversations that have taken place at the World Institute for Development Economics Research (WIDER), in which the anti-universalist position seemed to have alarming implications for women's lives.[20]

At a conference on 'Value and Technology', an American economist who has long been a left-wing critic of neo-classical economics delivers a paper urging the preservation of traditional ways of life in a rural area of Orissa, India, now under threat of contamination from Western development projects. As evidence of the excellence of this rural way of life, he points to the fact that, whereas we Westerners experience a sharp split between the values that prevail in the work-place and the values that prevail in the home, here, by contrast, there exists what the economist calls 'the embedded way of life', the same values obtaining in both places. His example: just as in the home a menstruating woman is thought to pollute the kitchen and therefore may not enter it, so too in the workplace a menstruating woman is taken to pollute the loom and may not enter the room where looms are kept. Some feminists object that this example is repellent, rather than admirable; for surely such practices both degrade the women in question, and inhibit their freedom. The first economist's collaborator, an elegant French anthropologist (who would, 1 suspect, object violently to a purity check at the seminar room door) replies: 'Don't we realise that there is, in these matters, no privileged place to stand? This, after all, has been shown by both Derrida and Foucault. Doesn't he know that he is neglecting the otherness of Indian ideas by bringing his Western essentialist values into the picture?'[21]

The same French anthropologist now delivers her paper. She expresses regret that the introduction of smallpox vaccination to India by the British eradicated the cult of Sittala Devi, the goddess to whom one used to pray in order to avert smallpox. Here, she says, is another example of Western neglect of difference. Someone (it might have been me) objects that it is surely better to be healthy rather than ill, to live rather than to die. The answer comes back: Western essentialist medicine conceives of things in terms of binary oppositions: life is opposed to death, health to disease.[22] But if we cast away this binary way of thinking, we will begin to comprehend the otherness of Indian traditions.

At this point Eric Hobsbawm, who has been listening to the proceedings in increasingly uneasy silence, rises to deliver a blistering indictment of the traditionalism and relativism that prevail in this group. He lists historical examples of ways in which appeals to tradition have been politically engineered to support oppression and violence (Hobsbawm and Ranger 1983).[23]

His final example is that of National Socialism in Germany. In the confusion that ensues, most of the relativist social scientists – above all those from far away, who do not know who Hobsbawm is – demand that Hobsbawm be asked to leave the room. The radical American economist, disconcerted by this apparent tension between his relativism and his affiliation with the left, convinces them, with difficulty, to let Hobsbawm remain.

We shift now to another conference two years later, a philosophical conference on the quality of life.[24] Members of the quality of life project are speaking of choice as a basic good, and of the importance of expanding women's spheres of choice. We are challenged by the radical economist of my first story, who insists that contemporary anthropology has shown that Non-Western people are not especially attached to freedom of choice. His example: a book on Japan has shown that Japanese males, when they get home from work, do not wish to choose what to eat for dinner, what to wear, etc. They wish all these choices to be taken out of their hands by their wives. A heated exchange follows about what this example really shows. I leave it to your imaginations to reconstruct it. In the end, the confidence of the radical economist is unshaken: we are victims of bad universalist thinking, who fail to respect 'difference'.[25]

The phenomenon is an odd one. For we see here highly intelligent people, people deeply committed to the good of women and men in developing countries, people who think of themselves as progressive and feminist and anti-racist, people who correctly argue that the concept of development is an evaluative concept requiring normative argument (Marglin 1990a) effectively eschewing normative argument and taking up positions that converge, as Hobsbawm correctly saw, with the positions of reaction, oppression and sexism. Under the banner of their fashionable opposition to universalism march ancient religious taboos, the luxury of the pampered husband, educational deprivation, unequal health care and premature death.

Nor do these anti-universalists appear to have a very sophisticated conception of their own core notions, such as 'culture', 'custom', and 'tradition'. It verges on the absurd to treat India as a single culture, and a single visit to a single Orissan village as sufficient to reveal its traditions. India, like all extant societies, is a complex mixture of elements (Nussbaum and Sen

1989; Sen 1997b: 33–40). Hindu, Muslim, Parsi, Christian, Jewish, atheist; urban, suburban, rural; rich, poor, and middle-class; high-caste, low-caste, and aspiring middle-caste; female and male; rationalist and mystical. It is renowned for mystical religion, but also for achievements in mathematics and for the invention of chess. It contains intense, often violent, sectarianism, but it also contains Rabindranath Tagore's cosmopolitan humanism and Mahatma Gandhi's reinterpretation of Hinduism as a religion of universal non-violence. Its traditions contain views of female whorishness and childishness that derive from the Laws of Manu (Verma 1995); but it also contains the sexual agency of Draupadi in the Mahabharata, who solved the problem of choice among Pandava husbands by taking all five: and it also contains the enlightened sensualism and female agency of the Kama Sutra, a sacred text that foreign readers wrongly interpret as pornographic. It contains women like Metha Bai, who are confined to the home; and it also contains women like Amita Sen (mother of Amartya Sen), who fifty years ago was among the first middle-class Bengali women to dance in public, in Rabindranath Tagore's musical extravaganzas in Santiniketan. It contains artists who disdain the foreign, preferring, with the Marglins, the 'embedded' way of life; and it also contains Satyajit Ray, that great Bengali artist and lover of local traditions, who could also write:

> I never ceased to regret that while I had stood in the scorching summer sun in the wilds of Santiniketan sketching simul and palash in full bloom, Citizen Kane had come and gone, playing for just three days in the newest and biggest cinema in Calcutta.
>
> (Ray 1976; 1994: 5)

What, then, is 'the culture' of a woman like Metha Bai? Is it bound to be that determined by the most prevalent customs in Rajasthan, the region of her marital home? Or might she be permitted to consider with what traditions or groups she wishes to align herself, perhaps forming a community of solidarity with other widows and women, in pursuit of a better quality of life? What is 'the culture' of Chinese working women who have recently been victims of the government's 'women go home' policy? Must it be the one advocated by Confucius, or may they be permitted to form new alliances – with one another, and with other defenders of women's human rights?[26] What is 'the culture' of General Motors employee Mary Carr? Must it be the one that says women should be demure and polite, even in the face of gross insults, and that an 'unladylike' woman deserves the harassment she gets? Or might she be allowed to consider what norms are appropriate to the situation of a woman working in a heavy metal shop, and to act accordingly? Real cultures contain plurality and conflict, tradition and subversion. They borrow good things from wherever they find them, none too worried about purity. We would never tolerate a claim that women in our own society must embrace traditions that arose thousands of years ago – indeed, we are proud that we have no such traditions. Isn't it condescending, then, to treat Indian and Chinese women as bound by the past in ways that we are not?

Indeed, as Hobsbawm suggested, the vision of 'culture' propounded by the Marglins, by stressing uniformity and homogeneity, may lie closer to artificial constructions by reactionary political forces than to any organic historical entity. Even to the extent to which it is historical, one might ask, exactly how does that contribute to make it worth preserving? Cultures are not museum pieces, to be preserved intact at all costs. There would appear, indeed, to be something condescending in preserving for contemplation a way of life that causes real pain to real people.

Let me now, nonetheless, describe the most cogent objections that might be raised by a relativist against a normative universalist project.

The attack on universalism

Many attacks on universalism suppose that any universalist project must rely on truths eternally fixed in the nature of things, outside human action and human history. Since some people believe in such truths and some do not, the objector holds that a normative view so grounded is bound to be biased in favour of some religious/metaphysical conceptions and against others.[27]

But universalism does not require such metaphysical support.[28] For universal ideas of the human do arise within history and from human experience, and they can ground themselves in experience. Indeed, those who take all human norms to be the result of human interpretation can hardly deny that universal conceptions of the human are prominent and pervasive among such interpretations, hardly to be relegated to the dustbin of metaphysical history along with recondite theoretical entities such as phlogiston. As Aristotle so simply puts it, 'One may observe in one's travels to distant countries the feelings of recognition and affiliation that link every human being to every other human being'.[29] Kwame Anthony Appiah makes the same point, telling the story of his bicultural childhood. A child who visits one set of grandparents in Ghana and another in rural England, who has a Lebanese uncle and who later, as an adult, has nieces and nephews from more than seven different nations finds, he argues, not unbridgeable alien 'otherness', but a great deal of human commonality, and comes to see the world as a 'network of points of affinity' (Appiah 1991: vii–viii).[30] But such a metaphysically agnostic, experiential and historical universalism is still vulnerable to some, if not all, of the objections standardly brought against universalism.

Neglect of historical and cultural differences

The opponent charges that any attempt to pick out some elements of human life as more fundamental than others, even without appeal to a trans-historical reality, is bound to be insufficiently respectful of actual historical and cultural differences. People, it is claimed, understand human life and humanness in widely different ways: and any attempt to produce a list of the most fundamental properties and functions of human beings is bound to enshrine certain understandings of the human and to demote others. Usually, the objector continues, this takes the form of enshrining the understanding of a dominant group at the expense of minority understandings. This type of objection, frequently made by feminists, can claim support from many historical examples in which the human has indeed been defined by focusing on actual characteristics of males.

It is far from clear what this objection shows. In particular it is far from clear that it supports the idea that we ought to base our ethical norms, instead, on the current preferences and the self-conceptions of people who are living what the objector herself claims to be lives of deprivation and oppression. But it does show at least that the project of choosing one picture of the human over another is fraught with difficulty, political as well as philosophical.

Neglect of autonomy

A different objection is presented by liberal opponents of universalism. The objection is that by determining in advance what elements of human life have most importance, the universalist project fails to respect the right of people to choose a plan of life according to their own lights, determining what is central and what is not.[31] This way of proceeding is 'imperialistic'. Such evaluative choices must be left to each citizen. For this reason, politics must refuse itself a determinate theory of the human being and the human good.

Prejudicial application

If we operate with a determinate conception of the human being that is meant to have some normative moral and political force, we must also, in applying it, ask which beings we take to fall under the concept. And here the objector notes that, all too easily, even if the conception itself is equitably and comprehensively designed – the powerless can be excluded. Aristotle himself, it is pointed out, held that women and slaves were not full-fledged human beings; and since his politics were based on his view of human functioning, the failure of these beings (in his view) to exhibit the desired mode of functioning contributed to their political exclusion and oppression.

It is, once again, hard to know what this objection is supposed to show. In particular, it is hard to know how, if at all, it is supposed to show that we would be better off without such determinate universal concepts. For it could be plausibly argued that it would have been even easier to exclude women and slaves on a whim if one did not have such a concept to contend with (Chomsky 1966).[32] On the other hand, it does show that we need to think not only about getting the concept right but also about getting the right beings admitted under the concept.

Each of these objections has some merit. Many universal conceptions of the human being have been insular in an arrogant way, and neglectful of differences among cultures and ways of life. Some have been neglectful of choice and autonomy and many have been prejudicially applied. But none of this shows that all such conceptions must fail in one or more of these ways. At this point, however, we need to examine a real proposal, in order both to display its merits and to argue that it can in fact answer these charges.

A conception of the human being: the central – human capabilities

The list of basic capabilities is generated by asking a question that from the start is evaluative: What activities[33] characteristically performed by human beings are so central that they seem definitive of a life that is truly human? In other words, what are the functions without which (meaning the availability of which) we would regard a life as not, or not fully, human?[34] We can get at this question better if we approach it via two somewhat more concrete questions that we often ask ourselves. First is a question about personal continuity. We ask ourselves what changes or transitions are compatible with the continued existence of that being as a member of the human kind, and what are not. Some functions can fail to be present without threatening our sense that we still have a human being on our hands; the absence of others seems to signal the end of a human life. This question is asked regularly, when we attempt to make medical definitions of death in a situation in which some of the functions of life persist, or to decide, for others or (thinking ahead) for ourselves, whether a certain level of illness or impairment means the end of the life of the being in question.[35]

The other question is a question about kind inclusion. We recognise other humans as human across many differences of time and place of custom and appearance. We often tell ourselves stories, on the other hand, about anthropomorphic creatures who do not get classified as human, on account of some feature of their form of life and functioning. On what do we base these inclusions and exclusions? In short, what do we believe must be there, if we are going to acknowledge that a given life is human?[36] The answer to these questions points us to a subset of common or characteristic human functions, informing us that these are likely to have a special importance for everything else we choose and do.

Note that the procedure through which this account of the human is derived is neither historical nor a priori. It is the attempt to summarise empirical findings of a broad and ongoing cross-cultural inquiry. As such, it is both open-ended and humble – it can always be contested and remade.

Nor does it claim to read facts of 'human nature' off from biological observation: the way it takes account of biology is as a relatively constant element in human experience.[37] It is because the account is evaluative from the start that it is called a conception of the good. It should also be stressed that, like John Rawls's account of primary goods (Rawls 1970: 62 ff., 90–5, 396–7), this list of good functions, which is in some ways more comprehensive than his own list, is proposed as the object of a specifically political consensus.[38] The political is not understood exactly as Rawls understands it, since the nation state is not assumed to be the basic unit, and the account is meant to have broad applicability to cross-cultural deliberations. This means, given the current state of world politics, that many of the obligations to promote the adequate distribution of these goods must rest with individuals rather than with any political institution, and in that way its role becomes difficult to distinguish from the role of other norms and goals of the individual. Nonetheless, the point of the list is the same as that of Rawlsian primary goods: to put forward something that people from many different traditions, with many different fuller conceptions of the good, can agree on, as the necessary basis for pursuing their good life. That is why the list is deliberately rather general.[39] Each of its components can be more concretely specified in accordance with one's origins, or religious beliefs, or tastes. In that sense, the consensus that it hopes to evoke has many of the features of the 'overlapping consensus' described by Rawls[40] (Rawls 1993: *passim*).

Having isolated some functions that seem central in defining the very presence of a human life, we do not rest content with mere bare humanness. We want to specify a life in which fully human functioning, or a kind of basic human flourishing, will be available. For we do not want politics to take mere survival as its goal; we want to describe a life in which the dignity of the human being is not violated by hunger or fear or the absence of opportunity. (The idea is very much Marx's idea, when he used an Aristotelian notion of functioning, to describe the difference between a merely animal use of one's faculties and a 'truly human use' [Sen 1995: 259–73; Becker 1995]). The list of basic capabilities is an attempt to specify this basic notion of the good: all citizens should have these capabilities, whatever else they have and pursue. I introduce this list as a list of capabilities to function, rather than of actual functionings, since I shall argue that capability, not actual functioning, should be the goal of public policy.

Central human capabilities

Life

Being able to live to the end of a human life of normal length; not dying prematurely, or before one's life is so reduced as to be not worth living.

Bodily health

Being able to have good health, including reproductive health; to be adequately nourished; to have adequate shelter.

Bodily integrity

Being able to move freely from place to place; to be secure against violent assault, including sexual assault and domestic violence; having opportunities for sexual satisfaction and for choice in matters of reproduction.

Senses, imagination, and thought

Being able to use the senses, to imagine, think, and reason – and to do these things in a 'truly human' way, a way informed and cultivated by an adequate education, including, but by no means limited to, literacy and basic mathematical and scientific training. Being able to use imagination and thought in connection with experiencing and producing works and events of one's own choice; religious, literary, musical, and so forth. Being able to use one's mind in ways protected by guarantees of freedom of expression with respect to both political and artistic speech, and freedom of religious exercise. Being able to have pleasurable experiences and to avoid non-beneficial pain.

Emotions

Being able to have attachments to things and people outside ourselves; to love those who love and care for us, to grieve at their absence; in general, to love, to grieve, to experience longing, gratitude, and justified anger. Not having one's emotional development blighted by fear and anxiety. (Supporting this capability means supporting forms of human association that can be shown to be crucial in their development).

Practical reason

Being able to form a conception of the good and to engage in critical reflection about the planning of one's life. (This entails protection for the liberty of conscience and religious observance).

Affiliation

A: being able to live with and toward others, to recognise and show concern for other human beings, to engage in various forms of social interaction; to be able to imagine the situation of another. (Protecting this capability means protecting institutions that constitute and nourish such forms of affiliation, and also protecting the freedom of assembly and political speech).

B: having the social bases of self-respect and non-humiliation; being able to be treated as a dignified being whose worth is equal to that of others. This entails provisions of non-discrimination on the basis of race, sex, sexual orientation, ethnicity, caste, religion, national origin.

Other species

Being able to live with concern for and in relation to animals, plants, and the world of nature.

Play

Being able to laugh, to play, to enjoy recreational activities.

Control over one's environment

A: political. Being able to participate effectively in political choices that govern one's life; having the right of political participation, protections of free speech and association.

B: material. Being able to hold property (both land and movable goods), and having property rights on an equal basis with others; having the right to seek employment on an equal basis with others; having the freedom from unwarranted search and seizure. In work, being able to work as a human being, exercising practical reason and entering into meaningful relationships of mutual recognition with other workers.

The 'capabilities approach' as I conceive it,[41] claims that a life that lacks any one of these capabilities, no matter what else it has, will fall short of being a good human life. So it would be reasonable to take these things as a focus for concern, in assessing the quality of life in a country and asking about the role of public policy in meeting human needs. The list is certainly general – and this is deliberate, in order to leave room for plural specification and also for further negotiation. But like (and as a reasonable basis for) a set of constitutional guarantees, it offers real guidance to policy makers, and far more accurate guidance than that offered by the focus on utility, or even on resources. The list is, emphatically, a list of separate components. We cannot satisfy the need for one of them by giving a larger amount of another one. All are of central importance and all are distinct in quality. This limits the trade-offs that it will be reasonable to make, and thus limits the applicability of quantitative cost-benefit analysis. At the same time, the items on the list are related to one another in many complex ways.

Employment rights, for example, support health, and also the freedom from domestic violence, by giving women a better bargaining position in the family. The liberties of speech and association turn up at several distinct points on the list, showing their fundamental role with respect to several distinct areas of human functioning.

Capability as goal

The basic claim I wish to make, concurring with Amartya Sen, is that the central goal of public planning should be the capabilities of citizens to perform various important functions. The question that should be asked when assessing quality of life in a country – and of course this is a central part of assessing the quality of its political arrangements: is, how well have the people of the country been enabled to perform the central human functions? And, have they been put in a position of mere human subsistence with respect to the functions, or have they been enabled to live well? Politics, we argue, (here concurring with Rawls) should focus on getting as many people as possible into a state of capability to function, with respect to the inter-locking set of capabilities enumerated by that list.[42] Naturally, the determination of whether certain individuals and groups are across the threshold is only as precise a matter as the determination of the threshold. I have left things deliberately somewhat open-ended at this point, in keeping with the procedures of the Human Development Report, believing that the best way to work toward a more precise determination, at present, is to focus on comparative information and to allow citizens to judge for themselves whether their policy makers have done as well as they should have. Again, we will have to answer various questions about the costs we are willing to pay to get all citizens above the threshold, as opposed to leaving a small number below and allowing the rest a considerably above-threshold life quality. It seems likely, at any rate, that moving all citizens above a basic threshold of capability should be taken as a central social goal. When citizens are across the threshold, societies are to a great extent free to choose the other goals that they wish to pursue. Some inequalities, however, will themselves count as capability failures. For example, inequalities based on hierarchies of gender or race will themselves be inadmissible on the grounds that they undermine self-respect and emotional development.

The basic intuition from which the capability approach starts, in the political arena, is that human capabilities exert a moral claim that they should be developed. Human beings are creatures such that, provided with the right educational and material support, they could become fully capable of the major human functions. That is, they are creatures with certain lower-level capabilities (which I call 'basic capabilities' (Nussbaum 1988)) to perform the functions in question. When these capabilities are deprived of the nourishment that would transform them into the high-level capabilities that figure on my list, they are fruitless, cut off in some way but a shadow of themselves. They are like actors who never get to go on the stage, or a person who sleeps all through life, or a musical score that is never performed. Their very being makes forward reference to functioning. Thus if functioning never arrives on the scene they are hardly even what they are. This may sound like a metaphysical idea, and in a sense it is (in that it is an idea

213

discussed in Aristotle's *Metaphysics*). But that does not mean that it is not a basic and pervasive empirical idea, an idea that underwrites many of our daily practices and judgements in many times and places. Just as we hold that a child who dies before getting to maturity has died especially tragically, for her activities of growth and preparation for adult activity now have lost their point, so too with capability and functioning more generally: we believe that certain basic and central human endowments have a claim to be assisted in developing, and exert that claim on others, and especially, as Aristotle saw, on government. Without some such notion of the basic worth of human capacities, we have a hard time arguing for women's equality and for basic human rights. Think, for example, of the remark of Catharine MacKinnon that I quoted as my epigraph. If women were really just trees or turtles or filing cabinets, the fact that their current status in many parts of the world is not a fully human one would not be, as it is, a problem of justice. In thinking of political planning we begin, then, from a notion of the basic capabilities and their worth, thinking of them as claims to a chance for functioning, which give rise to correlated political duties.

I have spoken both of functioning and of capability. How are they related? Getting clear about this is crucial in defining the relation of the capabilities approach to liberalism. For if we were to take functioning itself as the goal of public policy, the liberal would rightly judge that we were precluding many choices that citizens may make in accordance with their own conceptions of the good. A deeply religious person may prefer not to be well nourished, but to engage in strenuous fasting. Whether for religious or for other reasons, a person may prefer a celibate life to one containing sexual expression. A person may prefer to work with an intense dedication that precludes recreation and play. Am I saying that these are not fully human or flourishing lives? Does the approach instruct governments to nudge or push people into functioning of the requisite sort, no matter what they prefer?

Here we must answer: no, capability, not functioning, is the political goal. This is so because of the very great importance the approach attaches to practical reason, as a good that both suffuses all the other functions, making them human rather than animal (Nussbaum 1995b)[43] and figures, itself, as a central function on the list. It is perfectly true that functionings, not simply capabilities, are what render a life fully human: if there were no functioning of any kind in a life, we could hardly applaud it, no matter what opportunities it contained. Nonetheless, for political purposes it is appropriate for us to shoot for capabilities, and those alone. Citizens must be left free to determine their course after that. The person with plenty of food may always choose to fast, but there is a great difference between fasting and starving, and it is this difference that we wish to capture. Again, the person who has normal opportunities for sexual satisfaction can always choose a life of celibacy, and we say nothing against this. What we do speak against (for example) is the practice of female genital mutilation, which deprives individuals of the opportunity to choose sexual functioning (and indeed, the opportunity to choose celibacy as well). A person who has opportunities for play can always choose a workaholic life; again, there is a great difference between that chosen life and a life constrained by insufficient maximum-hour protections and/or the 'double day' that makes women unable to play in many parts of the world. The issue will be clearer if we recall that there are three different types of capabilities that figure in the analysis.[44] First, there are what we call basic capabilities: the innate equipment of individuals that is the necessary basis for developing the more advanced capabilities. Most infants have from birth the basic capability for practical reason and imagination, though they cannot exercise such functions without a lot more development and education. Second, there are internal capabilities: that is states of the person herself that are, so far as the person herself is concerned, sufficient conditions for the exercise of the requisite functions. A woman who has not suffered genital mutilation has the internal capability for sexual pleasure; most adult human beings everywhere have the internal capability to use speech and thought in accordance with their own conscience. Finally, we have combined capabilities, which we define as internal capabilities combined with suitable external conditions for the exercise of the function. A woman who is not mutilated but is secluded and forbidden to leave the house has internal but not combined capabilities for sexual expression (and work, and political participation). Citizens of repressive non-democratic regimes have the internal but not the combined capability to exercise thought and speech in accordance with their conscience. The aim of public policy is the production of combined capabilities. This means promoting the states of the person by providing the necessary education and care; and it also means preparing the environment so that it is favourable for the exercise of practical reason and the other major functions.[45]

This clarifies the position. The approach does not say that public policy should rest content with internal capabilities, but remain indifferent to the struggles of individuals who have to try to exercise these in a hostile environment. In that sense, it is highly attentive to the goal of functioning, and instructs governments to keep it always in view. On the other hand, we are not pushing individuals into the function: once the stage is fully set, the choice is up to them.

The approach is therefore very close to Rawls's approach using the notion of primary goods. We can see the list of capabilities as like a long list of opportunities for life functioning, such that it is always rational to want them whatever else one wants. If one ends up having a plan of life that does not make use of all of them, one has hardly been harmed by having the chance to choose a life that does (indeed, in the cases of fasting and celibacy it is the very availability of the alternative course that gives the choice its moral value). The primary difference between this capabilities list and Rawls's list of primary goods is its length and definiteness, and in particular its determination to place upon the list the social basis of several goods that Rawls has called 'natural goods' such as 'health and vigour, intelligence and imagination' (Rawls 1970: 62). Since Rawls has been willing to put the social basis of self-respect on his list, it is not at all clear why he has not made the same move with imagination and health.[46] Rawls's evident concern is that no society can guarantee health to its individuals – in that sense, saying that our goal is full combined capability may appear unreasonably idealistic. Some of the capabilities (e.g. some of the political liberties) can be fully guaranteed by society, but many others involve an element of chance and cannot be so guaranteed. We respond to this by saying that the list is a list of political goals that should be useful as a benchmark for aspiration and comparison. Even though individuals with adequate health support often fall ill, it still makes sense to compare societies by asking about actual health-capabilities, since we assume that the comparison will reflect the different inputs of human planning, and can be adjusted to take account of more and less favourable natural situations.

Earlier versions of the list appeared to diverge from the approach of Rawlsian liberalism by not giving as central a place as Rawls does to the traditional political rights and liberties – although the need to incorporate them was stressed from the start (Nussbaum 1990). This version of the list corrects that defect of emphasis. These political liberties have a central importance in making well-being human. A society that aims at well-being while overriding these has delivered to its members a merely animal level of satisfaction (Sen 1994: 38). As Amartya Sen has recently written:

> Political rights are important not only for the fulfilment of needs, they are crucial also for the formulation of needs. And this idea relates, in the end, to the respect that we owe each other as fellow human beings.
>
> (Nussbaum 1995b)

This idea has recently been echoed by Rawls: primary goods specify what citizens' needs are from the point of view of political justice (Rawls 1993: 187–8).

The capability view justifies its elaborate list by pointing out that choice is not pure spontaneity, flourishing independently of material and social conditions. If one cares about people's powers to choose a conception of the good, then one must care about the rest of the form of life that supports those powers, including its material conditions. Thus the approach claims that its more comprehensive concern with flourishing is perfectly consistent with the impetus behind the Rawlsian project, which has always insisted that we are not to rest content with merely formal equal liberty and opportunity, but must pursue their fully equal worth by ensuring that unfavourable economic and social circumstances do not prevent people from availing themselves of liberties and opportunities that are formally open to them.

The guiding thought behind this Aristotelian enterprise is, at its heart, a profoundly liberal idea,[47] and one that lies at the heart of Rawls's project as well: the idea of the citizen as a free and dignified human being, a maker of choices. Politics has an urgent role to play here, getting citizens the tools they need, both in order to choose at all and in order to have a realistic option of exercising the most valuable functions. The choice of whether and how to use the tools, however, is left up to them, in the conviction that this is an essential aspect of respect for their freedom. They are seen not as passive recipients of social planning, but as dignified beings who shape their own lives.[48] Let us now return to Mary Carr, and to Metha Bai. What would this universalist approach have to say about these concrete cases? For Metha Bai, the absence of freedom to choose employment outside the home is linked to other capability failures, in the areas of health, nutrition, mobility, education, political voice. Unlike the type of liberal view that focuses on resources alone, my view enables us to focus directly on the obstacles to self-realisation imposed by traditional norms and values, and thus to justify special political action to remedy the unequal situation. No male of Metha Bai's caste would have to overcome threats of physical violence in order to go out of the house to work for life-sustaining food. In Mary Carr's case, the men's harassing behaviour limited her capability to work and her mental freedom, in a way that her occasional use of a swearword did not limit or threaten them. Indeed it was this 'asymmetry of positions' that Judge Richard Posner emphasised when he overruled the lower court judge, finding in Carr's favour. The core issue Title VII invited him to consider was, in effect, one of human capability: did their action create an environment that a reasonable person would find hostile to normal functioning? In finding that it did, Posner noted that her vulgar language 'cannot be compared to those of the men and used to justify their conduct and exonerate their employer'.

Answering the objections: human functioning and pluralism

We still need to show that this approach has answers to the legitimate questions that confronted it. Concerning neglect of historical and cultural difference, we can begin by insisting that this normative conception of human capability is designed to make room for a reasonable pluralism in specification. The capabilities approach urges us to see common needs, problems, and capacities: but it also reminds us that each person and group faces these problems in a highly concrete context. The list claims to have identified in a very general way some components that are fundamental to any human life. But it makes room for differences of context in several ways. First, it is open-ended and non-exhaustive. It does not say that these are the only important things, or that there is anything non-important (far less, bad) about things not on the list. It just says that this is a group of especially important functions on which we can agree to focus for political purposes.

Further, the list allows in its very design for the possibility of multiple specifications of each of the components. Good public reasoning about the list will retain a rich sensitivity to the concrete context, to the characters of the agents and their social situation. Sometimes what is a good way of promoting education in one part of the world will be completely ineffectual in another. Forms of affiliation that flourish in one community may prove impossible to sustain in another. Arriving at the best specification will most reasonably be done by a public dialogue with those who are most deeply immersed in those conditions. We should use the list to criticise injustice; but we should not say anything at all without rich and full information.

For example, Metha Bai's is the story of age-old traditions regarding widowhood in India.[49] Any approach to her situation would have to be based on an understanding of these traditions and their special connection with issues of caste in an upwardly mobile Hindu family. Talk of 'the right to work' would have been no use without a concrete local understanding. On the other hand, if the workers in the widows project had simply backed off, saying that the local values did not include a value of right to work for widows, they would have missed the depth at which Metha Bai herself longed for choice and autonomy, both as means to survival for herself and her children and as means to selfhood. These are typical examples of the fruitful ways in which an abstract value can be instantiated in a concrete situation, through rich local knowledge. One further observation is in order. This objector is frequently worried about the way in which universalist projects may erode the values that hold communities together. We have already seen that traditional community values are not always so good for women. We can now add that universalist values build new types of community. In Martha Chen's related study of a rural literacy project in Bangladesh, all the women studied stressed the solidarity promoted by the project, the comfort and pleasure they had in consulting with a group of women (some local, some from the development project), rather than each being isolated in the home. Mallika, a young widow in Dapunia, vigorously expresses this idea.

> The group helped us and taught us many things. I have learned how to live unitedly. Before, if any rich person abused or criticised, we could not reply. But now if anybody says anything bad, we, the seventeen members of the group, go together and ask that person why he or she passed this comment. This is another kind of help we have gotten. Before we did not know how to get together and help each other. Each one was busy with their own worries and sorrows, always thinking about food for their children and themselves. Now we, the seventeen members of the group, have become very close to one another.
>
> (Chen 1983: 216)

This story is no isolated phenomenon. In women's groups I have visited in both India and China, the first benefit that is typically mentioned is that of affiliation and friendship with other women in pursuit of common goals. This shows us something highly pertinent to the Marglins' nostalgic tale of embeddedness. We do not have to choose between 'the embedded life' of community and a de-racinated type of individualism. Universal values build their own communities, communities of resourcefulness, friendship, and agency, embedded in the local scene but linked in complex ways to groups of women in other parts of the world. For these women the new community was a lot better than the one they had inhabited before.

The liberal charges the capability approach with neglect of autonomy, arguing that any such determinate conception removes from the citizens the chance to make their own choices about the good life. We have already said a good deal about this issue, but let us summarise, stressing three points. First, the list is a list of capabilities, not a list of actual functions, precisely because the conception is designed to leave room for choice. Government is not directed to push citizens into acting in certain valued ways; instead, it is directed to make sure that all human beings have the necessary resources and conditions for acting in those ways. By making opportunities available, government enhances, and does not remove, choice.[50] It will not always be easy to say at what point someone is really capable of making a choice, especially where there are traditional obstacles to functioning. Sometimes our best strategy may well be to look at actual functioning and infer negative capability (tentatively) from its absence.[51] But the conceptual distinction remains critical. Even in the rare case in which the approach will favour compulsory measures – particularly in primary and secondary education – it does so because of the huge role education plays in opening other choices in life.

Second, this respect for choice is built deeply into the list itself, in the role it gives to practical reasoning, to the political liberties, and also to employment, seen as source of opportunity and empowerment. One of the most central capabilities promoted by the conception will be the capability of choosing itself.[52]

Finally, the capability view insists that choice is not pure spontaneity, flourishing independently of material and social conditions. If one cares about autonomy, then one must care about the rest of the form of life that supports it, and the material conditions that enable one to live that form of life. Thus the approach claims that its own comprehensive concern with flourishing is a better way of promoting choice than is the liberal's narrower concern with spontaneity alone, which sometimes tolerates situations in which individuals are cut off from the fully human use of their faculties.

We now face the objection about prejudicial application. Catharine MacKinnon once claimed that 'being a woman is not yet a way of being a human being'.[53] As this remark suggests, most traditional ways of categorising and valuing women have not accorded them full membership in the human species, as that species is generally defined. If this is so, one might well ask, of what use is it to identify a set of central human capabilities? For the basic (lower-level) capacity to develop these can always be denied to women even by those who grant their centrality – for example, by denying women 'rational nature', or by asserting that they are connected to dangerous or unclean animality. Does this problem show that the human functioning idea is either hopelessly in league with patriarchy or, at best, impotent as a tool for justice?

I believe that it does not. For if we examine the history of these denials we see, I believe, the great power of the conception of the human as a source of moral claims. Acknowledging the other person as a member of the very same kind would have generated a sense of affiliation and a set of moral and educational duties. That is why, to those bent on shoring up their own power, the stratagem of splitting the other off from one's own species seems so urgent and so seductive. But to deny humanness to beings with whom one lives in conversation and interaction is a fragile sort of self-deceptive stratagem, vulnerable to sustained and consistent reflection, and also to experiences that cut through self-deceptive rationalisation. Any moral conception can be withheld out of ambition or hatred or shame. But the conception of the human being, spelled out, as here, in a roughly determinate way, seems much harder to withhold than others that have been made the basis for ethics, such as 'rational being' or 'person'.

Women and men: two norms or one?

But should there be a single norm of human functioning for men and women? One might grant that human capabilities cross cultures while still maintaining that in each culture a division of labour should be arranged along gender lines.

One such position, which I shall call Position A, assigns to both males and females the same general normative list of functions, but suggests that males and females should exercise these functions in different spheres of life: men in the public sphere, for example, and women in the home. The second, which I shall call Position B, insists that the list of functions, even at a high level of generality, should be different: for men, citizenship and rational autonomy, for women, family love and care.

Position A is compatible with a serious interest in equality and in gender justice. For what it says, after all, is that males and females have the same basic needs for capability development and should get what they need. It is determined to ensure that both get to the higher (developed) level of capability with respect to all the central functions. It simply holds that this can (and perhaps should) be done in separate spheres. Is this any more problematic than to say that human functioning in India can, and even should, take a different concrete form from functioning in England? Or that some people can realise musical capacities by singing, others by playing the violin?

The trouble comes when we notice that Position A usually ends up endorsing a division of duties that is associated with traditional forms of hierarchy. Even Mill, who made so many fine arguments against women's subordination, did not sufficiently ask how the very perpetuation of separate spheres of responsibility might reinforce subordination.

It is hard to find plausible good reasons for perpetuating functional distinctions that coincide with traditional hierarchy. Even in the fourth century BC, Plato was able to see that women's role in childbearing does not require, or even suggest, that women be confined to the home.[54] Advances in the control of reproduction are making this less and less plausible. The disability imposed by childbearing on a member of the labour force is to a large extent socially constructed, above all by the absence of support for childcare, from the public sphere, from employers, and from male partners.

Sometimes clinging to traditional divisions is a prudent way of promoting social change. Neither Chen nor her colleagues proposed to jettison all gender divisions within the Bangladeshi villages. Instead, they found 'female jobs' for the women that were somewhat more dignified and important than the old jobs, jobs that looked continuous with traditional female work but were outside the home and brought in wages. The revolution in women's quality of life never would have taken place but for the caution of the women, who at each stage gave the men of the village reason to believe that the transformations were not overwhelmingly threatening and were good for the well-being of the entire group. But such pragmatic decisions in the face of recalcitrant realities do not tell us how things ought to be. And it is likely that women's subordination will not be adequately addressed as long as they are confined to a sphere traditionally devalued, linked with a low 'perceived well-being contribution'.[55] The Human Development Reports' Gender Empowerment Measure rightly focuses, therefore, on the ability of women to win entry into the traditional male spheres of politics and administration.

I turn, then, to Position B, which has been influentially defended by many philosophers, including Rousseau and some of his followers in today's world.[56] Insofar as B relies on the claim that there are two different sets of basic innate capacities, we should insist, with J. S. Mill, that this claim has not been borne out by any responsible scientific evidence. Experiments that allegedly show strong gender divisions in basic (untrained) abilities have been shown to contain major scientific flaws; these flaws removed, the case for such differences is altogether inconclusive.[57] Experiments that cross-label babies as to sex have established that children are differentially handled, played with, and talked to straight from birth, in accordance with the handler's beliefs about the child's biological sex. It is therefore impossible at present to separate 'nature' from 'culture' (Fausto-Sterling 1992). There may be innate differences between the sexes, but so far we are not in a position to know them – any more than we were when Mill first made that argument in 1869 (Mill 1869).

Second, we should note that even what is claimed without substantiation in this body of scientific material does not usually amount to a difference in what I have been calling the central basic capabilities. What is alleged is usually a differential statistical distribution of some specific capacity for a high level of excellence, not for crossing a basic threshold, and excellence in some very narrowly defined function (say, geometrical ability), rather than in one of our large-scale capabilities such as the capability to perform practical reasoning. So, even if the claim were true it would not be a claim about capabilities in our capacious sense; nor, since it is a statistical claim, would it have any implications for the ways in which individuals should be treated. The political consequences of such alleged sex differences in our scheme of things, even had they been established, would be nil.

But we can also criticise Position B in a different way, arguing that the differentiated conceptions of male and female functioning characteristically put forward by B are internally inadequate, and fail to give us viable norms of human flourishing.[58] What do we usually find, in the versions of B that our philosophical tradition bequeaths to us? (Rousseau's view is an instructive example). We have, on the one hand, males who are 'autonomous', capable of practical reasoning, independent and self-sufficient, allegedly good at political deliberation. These males are brought up not to develop strong emotions of love and feelings of deep need that are associated with the awareness of one's own lack of self-sufficiency. For this reason they are not well equipped to care for the needs of their family members, or, perhaps, even to notice those needs. On the other hand, we have females such as Rousseau's *Sophie* (Rousseau, 1979: Book V) brought up to lack autonomy and self-respect, ill equipped to rely on her own practical reasoning, dependent on males, focused on pleasing others, good at caring for others. Is either of these viable as a complete life for a human being?

It would seem not. The internal tensions in Rousseau's account are a good place to begin.[59] Rousseau places tremendous emphasis on compassion as a basic social motivation. He understands compassion to require fellow feeling, and a keen responsiveness to the sufferings of others. And yet, in preparing Emile for autonomous citizenship, he ultimately gives emotional development short shrift, allocating caring and responsiveness to the female sphere alone. It appears likely that Emile will be not only an incomplete person but also a defective citizen, even by the standards of citizenship recognised by Rousseau himself.

With Sophie, things again go badly. Taught to care for others, but not taught that her life is her own to plan, she lives under the sway of external influences and lacks self-government. As Rousseau himself shows, in his fascinating narrative of the end of her life,[60] she comes to a bad end through her lack of judgement. Moreover, in the process she proves to be a bad partner and deficient in love. For love, as we come to see, requires judgement and constancy. So each of them fails to live a complete human life; and each fails, too, to exemplify fully and well the very functions for which they were being trained, since those functions require support from other functions for which they were not trained. The text leads its thoughtful reader to the conclusion that the capabilities that have traditionally marked the separate male and female spheres are not separable from one another without a grave functional loss. Society cannot strive for completeness by simply adding one sphere to the other. It must strive to develop in each and every person the full range of the human capabilities.

This more inclusive notion of human functioning admits tragic conflict. For it insists on the separate value and the irreplaceable importance of a rich plurality of functions. And the world does not always guarantee that individuals will not be faced with painful choices among these functions, in which, in order to pursue one of them well they must neglect others (and thus, in many cases, subvert the one as well). But this shows once again, I believe, the tremendous importance of keeping some such list of the central functions before us as we assess the quality of life in the countries of the world and strive to raise it. For many such tragedies – like many cases of simple capability failure – result from unjust and unreflective social arrangements. One can try to construct a society in which the tragic choices that faced Emile and Sophie would not be necessary, in which both males and females could learn both to love and to reason.

In April 1994, Metha Bai went to Bangalore for a nation-wide widows' conference. She met widows from all over India, and they spent a week discussing their common problems. During that week, Metha Bai began to smile a lot. She bought beads in the forbidden colour of blue, and she seemed pleased with the way she looked. With advice from a local NGO involved in the conference, she applied for and obtained a loan that enabled her to pay off the mortgage on the small property she still owns. Although her economic situation is not secure and she still does not hold a job outside the home, she has managed to stave off hunger. Like many women all over the world, she is fighting for her life, with resilience and fortitude.[61]

Women belong to cultures. But they do not choose to be born into any particular culture, and they do not really choose to endorse its norms as good for themselves, unless they do so in possession of further options and opportunities – including the opportunity to form communities of affiliation and empowerment with other women. The contingencies of where one is born, whose power one is afraid of, and what habits shape one's daily thought are chance events that should not be permitted to play the role they now play in pervasively shaping women's life chances. Beneath all of these chance events are human powers, powers of choice and intelligent self-formation. Women in much of the world lack support for the most central human functions, and this denial of support is frequently caused by their being women. But women, unlike rocks and plants and even dogs and horses, have the potential to become capable of these human functions, given sufficient nutrition, education, and other support. That is why their unequal failure in capability is a problem of justice. It is up to all human beings to solve this problem. I claim that a conception of human functioning gives us valuable assistance as we undertake this task.

Notes

1 A different form of the present paper appears in Nussbaum 1999. This paper is also related to several others in which I have discussed human capabilities: see Nussbaum (1988, 1990, 1992, 1993, 1995a and b).
2 Oral communication, participants at conference on Chinese Women and Feminist Philosophy organised by the Ford Foundation and the Chinese Academy of Social Sciences, Beijing, June 1995.
3 For this case and others like it, see Chen (1995: 37–57). See also Chen (forthcoming).
4 *Human Development Report* (1996). See also the 1995 report, which focuses on gender. The countries where women do best in life quality, according to the GDI, a measure using the same variables as the HDI (Human Development Index), but adjusted according to disparities between the sexes see (*Human Development Report*: 107) for the technical formulation are, in order, Sweden, Canada, Norway, the USA, Finland, Iceland, Denmark, France, Australia, New Zealand, the Netherlands, Japan, Austria, the United Kingdom and Belgium.
5 If we subtract the GDI rank from the HDI rank, we get 10 for Spain, 9 for Japan, 8 for Sweden, 10 for Denmark and 4 for New Zealand.
6 These include percentage shares of administrative and managerial positions, percentage shares of professional and technical jobs, and percentage shares of parliamentary seats.
7 The ranking at the top: Norway, Sweden, Denmark, Finland, New Zealand, Canada, Germany, the Netherlands, the USA, Austria, Barbados, Switzerland. Spain ranks 25, Japan 37, France 40, Greece 60.
8 These data are from *Human Development Report* (1993); later reports disaggregate employment data into jobs of various specific kinds, and no longer count unpaid agricultural labour as employment.
9 Again, these are 1993 data; the 1996 report gives the absolute percentages, which are, for these examples, Sierra Leone 16.7 per cent, Afghanistan 13.5 per cent, Sudan 32 per cent, Nepal 13.0 per cent. Nations in which the female literacy rate is strikingly out of step with the general level of economic development include Saudi Arabia, 47.6 per cent, Algeria, 45.8 per cent, Egypt 37.0 per cent, Iraq 42.3 per cent, Pakistan 23.0 per cent, India 36.0 per cent. Striking progress in female literacy, on the other hand, if one can rely on the figures, has been made in Cuba, 94.6 per cent, Sri Lanka, 86.2 per cent, Philippines, 93.9 per cent, most of the former constituent states of the Soviet Union, in the 1990s, Vietnam, 89.5 per cent, China, 70.9 per cent. On the disparity of achievement between China and India, see Drèze and Sen (1996).
10 Numbers of female students in tertiary education per 100,000 people: Hong Kong 1022, Barbados 1885, Republic of Korea 2866, Philippines 3140, Egypt 499, China 132, Iran 764, Laos 60, Pakistan 149, Ethiopia 24, Rwanda 19.
11 Countries where women hold a high percentage of parliamentary seats: Norway 39.4 per cent, Sweden 40.4 per cent, and Denmark 33.0 per cent. Bangladesh at

10.6 per cent is ahead of the USA at 10.4 per cent, and India at 8.0 per cent is ahead of Japan at 6.7 per cent.

12 The statistics in this paragraph are taken from Drèze and Sen (1989).

13 This is very likely due to the central role women play in productive economic activity. For a classic study of this issue, see Boserup (1970). For a set of valuable responses to Boserup's work, see Tinker (1990).

14 See Drèze and Sen (1996) for graphic evidence of the relative independence of educational and health attainment from economic growth in comparative regional studies.

15 See Sen (1990), Dasgupta (1993: chapter 11); on food allocation, see Chen, L.C.E., Huq. E. and D'Souza, S. (1981: 55–70). Bargaining models of the family are now proliferating; for two valuable recent examples, see Lundberg, S. and Pollak, R. (1996: 139–58), and Lundberg, S., Pollak, R. and Wales, T.J. (forthcoming).

16 See now Becker (1995: 647) on the role of childhood experiences in shaping preferences.

17 Sen (1990) argues that Becker's account is much stronger as an account of actual preferences in the household than as an account of the real interests (life and death, good and bad health, good and bad nutrition) that underlie the preferences. (He provides evidence that people's perception of their health and nutritional status may be severely distorted by informational deficiencies.)

18 Becker now admits deficiencies in the model: 'Many economists, including me, have excessively relied on altruism to tie together the interests of family members'. Motives of obligation, anger, and other attitudes usually neglected by theories of rational behaviour should be added to the models (Becker 1995: 648); elsewhere, he mentions guilt, affection, and fear – his example being a woman's habitual fear of physical abuse from men (Becker 1995: 647). It is unclear whether he still supports an organic one-actor model, with a more complicated motivational structure, or a 'bargaining model', of the sort increasingly used by family economists.

19 The 'capabilities approach' was pioneered within economics by Amartya Sen, and has been developed by both Sen and me in complementary but not identical ways: for an overview, see Crocker (1995: 152–98).

20 Much of the material described in these examples is now published in Marglin and Marglin (1990). The issue of 'embeddedness' and menstruation taboos is discussed in Marglin (1990b: 217–82) and related issues are discussed in Marglin (1990a: 1–28). On Sittala Devi, see Marglin (1990: 102–44); and for related arguments see Nandy and Visvanathan (1990: 144–84). I have in some cases combined two conversations into one; otherwise things happened as I describe them.

21 For Sen's own account of the plurality and internal diversity of Indian values, one that strongly emphasises the presence of a rationalist and critical strand in Indian traditions, see Nussbaum and Sen (1989: 299–325), a paper originally presented at the same WIDER conference and refused publication by the Marglins in its proceedings; and Sen (1993a). See also Matilal (1989), a fundamental study of Indian traditions regarding knowledge and logic, and Matilal (1989: 339–62).

22 Marglin (1990a: 22–3), suggests that binary thinking is peculiarly Western. But such oppositions are pervasive in Indian, Chinese, and African traditions Nussbaum (1993). To deny them to a culture is condescending: for how can one utter a definite idea without bounding off one thing against another?

23 In his *New Republic* piece, Sen makes a similar argument about contemporary India: the Western construction of India as mystical and 'other' serves the purposes

of the fundamentalist BJP, who are busy re-fashioning history to serve the ends of their own political power. An eloquent critique of the whole notion of the 'other', and of the associated 'nativism', where Africa is concerned, can be found in Appiah (1991).

24 The proceedings of this conference are published as Nussbaum and Sen (1993).

25 Marglin has since published this point in Marglin (1990a: 1–28). His reference is to Doi (1971).

26 At the conference mentioned above, a paper by Julia Tao of Hong Kong University that defended Confucian values as good for women was received very critically by the Chinese women, who called it 'a Western paper', and commented that she would not have spoken that way had she not been from Hong Kong. Their own preferences ran to Mill, whose *The Subjection of Women* was translated into Chinese early in the twentieth century.

27 Note that this objection itself seems to rely on some universal values such as fairness and freedom from bias.

28 See Nussbaum (1992) for a longer version of this discussion.

29 Aristotle, *Nicomachean Ethics* VIII.I. I discuss this passage in Nussbaum (1995b) and Nussbaum (1993).

30 'If my sisters and I were "children of two worlds", no one bothered to tell us this; we lived in one world, in two "extended" families divided by several thousand miles and an allegedly insuperable cultural distance that never, so far as I can recall, puzzled or perplexed us much'. Appiah's argument does not neglect distinctive features of concrete histories; indeed, one of its purposes is to demonstrate how varied, when concretely seen, histories really are. But his argument, like mine, seeks a subtle balance between perception of the particular and recognition of the common.

31 This point is made by the Marglins, as well as by liberal thinkers; but can they consistently make it, while holding that freedom of choice is just a parochial Western value? It would appear not; on the other hand, F. A. Marglin (here differing, 1 believe, from S. A. Marglin) also held in oral remarks delivered at the 1986 conference that logical consistency is simply a parochial Western value.

32 Chomsky argues that Cartesian rationalism, with its insistence on innate essences, was politically more progressive, more hostile to slavery and imperialism, than empiricism, with its insistence that people were just what experience had made of them.

33 The use of this term does not imply that the functions all involve doing something especially, 'active'. See here Sen (1993b). In Aristotelian terms, and in mine, being healthy, reflecting, being pleased, are all 'activities'.

34 For further discussion of this point, and examples, see Nussbaum (1995b).

35 Could one cease to be one's individual self without ceasing to be human? Perhaps, in cases of profound personality or memory change, but I shall leave such cases to one side here. This is ruled out, I think, in Aristotle's conception, but is possible in some other metaphysical conceptions.

36 See Nussbaum (1995b) for a more extended account of this procedure and how it justifies.

37 Nor does it deny that experience of the body is shaped by culture: see Nussbaum (1993).

38 This was implicit in (1990), but has become more prominent in recent papers: see Sen (1994: 31–8) and Nussbaum (1998).

39 In Nussbaum (1990). I call it 'the thick vague theory of the good'.

40 Note that the consensus is defined in terms of a normative notion of reasonableness: thus the failure of some real individuals to agree will not be fatal to the view.

41 Sen has not endorsed any such specific list of the capabilities.

42 With Sen, I hold that the capability set should be treated as an interlocking whole: for my comments on his arguments, see Nussbaum (1988).

43 This is the core of Marx's reading of Aristotle.

44 See Nussbaum (1988), referring to Aristotle's similar distinctions.

45 This distinction is related to Rawls's distinction between social and natural primary goods. Whereas he holds that only the social primary goods should be on the fist, and not the natural (such as health, imagination), we say that the social basis of the natural primary goods should most emphatically be on the list.

46 Rawls comments that 'although their possession is influenced by the basic structure, they are not so directly under its control', primary goods Rawls (1970: 62). This is of course true if we are thinking of health, but if we think of the social basis of health, it is not true. It seems to me that the case of putting these items on the political list is just as strong as the case for the social respect. In 'The Priority of Right', Rawls suggests putting health on the list.

47 Though in one form Aristotle had it too.

48 Compare Sen (1994: 38). 'The importance of political rights for the understanding of economic needs turns ultimately on seeing human beings as people with rights to exercise, not as parts of a "stock" or a "population" that passively exists and must be looked after. What matters, finally, is how we see each other'.

49 See the account of these in Chen (forthcoming).

50 Sen has stressed this throughout his writing on the topic. For an overview see Nussbaum (1997) and for some complications, see my Nussbaum (1998).

51 This is the strategy used by Robert Erikson's Swedish team, when studying inequalities in political participation: see 'Descriptions of Inequality' in Nussbaum and Sen (1993).

52 Rawls proceeds in a similar way, insisting that satisfactions that are not the outgrowth of one's very own choices have no moral worth. He conceives of the 'two moral powers' (analogous to our practical reasoning), and of sociability (corresponding to our affiliation) as built into the definition of the parties in the original position, and thus as necessary constraints on any outcome they will select Nussbaum (1990).

53 The remark was cited by Richard Rorty (1998: 205). It has since been confirmed and repeated by MacKinnon herself.

54 Plato, *Republic*, Book V. Although Plato's proposal is theoretical and utopian, it is closely based on observation of the functioning of women in Sparta: see Halliwell (1994).

55 See Sen (1990).

56 In Rousseau, see Okin (1979) and Martin (1985). On some related recent arguments, for example those of Allan Bloom, see Okin (1989: chapter 1).

57 See the convincing summary in Ame Fausto-Sterling (1992).

58 Here I am in agreement with the general line of argument in Okin (1979), Martin (1985) and Chodorow (1978).

59 See Okin (1989) and Martin (1985).

60 See the discussion in Okin (1979).

61 Chen, oral communication.

10

ETHNOCULTURAL MINORITIES IN LIBERAL DEMOCRACIES

Will Kymlicka
and
Raphael Cohen-Almagor

Introduction

One of the most pressing issues facing liberal democracies today is the politi-cisation of ethnocultural diversity. Minority cultures are demanding greater public recognition of their distinctive identities, and greater freedom and opportunity to retain and develop their distinctive cultural practices. In response to these demands, new and creative mechanisms are being adopted in many countries for accommodating difference. This paper discusses some of the issues raised by these demands, focusing in particular on the difficul-ties that arise in North America and Israel when the minority seeking accom-modation is illiberal.

Historically, liberal democracies have hoped that the protection of basic individual rights would be sufficient to accommodate ethnocultural minori-ties. And indeed the importance of individual civil and political rights in pro-tecting minorities cannot be underestimated. Freedom of association, religion, speech, mobility and political organisation enable individuals to form and maintain groups and associations, to adapt these groups to changing cir-cumstances, and to promote their views and interests to the wider population.

However, it is increasingly accepted that these common rights of citizen-ship are not sufficient to accommodate all forms of ethnocultural diversity. In some cases, certain 'collective' or 'group-differentiated' rights are also required. And indeed there is a clear trend within liberal democracies towards the greater recognition of such group-differentiated rights. Yet this trend raises a number of important issues, both theoretical and practical. How are these group rights related to individual rights? What should we do if group rights come into conflict with individual rights? Can a liberal democracy allow minority groups to restrict the individual rights of their members, or should it insist that all groups uphold liberal principles?

These are genuinely difficult questions. Ethnocultural relations are often full of complications that defy simple categories or easy answers. However, we can make some progress if we draw some distinctions between different kinds of groups, and different kinds of 'group rights'. In this paper we first make a distinction between two forms of cultural pluralism: multinational states and polytechnic states, and then make a further distinction between internal restrictions and external protections. The concept of internal restrictions concerns the right of a group against dissenting members of the same group; whereas the concept of external protections concerns the rights of a group against the society at large. We proceed by probing the nature of liberal tolerance and then delineate the limits of state intervention.

Two kinds of minority cultures

Virtually all liberal democracies contain some degree of ethnocultural diversity. They can all be described, therefore, as 'multicultural'. But the patterns of ethnocultural diversity vary dramatically between countries, and these variations are important in understanding the claims of minority cultures. A complete typology of the different forms of ethnocultural diversity would be an immensely complicated task, but for the purposes of this chapter, we outline a very basic distinction between two forms of cultural pluralism – 'multinational' states versus 'polytechnic' states.

Multinational states

In everyday parlance, we often describe independent countries as 'nation-states'. But many countries are in fact multinational; they contain more than one nation. By 'nation' we mean a historical community, more or less institutionally complete, occupying a given territory or homeland, sharing a distinct language and culture. A 'nation' in this sociological sense is closely related to the idea of a 'people' or a 'culture' – indeed, these concepts are often defined in terms of each other.

If a nation's homeland becomes incorporated into a larger state, then it becomes what we will call a 'national minority'. The incorporation of national minorities into a larger state has typically been an involuntary process. Some national minorities have been invaded and conquered by another nation; others have been ceded from one imperial power to another; yet others have had their homeland overrun by colonising settlers. But some multinational states have arisen voluntarily, when different cultures agree to form a federation for their mutual benefit.[1]

Israel is a binational state. It is comprised of Jews and Palestinians who try to live in coexistence. The liberal formula they seek to advance is 'live and let live'. Israeli-Jews are mostly concerned with their security. Once they feel that the Israeli-Palestinians do not threaten their very existence they would allow Palestinians to further their own conception of the good.[2] With the exception of a few cities where we may find Jews and Palestinians living together, the two groups do not strive to intermingle. They live in their own communities and generally speaking do not try to overcome the dissimilarities. Both nations have different interpretations of history regarding the events that brought about the current situation. While most Jews claim that they took over the land via just means, many of the Palestinian people complain of colonisation and deportations. With regard to the current state of affairs, Palestinians often claim that they are being discriminated against, and that they do not feel 'at home' in Israel (Cohen-Almagor 1991: 34). Israeli-Jews argue in response that the Palestinians are equal citizens. In this context a distinction could be made between formal and full citizenship.

The notion of citizenship is commonly perceived as an institutional status from within which a person can address governments and other citizens and make claims about human rights. All who possess the status are equal with respect to rights and duties with which the status is endowed. The Israeli-Jews can be said to enjoy full citizenship, i.e. they enjoy equal respect as individuals, and they are entitled to equal treatment by law and in its administration. The situation is different with regard to the Israeli-Palestinians, who constitute today some 19 per cent of the population. Although formally the Israeli-Palestinians are considered to enjoy liberties equal to those of the Jewish community, in practice they do not share and enjoy the same rights and burdens. Moreover, they have to live with some limitations on their freedoms which the Jewish majority does not bear (Cohen-Almagor 1991: 33).[3]

In North America national minorities include the American Indians, Puerto Ricans and descendants of the Mexicans living in the Southwest before 1848 in the United States, and the Aboriginal peoples and the Quebecois in Canada. In Europe some countries are multinational, either because they have forcibly incorporated indigenous populations (e.g. Norway and Finland which contain communities of Lapps, known also as Sami. In Norway the Sami community is considerably larger), or because they were formed by the more or less voluntary federation of two or more European cultures (e.g. Belgium and Switzerland). However they were incorporated, national minorities have typically sought to maintain or enhance their political autonomy, either through outright secession, or through some form of regional autonomy. And they typically mobilise along nationalist lines, using the language of 'nationhood' to describe and justify these demands for self-government.

While the ideology of nationalism has typically seen fully-fledged independence as the 'normal' or 'natural' end-point, economic or demographic reasons may make this unfeasible for some national minorities. Moreover, the historical ideal of a fully sovereign state is increasingly obsolete in today's world of globalised economics and transnational institutions. Hence there is a growing interest in exploring other forms of self-government, such as federalism. Indeed, some commentators argue that we are currently witnessing a 'federalist revolution' around the world, precisely because federalism has proven the most effective way to accommodate minority nationalisms within larger states (Elazar 1987; Kymlicka 1996a).

Polyethnic states

A second source of diversity is immigration, particularly where large numbers of individuals and families are admitted from other countries, and allowed to maintain some of their ethnic particularity. An increasing number of countries now contain sizeable immigrant communities, but it is the New World 'countries of immigration' which have the greatest experience in this area – particularly Australia, Canada and the United States.

Until the 1960s, all three of these countries adopted an 'Anglo-conformity' model of immigration. That is, immigrants were expected to assimilate to existing cultural norms, and, over time, become indistinguishable from native-born citizens in their speech, dress, leisure activities, cuisine, family size and so on. However, beginning in the 1970s, it was increasingly accepted that this assimilationist model was unrealistic and unjust. All three countries gradually adopted a more tolerant or 'multicultural' approach which allows and indeed encourages immigrants to maintain various aspects of their ethnic heritage. Immigrants are free to maintain some of their old customs regarding food, dress, recreation, religion, and to associate with each other to maintain these practices. This is no longer seen as unpatriotic, 'un-American' or 'un-Australian'.

In Israel, too, we find a gradual adaptation of the multicultural approach regarding the different Jewish cultures that came to live in the newly established state from all corners of the world. Israel, established in 1948, is an immigrant society. During the 1950s the aspiration was to create 'an Israeli-Jewish life-style' which really meant to create a unified, western life-style. Israel's first prime minister, David Ben-Gurion, declared that '[W]e shall not shut ourselves up in our shell. We shall be open to take in all the cultures of the world, all the conquests of the spirit' (Ben-Gurion 1959: 339). In practice, however, some cultures were rejected during the formative years and efforts were made to curtail their legitimacy, perhaps because they were not conceived at that time (the 1950s) as conquests of the spirit of the Israeli-Jew. Instead of encouraging pluralism, cultural pluralism was viewed as a threat to the founding elite. Feelings of ethnocentrism and paternalism, mixed with intolerance, impermeability and sometimes even pure cruelty brought about the notion of 'us' and 'them'. The Middle-Eastern tradition was looked upon as a threat to progress, development and to Israeli democracy as such. It was acknowledged that the Middle-Easterners conceived their culture in a positive light and did not realise how harmful it was. In due course, however, the Middle-Easterners will comprehend the western values and then, so it was believed, 'they' will thank 'us' (the Ashkenazi European elite) for helping them to accommodate to the western life-style. The enunciated view was that 'we' were benevolent people who brought the Middle-Easterners to an upper stage of development, and that it was for their own advantage to change their culture. As a result efforts were made to upgrade the 'backward primitives' and to reshape their entire being and thinking in the European image. Those 'primitives' were expected to switch worlds, and to start a new life according to a new set of values that included socialist, modern nationalistic, secular as well as democratic notions and norms. Upon this set of values the legitimation of the state and the national consensus were to be founded. That many of these values were remote from the Middle-Easterners' conception of the good was not considered to constitute a major obstacle. They would have to accommodate themselves, forget their old world and accept values that coincide with the nation-building ideology. The acculturation process left no room for preserving the tradition and culture prior to the ascension to Israel (Cohen-Almagor 1995a).

In the mid-1960s the concept of integration through *mizug galuyot* – a euphemism for the assimilation of the Middle-Easterners to the Europeans – was dropped by government and Jewish Agency leaders in favour of 'cultural pluralism'. The Israeli culture was no longer to be envisaged monolithically, but as the sum total of numerous subcultures, Western and Eastern alike, each with its own distinction and legacy. Yet the patronising attitude did not disappear and the trend of thinking that prefers the making of a 'standard' Israeli, who bears the Sabra image over cultural pluralism, still continued to prevail.

During the 1970s attempts were made to extend the scope of symbols and landmarks of the civil religion. We witnessed a growing emphasis on ethnicity and ethnic celebrations. This development legitimised and celebrated the distinctive customs and traditions of a variety of Oriental ethnic groups, like the Kurdish (the Saharane celebrations) and the North African (the maimounah celebrations) (Liebman and Don-Yehiya 1982; Deshen and Shokeid 1974). Recently voices proposing the inclusion of the maimounah celebrations within the calendar of national festivals were heard.

In 1977 the Likud came to power. The deprivation of the Middle-Easterners in the cultural sphere and their institutional discrimination in the economic sphere played a significant role in the emergence of the leading opposition party. Many felt that by voting for the Likud they could retain some of their dignity and pride. Although the Likud did not succeed in eliminating economic differences, it did succeed in raising the self-esteem of the Middle-Easterners. The Likud had promoted a sense of psychological equality between the two major ethnic groups in Israeli society, Ashkenazim and Middle-Easterners. It had done so, *inter alia*, by giving an institutional legitimation to traditional norms and to folklorist behaviour. People of Middle-Eastern origin who were previously ashamed of certain expressions of traditional beliefs, who were made to feel uncomfortable in regard to them, no longer felt a sense of uneasiness in performing them in public. Thus, for instance, since 1977 we increasingly witness the revival of cults that praise saints and of *hiluloth* (celebrations) at tombs and sites consecrated to these saints.

From a psychological perspective, this constituted a fundamental difference. Traditional behaviour, technological modernism and the appeal to the west emerged as legitimate factors that could be sustained alongside each other. It was not that Israel had to decide between modernism and traditionalism, and that one should come at the expense of the other in all times at all spheres through the implementation of coercive means. Rather, one could be compatible with the other if a balance was drawn through the promotion of tolerance, understanding of different needs of different sectors, and the making of compromises. The negative attitude to multiculturalism that prevailed in the 1950s was replaced in the 1980s by a positive attitude, acknowledging that both western and eastern cultures are legitimate within the society (Cohen-Almagor 1995a).

In Israel the national divide is far more prominent than the cultural. Though we do not underestimate the feelings of hostility and mistrust that still prevail among Middle-Easterners against Ashkenazim for years of deprivation and discrimination, still considerations of security are the most prominent. The first and foremost worry is to secure the Israeli borders and mitigate the Israeli-Palestinian conflict in a way that would accommodate the interests of both sides. We should also note that the cultural character of Israel is in process of change as a result of waves of immigration that continue to arrive, especially from eastern Europe and more particularly from the former republics of the Soviet Union. It is estimated that since 1989 more than 700,000 people arrived in Israel from the former Soviet republics.

In the Anglo-Saxon societies considerations of security are far less dominant. Here some people worry that the 'multicultural' approach to immigration is encouraging immigrant groups to develop the same attributes and ambitions as national minorities – i.e. to start thinking of themselves as 'nations' with the right to govern themselves, and to develop a more or less full set of separate institutions operating in their own language (Schlesinger 1992; Bissoondath 1994). But this is neither the intention nor the effect of existing policies in the three major immigrant countries. In public life, immigrant groups still participate overwhelmingly within the institutions of the larger society. They mix with native-born citizens in common educational, economic, legal and political institutions, all of which operate in the majority's language. Their distinctiveness, therefore, is manifested primarily in their family lives and in voluntary associations. Because they lack separate institutions operating in their own language, and because they do not occupy homelands, few if any immigrant groups think of themselves as 'nations', or claim rights to self-government.

Multiculturalism for immigrants, therefore, is best understood not as a rejection of linguistic and institutional integration, but as a change in the terms of integration. Immigrants are still expected to learn the majority's language, and to integrate into common institutions. Indeed, learning English is a mandatory part of children's education in Australia and the United States.[4] Similarly, in Israel the Hebrew language is mandatory in Jewish schools and in Canada children must learn either of the two official languages (French or English). Multiculturalism holds that it is neither necessary nor fair to insist that institutional and linguistic integration be accompanied by a more extensive cultural assimilation. On the contrary, for the government to require linguistic and institutional integration is only fair if, in return, these common institutions are reformed so as to accommodate the identity of immigrant groups (Kymlicka 1998).

As a result of extensive immigration, combined with the increased toleration of ethnic identities, the United States and Australia have a number of 'ethnic groups' as loosely aggregated subcultures within the larger English-speaking society, and so exhibit what we will call 'polyethnicity'. Similarly, Canada has a number of ethnic groups as loosely aggregated subcultures within both the English- and French-speaking societies. In Israel we find this phenomenon especially among Ethiopian and Russian immigrants who made *aliya* (came to live in the Jewish state) during the past fourteen years or so. Many of these immigrants prefer to live in their own cultural communities. Living together answers some of their most basic needs: it gives them a sense of familiarity, of unity and of security. They also share their financial problems and could consult in their own language with people they know, people who belong to the same community and could understand, sympathise and identify with their difficulties.

To summarise: some countries are 'multinational' (as a result of colonisation, conquest, and confederation), others are 'polyethnic' (as a result of immigration), and some countries, like Canada, the United States and Israel are both. Of course, there are other kinds of ethnocultural diversity; many groups are neither immigrants nor national minorities (e.g. African-Americans;[5] gypsies;[6] Turkish guest-workers in Germany;[7] guest-workers from all over the world in Israel).[8] But we will focus on these two types, partly because they are the most common in liberal democracies, and also because liberal democracies have, over the years, learned a great deal about how to accommodate these forms of diversity. Both immigration and minority nationalisms continue to raise many conflicts and challenges for liberal democracies. But we can also see some familiar patterns in how these conflicts and challenges are dealt with, and we can begin to trace the outlines of a liberal-democratic approach to the rights of these minority cultures.

Two kinds of group rights

Both immigrant groups and national minorities are, in different ways, seeking legal recognition of their ethnocultural identities and practices. These demands are often described, by both their defenders and critics, in the language of 'group rights'. Defenders, however, typically describe group rights as supplementing individual rights, and hence as enriching and extending traditional liberal principles to deal with new challenges, whereas critics tend to assume that group rights involve restricting individual rights, and hence as threatening basic liberal democratic principles.

What then is the relationship between individual rights and group rights – are they mutually reinforcing, or mutually antagonistic? The answer to this question is not a simple one and we need to take into account the different claims that are involved. Consider two kinds of rights that a group might claim: the first involves the right of a group against its own members; the second involves the right of a group against the larger society. Both kinds of collective rights can be seen as protecting the stability of national, ethnic or religious groups. However, they respond to different sources of instability. The first kind is intended to protect the group from the destabilising impact of internal dissent (e.g. the decision of individual members not to follow traditional practices or customs), whereas the second is intended to protect the group from the impact of external pressures (e.g. the economic or political decisions of the larger society). To distinguish these two kinds of group rights, we will call the first 'internal restrictions', and the second 'external protections'.[9]

Of course, all forms of government involve restricting the liberty of citizens (e.g. paying taxes, undertaking jury duty or military service). Even the most liberal of democracies imposes such restrictions in order to uphold individual rights and democratic institutions. But some groups seek to impose much greater restrictions, not in order to maintain liberal institutions, but rather to protect religious orthodoxy or cultural tradition. A sociological look at different societies reveals that many groups seek the right to legally restrict the freedom of their own members in the name of group solidarity or cultural purity. When one looks at rituals around the globe, it is almost always the case that women are being discriminated against: suttee, arranged marriage, female infanticide, as well as female circumcision and murder for family honour are such examples. Women are required to pay a high price for the norm of male dominance. Group rights are invoked by theocratic and patriarchal cultures where women are oppressed and religious orthodoxy enforced. This obviously raises the danger of individual oppression. At the same time there is also a danger that claims for groups' rights might override law and order. In the name of preserving culture and protecting a sense of community, a demand is raised against society not to interfere even when the most atrocious things take place.

On our view, such internal restrictions are almost always unjust. Groups are free, of course, to impose certain restrictions as conditions for membership in voluntary associations, but it is unjust to use governmental power, or the distribution of public benefits, to restrict the liberty of members. From a liberal point of view, whoever exercises political power in a community must respect the civil and political rights of its members. Furthermore, members of cultural groups should enjoy the liberty to leave their groups upon reaching the conclusion that they no longer like to associate themselves with the group. People in democratic societies should be free to move in and out of their cultural communities and should not be coerced to stay in order to serve the partisan interests of others. This, as we said, is especially true for women who live in a chauvinist, discriminatory environment.

Look, for instance, at the practice of murder for family honour that is employed by some cultural communities in Israel, most notably in the Bedouin and Druze but sometimes also in the Christian community. On most occasions its victims are women who are perceived to be 'misbehaving'. In these communities, honour is frequently more important than life, and culture more important than law. Reports show that women were assassinated because they were accused of not conforming to prevailing moral codes (Kressel 1981). Violation of the sexual norm by a married woman automatically calls for her murder. For single women, accusation is always based on the breach of the norm that a girl or unmarried woman who has 'sinned' must be punished by death unless she marries the partner in intercourse. By murdering their daughters or sisters the men prove the control that the natal family has over its women (Cohen-Almagor 1996: 178).

Many men of these communities conceive such instances of murder for family honour as 'internal matters', meaning that society should not interfere. In these communities, a conspiracy of silence surrounds the issue. Of the victims who escaped death, only a few were prepared to testify against their families. On some occasions, the act of murder is disguised as a suicide, and it needs some investigation to clear things up and resolve the case. When girls do not step forward and acts of murder are committed, often the police show reluctance to interfere, perceiving these crimes as what the decision-makers of these communities want, i.e. as 'internal affairs' that have to be resolved within the community. *Ipso facto*, the result of this outlook might be that an offence against family honour (*intihak el-hurma*) serves as an adequate justification for taking life.

The problem is that in the Muslim and Druze communities no powerful organisations exist to safeguard the most fundamental right: the right to life where 'problematic' girls are concerned. Girls who flee for fear because they betrayed their family honour are usually returned to their families by the police or turned over to a respectable figure, a sheikh, qadi or mukhtar, or to a tribal chief. The regime reinforces the patriarchal tradition at the expense of women. Women are left unprotected and a mere rumour might be sufficient to end the life of one suspected of indecent conduct (Cohen-Almagor 1996: 182).

It is our contention that some things lie beyond the ability of liberal democracies to tolerate. Democracy cannot endure norms that deny respect to people and that are designed to harm others, although they might be dictated by some cultures. Some norms are considered by liberal standards to be intrinsically wrong, wrong by their very nature; for example those which result in physical harm to women and babies – widow burning, female infanticide, harsh forms of female circumcision,[10] and murder for family honour.

The right of a group against its own members is not absolute. Sometimes society is justified in interfering and imposing restrictions on certain cultural practices. This, however, does not mean that cultural groups do not have rights against the larger society on matters that do not entail considerable harm to others. Let us now examine when external protections are justified.

The second kind of collective rights, external protections, are defensible when groups seek to protect their identity by limiting their vulnerability to the decisions of the larger society. For example, reserving land for the exclusive use of a minority group ensures that it will not be outbid for the land by the greater wealth of outsiders. Guaranteeing representation for a minority on advisory or legislative bodies reduces the chance that the group will be outvoted on decisions that affect the community. Devolving power to local levels enables the group to make certain decisions on its own. These sorts of external protections are often consistent with liberal democracy, and may indeed be necessary for justice. They help put the different groups in a society on a more equal footing, by reducing the extent to which minorities are vulnerable to the larger society.

Some claims for external protections are unjust. Apartheid, where a certain minority takes over the wealth of the country while discriminating against the majority, monopolises all the political power and imposes their language on other groups, is manifestly unjust. The South African apartheid where whites who constituted less than 20 per cent of the population demanded 87 per cent of the land mass of the country, monopolised all the political power, and imposed their language on other groups, was manifestly unjust and made South Africa the second country in history to base its constitution on racism (Richardson 1978). In democracies the minority usually has no ability or desire to dominate larger groups. The external protections they seek would not deprive other groups of their fair share of economic resources, political power or language rights. As a rule, minorities simply seek to ensure that the majority cannot use its superior numbers and wealth to deprive the minority of the resources and institutions needed to sustain their community. And that, we think, is a legitimate demand.

So, whereas internal restrictions are almost inherently in conflict with liberal democratic norms, external protections are not, as long as they promote equality between groups, rather than allowing one group to dominate or oppress another. It is important, therefore, to determine whether the claims of ethnocultural groups involve internal restrictions or external protections, and what are the grounds for each claim. This is not always an easy question to answer, particularly since self-government rights can be used either to secure external protections or to impose internal restrictions. But it is worth noting that some ethnocultural groups are only interested in external protections. Some national minorities and immigrant groups are concerned with ensuring that the larger society does not deprive them of the conditions necessary for their survival, but not with controlling the extent to which their own members engage in untraditional or unorthodox practices.

We emphasise this because some commentators assume that if a minority is itself liberal, and respects the rights of its individual members, then it has no need for group-differentiated rights.[11] If a minority seeks group-differentiated rights beyond the common rights of liberal citizenship, this is seen as evidence that it must somehow be illiberal. But even the most liberal minority can still wish for external protections – such as land claims, guaranteed representation, self-government rights, or exemptions from particular laws – in order to limit their vulnerability to the economic or political power of the larger society. There is no inconsistency in seeking such external protections while respecting the rights of members within the group. Indeed, such groups may adopt internal constitutions which guarantee civil and political rights for their members.

However, these are the easy cases, at least in principle. Even if many liberal theorists and commentators have historically opposed demands for external protections, there is no reason in principle why liberal democracies cannot accommodate the demands of ethnocultural groups which are themselves liberal.[12] The more difficult cases concern groups which are illiberal – i.e. groups which are concerned with controlling internal dissent, and so seek to impose internal restrictions short of inflicting physical harm on their members. We have mentioned cultural minorities in Israel which exhibit intolerant and harmful attitudes towards their women. Now we wish to probe the more difficult issues that involve some restrictions on group members but which do not amount to severe physical harm.

One example is concerned with some Pueblo Indians communities in the United States who enjoy extensive rights of self-government and discriminate against members who have abandoned the traditional tribal religion in the distribution of housing. They also discriminate against women who have married outside the tribe.[13] Similarly, some immigrant groups and religious minorities use 'multiculturalism' as a pretext for imposing traditional patriarchal practices on women and children. Some immigrant and religious groups may demand the right to stop their children (particularly girls) from receiving a proper education, so as to reduce the chances that the child will leave the community; or the right to continue traditional customs such as compulsory arranged marriages that is common among certain immigrant cultural communities in North America and Israel.[14]

The nature of liberal tolerance

How should liberal states respond to these cases in which immigrant, cultural and national groups demand the 'right' to protect their historical customs by limiting the basic civil liberties of their members and at the same time refrain from using violence? Some of these cases are difficult. It is easy for liberal states to accommodate the demands of groups which are themselves liberal, but surely what some minorities desire is precisely the ability to reject liberalism, and to organise their society along traditional, non-liberal lines? Isn't this part of what makes them culturally distinct? If the members of a minority lose the ability to enforce religious orthodoxy or traditional gender roles, haven't they lost part of the *raison d'être* for maintaining themselves as a distinct society? Isn't the insistence on respect for individual rights a new form of ethnocentrism, which sets the (liberal) majority culture as the standard to which other cultures must adhere? Indeed, isn't it fundamentally intolerant to force a national minority or religious sect to reorganise their community according to 'our' liberal principles?

These difficult questions have given rise to important conflicts, not only between liberals and non-liberals, but also within liberalism itself. For tolerance is itself a quintessential liberal value, alongside other liberal values like individual freedom and personal autonomy. The problem, of course, is that these values can conflict: promoting individual freedom may entail intolerance towards illiberal groups, while promoting tolerance of illiberal groups may entail accepting restrictions on the freedom of individuals. What should be done in such cases?

If an illiberal minority is seeking to oppress other groups, then most liberals would agree that intervention is justified in the name of self-defence (Rawls 1971: 216–21). Hence the secular majority in Israel has every right to object to attempts which aim to narrow its freedom of conscience and to broaden the authority of religious orthodoxy. But what if the group has no interest in ruling over others or depriving them of their resources, and instead simply wants to be left alone to run its own community in accordance with its traditional non-liberal norms? In such cases, some liberals may think that tolerance should take precedence over autonomy so long as the practice in question does not contravene the rule of law.[15] If these minorities do not want to impose their values on others, shouldn't they be allowed to organise their society according to their culture and within the general ambit of the law, even if this involves limiting the liberty of their own members?

There is a growing debate amongst liberals about whether autonomy or tolerance is the fundamental value within liberal theory.[16] Defenders of tolerance argue that there are many groups within the boundaries of liberal states which do not value personal autonomy, and which restrict the ability of their members to question and dissent from traditional practices. Basing liberal theory on autonomy threatens to alienate these groups, and undermine their allegiance to liberal institutions, whereas a tolerance-based liberalism can provide a more secure and wider basis for the legitimacy of government. On a tolerance-based view, liberals should seek to accommodate illiberal groups, so long as they do not seek any support from the larger society, and do not seek to impose their values on others.

Defenders of the tolerance-based view often argue that liberalism emerged out of the idea of religious toleration. Religious tolerance developed in the West when both Catholics and Protestants realised that a stable constitutional order could rest on a shared religious faith; liberals have simply extended the principle of tolerance to other controversial questions about the 'meaning, value and purpose of human life' (Rawls 1993: xxv–xxix).

There is some truth to this claim that liberalism is an extension of the principle of religious tolerance, but this connection, paradoxically, does not exclusively support the tolerance-based view. For the sort of religious tolerance which emerged in the West, and which was subsequently generalised, was precisely an autonomy-based conception of tolerance. Religious toleration in the West was based on the idea of individual freedom of conscience. Tolerance was achieved by giving each individual the right to worship freely, to propagate one's religion, to change one's religion, or indeed to renounce religion altogether. Indeed, to restrict an individual's exercise of these liberties is now seen as a violation of a fundamental human right.

There are other forms of religious toleration which are not based on individual freedom and autonomy. They are based on the idea that each religious group should be free to organise its community as it sees fit, including along non-liberal lines. In the 'millet system' of the Ottoman Empire, for example, Muslims, Christians and Jews were all recognised as self-governing units (or 'millets'), and allowed to impose restrictive religious laws on their own members. This was a group-based form of toleration, which did not recognise any principle of individual freedom of conscience.[17]

So when liberals extended the principle of religious tolerance to other areas of life, they were extending an individual freedom-based notion of tolerance. This is why a genuinely liberal conception of tolerance will deny the legitimacy of internal restrictions which limit the right of individuals within the group to revise their conceptions of the good. For example, liberalism opposes attempts by a religious minority to legally prohibit apostasy and proselytisation, or to prevent their children learning about other ways of life.[18]

Let us reflect on two different examples of this conflict. First, consider the Canadian case of *Hofer* v. *Hofer*, which dealt with the powers of the Hutterite Church over its members (*Hofer et al.* v. *Hofer et al.* 1970: 13 DLR (3d) 1). The Hutterites live in large agricultural communities called colonies, within which there is no private property. Members of the Hofer family, life-long members of a Hutterite colony, were expelled for apostasy. They demanded their share of the colony's assets, which they had helped create with their years of labour. When the colony refused, the two ex-members sued in court. They objected to the fact that they had 'no right at any time in their life to leave the Colony where they are living unless they abandon literally everything ... even the clothes they are wearing' (*Hofer et al.* v. *Hofer et al.* 1970: 21). The Hutterites defended this practice on the grounds that freedom of religion protects a congregation's ability to live in accordance with its religious doctrine, even if this limits individual freedom.

The Canadian Supreme Court in a 6 to 1 decision accepted this Hutterite claim. The majority opinion (Cartwright CJC, Martland, Judson, Ritchie, Hall, and Spence JJ) did not regard this as a case in which the Court can be asked to relieve against a forfeiture, for by the terms of the articles signed by the Hutterite members, the appellant never had any individual ownership of any of the assets of the Colony. Cartwright CJC added that the 'principle of freedom of religion is not violated by an individual who agrees that if he abandons membership in a specified church he shall give up any claim to certain assets' (*Hofer et al.* v. *Hofer et al.* 1970: 4).

Justice Pigeon noted in dissent that the usual liberal notion of freedom of religion 'includes the right of each individual to change his religion at will'. Hence churches 'cannot make rules having the effect of depriving their members of this fundamental freedom'. The proper scope of religious authority is therefore 'limited to what is consistent with freedom of religion as properly understood, that is freedom for the individual not only to adopt a religion but also to abandon it at will'. Pigeon thought that it was 'as nearly impossible as can be' for people in a Hutterite colony to reject its religious teachings, due to the high cost of changing their religion, so they were effectively deprived of freedom of religion (*Hofer et al.* v. *Hofer et al.* 1970: 21).

Justice Pigeon's dissent is the proper liberal approach. Pigeon starts with the liberal presumption that people have a basic interest in their capacity to form and revise their conception of the good. Hence, he concludes, the power of religious communities over their own members must be such that individuals can freely and effectively exercise that capacity. If we accept this view, then we must interpret freedom of religion in terms of an individual's capacity to form and revise her religious beliefs.

The second example is the *Wisconsin* v. *Yoder* case in the US which dealt with the power of the Amish community over its members (*Wisconsin* v. *Yoder* 1972: 406 US 205, 92 S.Ct 1526). The Amish wanted to withdraw their children from the state educational system before the age of 16, arguing that formal high school education beyond the eight grade is contrary to their beliefs, not only because it places the Amish children in an environment hostile to their beliefs but also because it takes them away from their community, physically and emotionally, during the crucial and formative adolescent period of life. Undoubtedly, this would severely limit the extent to which the children learn about the outside world. The Amish, like the Hutterite, defended this by arguing that freedom of religion protects a group's freedom to live in accordance with its doctrine, even if this limits the individual freedom of children. The American Supreme Court, led by Burger CJ accepted the Amish claim, but here again the claim seems inconsistent with basic liberal principles. We should emphasise that our objection to the decision is not to the actual conclusion, but rather to the conception/interpretation which the Court gave to the right of freedom of religion. The Court defined freedom of religion primarily in terms of the group's ability to live in accordance with its doctrine, rather than the individual's ability to form and revise his or her religious beliefs. This is not to say that the Amish necessarily deny this latter individual freedom. Our point is that the Court never really even addressed that question systematically, since it defined freedom of religion in a non-liberal, group-based way. We are not saying that group-imposed restrictions on education are necessarily inconsistent with individual freedom of choice, but that for a liberal interpretation of freedom of religion, this is what needs to be examined. The demands of the group must be consistent with the real and ongoing capacity for choice by individuals.

Hence, our concern is less with the Amish *per se* than with the test the Court invoked to assess the Amish situation. Of course, one could argue that the Amish should be exempted from the usual liberal conception of freedom of religion, on the grounds that they, like the Pueblo, do not fall under the jurisdiction of the Bill of Rights. But that was not the argument that the Amish made, nor was it the basis for the Court's decision. So long as the Amish appeal to the right of freedom guaranteed in the constitution, the liberal state should interpret that right as one which protects and defends the capacity of individuals to form and revise their religious beliefs.[19]

In sum: in both the Hutterite and the Amish cases, the courts supported the claims of illiberal groups, in the name of 'tolerance' and 'freedom of religion'. But the courts interpreted these ideals in non-liberal ways, rather than insisting on a distinctively liberal interpretation of tolerance and freedom. Hence it seems that the appeal to 'tolerance' does not resolve the conflict between liberal values and illiberal minorities. Since liberal tolerance is individual freedom-based, not group-based, it cannot justify internal restrictions that limit individual freedom of conscience.

The limits of intervention

The question of identifying a defensible liberal theory of minority rights is separate from that of imposing that liberal theory. Internal restrictions may be inconsistent with liberal principles, but it does not yet follow that liberals should impose their views on minorities which do not accept some or all of these liberal principles.

In the case of immigrants who come to a country knowing its laws, we see no objection to imposing liberal principles. This can be seen as part of the terms of admission to a liberal polity, and immigrants have no basis for denying that the state has legitimate authority over them.[20] But the situation is more complicated with national minorities, particularly if (a) they were involuntarily incorporated into the larger state (as the Palestinians claim with regard to their incorporation into the Jewish state), and (b) they have their own formalised governments, with their own internal mechanisms for dispute resolution. In these circumstances, the legitimate scope for coercive intervention by the state may be limited.

Recall the case of some Pueblo Indians communities in the United States, whose tribal council violates the rights of its members by limiting freedom of conscience, and by employing sexually discriminatory membership rules. Liberal principles tell us that the Pueblo tribal government is acting unjustly, since individuals have certain claims which their government must respect, such as individual freedom of conscience. But if the Pueblo government fails to respect those claims, does the American federal government have the authority to step in and force compliance?

Many liberals have assumed that all governments within a country should be subject to a single Bill of Rights, adjudicated and enforced by a single Supreme Court. Hence many American liberals supported legislation to make tribal governments subject to the federal Bill of Rights, even though Indian tribes have historically been exempt from having to comply with the Bill of Rights, and their internal decisions have not been subject to Supreme Court review (Svensson 1979: 421–39).

This legislation was widely opposed by Indian groups, and for under-standable reasons.[21] The assumption that all governments within a country should be subject to a single Bill of Rights, enforced by a common Supreme Court, is inappropriate in the case of the Pueblo and other incorporated national minorities. For one thing, the federal constitution and courts may have no legitimacy in the eyes of an involuntarily-incorporated national minority. After all, the American Supreme Court legitimised the acts of colonisation and conquest which dispossessed the Pueblo of their property and political power.[22] Furthermore, the Pueblo have never had any represen-tation in the Supreme Court. Why should the Pueblo agree to have their internal decisions reviewed by a body which is, in effect, the courts of their conquerors?

Moreover, it is important to note that the Pueblo have their own internal constitution and courts which prevent the arbitrary exercise of political power. To be sure, the Pueblo constitution is not a fully liberal one, but it is a form of constitutional government, and so should not be equated with mob rule or despotism. As Graham Walker (1997) notes, it is a mistake to conflate the ideas of liberalism and constitutionalism. There is a genuine cat-egory of non-liberal constitutionalism, which provides meaningful checks on political authority and preserves the basic elements of natural justice, and which thereby helps ensure that governments maintain their legitimacy in the eyes of their subjects.[23]

The non-liberal constitutionalism of the Pueblo is obviously unsatisfactory from the point of view of liberal principles. After all, the Pueblo courts upheld the rules which discriminated against women as well as Christians. But for the federal courts to overturn the decisions of the Pueblo courts and impose liberal principles is a dangerous move. To impose liberalism on such an involuntarily incorporated and self-governing group is to denigrate the group's own system of government and courts, even though it has high levels of legitimacy in the eyes of its members; and to impose instead a court system which has no legitimacy, since it has historically justified the dispossession of the Pueblo, and has never had a Pueblo member of the Supreme Court. We should emphasise, however, that we would find intervention justified should the Pueblo inflict bodily harm on women or members of other religions.

For these reasons, imposing liberal principles on self-governing national minorities is not unlike imposing liberalism on other countries. In both cases, attempts to impose liberal principles by force often backfire, since they are perceived as a form of aggression or paternalistic colonialism. The experience of post-colonial Africa shows that liberal institutions are unlikely to be stable when they have arisen as a result of external imposition rather than internal reform. In the end, liberal institutions can only work if liberal beliefs have been internalised by the members of the self-governing society, be it an independent country or a national minority.[24]

Insofar as it is illegitimate to impose liberalism in these cases, the liberal state and the illiberal national minority will have to come to some sort of *modus vivendi*. This means that the majority will be unable to prevent the violation of some individual rights within the minority community. At the same time we should not infer that liberals should stand by and do nothing. There are several things which liberals can do to promote respect for individual rights within non-liberal minority groups. Since a national minority which rules in an illiberal way acts unjustly, liberals have a right – indeed a responsibility – to speak out against such injustice, and to support any efforts the group makes to liberalise their culture. Since the most enduring forms of liberalisation are those that result from internal reform, the primary focus for liberals outside the group should be to provide this sort of support.

Moreover, incentives can be provided, in a non-coercive way, for liberal reforms. In this context consider the case of female circumcision as it is conducted among some Bedouin tribes in Israel involving a minor ritual procedure. On most (if not all) occasions, girls of these tribes experience a very moderate form of circumcision. The ceremony takes place between the ages 12 to 17, some time before the girl's marriage. Physical examinations of prenatal women show only a tiny scar on the labia (Cohen-Almagor 1996:

176). Bedouin women believe that this conduct contributes to their tidiness and purifies them. Women who did not undergo circumcision are said not to be good bakers and cooks. Since there are hardly any complaints, on the whole no complications, and the overwhelming majority of girls do not feel they are being coerced, we would do better to leave the matter as it is and not interfere to try and stop it. The state should intervene to help those girls who do not wish to go through this small operation and feel that they are being coerced to undergo it. To eliminate the possibility of infection and severe bleeding (few cases were reported) we may also try to convince the old ladies performing this conduct to use sterilised knives instead of the instruments they use today (often razors but sometimes knives and even glass). We suggest this restricted pattern of interference only because current data indicates that the possibilities of severe bodily damage (physical and psychological) and the risk of death are low, and we do not think that we should hypothesise on the basis of it. It is almost impossible to refute hypotheses that suggest a very low risk, and we should not waste our time in trying to do so. The reader should not infer from this attitude that we see moderate forms of female circumcision as morally justifiable. We do not. From a principled point of view we find this practice morally repugnant. Thus, we justify interference to help those who feel the same. But since in most cases no coercion is involved, and since we are not able to say that our value judgement should prevail over the Bedouins' (i.e. that our liberal view that female circumcision is morally repugnant is truer than the power of tradition), interference in the Bedouin cultural life seems to be more harmful than the performance of female circumcision in its existing form. The state may also take two additional steps: it could send social workers to have discussions with all the Bedouin women about their health. This could be done by approaching the tribe's decision makers, i.e. the men, asking their permission to have access to the women of the tribe in order to find ways to promote their health. The idea is to persuade the men that the health of their families could be improved by such discussions. After gaining permission and access, one or more of the sessions could concern traditional codes that undermine health. The issue of circumcision will be raised in that context, aiming to separate facts from fiction and to show that female circumcision has no bearing – good or bad – on the food, and that it might have a negative bearing on the health of women. A sincere and open discussion might help women realise that the ritual does not in any sense improve their position but rather mutilates their bodies. A careful, well designed plan, with the co-operation of the people concerned, might bring about change of custom. We stress that the precondition for the success of this plan is to gain the consent of both men and women. Such educational methods could be useful only if the permission of the tribe is granted.

Another step that the state could adopt is to offer to train Bedouin women and grant them official authorisation as circumcisers. The training will include, *inter alia*, studies of sterilisation and methods to reduce pain and handle severe bleeding. The government could offer to pay the trained circumcisers for each circumcision as an incentive, just as it pays maternity grants to Bedouin women who have their babies in hospital. Since this grant was made, the number of Bedouin women preferring to give birth in state hospitals has increased significantly. From this we may infer that the Bedouins may view such a suggestion favourably. This solution may be adopted throughout the world wherever female circumcision is being conducted. Such a moderate suggestion could end the tragedy of mutilation while respecting tribal traditions (Asali *et al*, draft paper; Belmaker 1994: 5C). It is necessary, however, to continue research on this issue and review this tolerant suggestion from time to time in order to ensure that the recorded mild form of female circumcision is not being radicalised, and that no significant harm, both physically and psychologically, is involved. The issue has to be put on the public agenda. Upon reaching the conclusion that the best interests of the circumcised girls justify state intervention (because, for instance, complaints about coercion are becoming frequent), then these interests should serve as a trump card to override tradition and cultural considerations. The current lenient attitude is suggested here only because it seems that the best interests of the girls are better served by abstention from interference.

Before we close we also wish to recommend liberals to promote the development of regional or international mechanisms for protecting human rights. Many national minorities have expressed a willingness to abide by international declarations of human rights, and to answer to international tribunals for complaints of rights violations within their community. Indeed, minorities have often shown greater willingness to accept this kind of international review than majority groups, which jealously guard their sovereignty in domestic affairs.[25]

So there are many ways to strengthen mechanisms for respecting individual rights in a consensual way, without simply imposing liberal values on national minorities. This is not to say that coercive intervention in the internal affairs of a national minority is never justified. Intervention is justified in the case of gross and systematic violation of human rights, such as slavery or murder or inflicting severe bodily harms on certain individuals or expulsions of people. A number of factors are relevant in deciding when intervention is warranted, including the severity of rights violations within the minority community; the extent to which mechanisms of formalised dispute resolution exist within the community, and the extent to which these mechanisms are seen as legitimate by group members; the ability of dissenting group members to leave the community if they so desire; and the existence of historical agreements which base the national minority's claim for some sort of autonomy (Kymlicka 1995: 165–70; Cohen-Almagor 1994: chapter 4). For example, whether it is justified to intervene in the case of an Indian tribe that restricts freedom of conscience surely depends on whether it is governed by a tyrannical dictator who lacks popular support and prevents people leaving the community, or whether the tribal government has a broad base of support and religious dissidents are free to leave.[26]

Conclusion

Liberal democracies have a long history of seeking to accommodate ethno-cultural differences. We have focused on two particular aspects of this history. With respect to national minorities, liberal democracies have typically accorded these groups some degree of regional political autonomy, so that they can maintain themselves as separate and self-governing, culturally and linguistically distinct, societies. With respect to immigrants, liberal democracies have typically expected that these groups will integrate into mainstream institutions, but have become more tolerant of the expression of immigrant identities and practices within these institutions.

Liberal democracies have been surprisingly consistent in following these general patterns. Yet this distinction between immigrant groups and national minorities remains remarkably unexplored at the level of normative liberal democratic theory. It is difficult to identify a single major liberal political scientist or philosopher who has seriously examined or evaluated these differences in the way that immigrants and national minorities have been treated historically by liberal democratic states. As a result, we do not yet have an adequate theory of the moral justification for, or the moral limitations on, the rights of ethnocultural minorities. Developing such a liberal theory of minority rights is of the utmost importance for the future of liberal democracies, particularly for newly democratising countries in Eastern Europe, Asia and Africa. At present, the fate of ethnic and national groups around the world is in the hands of xenophobic nationalists, religious extremists, and military dictators. If liberalism is to have any chance of taking hold in these countries, it must explicitly address the needs and aspirations of ethnic and national minorities.[27]

Notes

1 For further discussion see Cohen-Almagor (1994: 68–76).
2 By 'conception of the good' is meant a more or less determinate scheme of ends that the doer aspires to carry out for their own sake, as well as of attachments to other individuals and loyalties to various groups and associations. It involves a mixture of moral, philosophical, ideological and religious notions, together with personal values that contain some picture of a worthy life.
3 For example, Israeli-Palestinians pay more income tax than Jews since they do not enjoy discounts given to those who serve in the army. Palestinians will find it more difficult than Jews to obtain licences for extending their flats, or for building new ones. They also find it difficult to buy, or even to rent, a flat, in a Jewish neighbourhood. Furthermore, budgets of Arab municipalities stand in no comparison

to those of Jewish municipalities. There are not enough classes in Arab towns and villages. Arabs who graduate find it difficult to get a job in government offices. In addition, being a Palestinian-Arab in many cases 'guarantees' that a worker's salary would be lower than that of a Jew who is doing the same work.

4 The language requirements for citizenship are waived for elderly immigrants.

5 African-Americans do not fit the voluntary immigrant pattern, not only because they were brought to America involuntarily as slaves, but also because they were prevented (rather than encouraged) from integrating into the institutions of the majority culture (e.g. racial segregation; laws against miscegenation and the teaching of literacy). Nor do they fit the national minority pattern, since they do not have a homeland in America or a common historical language. They came from a variety of African cultures, with different languages, and no attempt was made to keep together those with a common ethnic background. On the contrary, people from the same culture (even from the same family) were typically split up once in America. Moreover, before emancipation, they were legally prohibited from trying to recreate their own cultural structure (e.g. all forms of black association, except churches, were illegal). The situation of African-Americans, therefore, is virtually unique.

6 The situation of gypsies in Europe is also exceptional because their homeland is everywhere and nowhere.

7 Recent changes in Germany's citizenship laws give the children of Turkish guest-workers the right to acquire citizenship, depending on their age and length of residence. However, for older guest-workers, the process of obtaining citizenship is a costly and uncertain process, with the decision left entirely to the discretion of government officials. They have no right to gain citizenship, no matter how long they have lived in Germany, and no matter how fluent their German is. For a comparative discussion of Germany's citizenship laws, see (Dilek Cinar 1994: 49–72).

8 The guest-workers in Israel were admitted solely as temporary workers and have no right to citizenship.

9 The distinction between these two kinds of collective rights is developed in depth in Kymlicka (1995: chapter 3).

10 We emphasise that we speak of harsh forms of female circumcision, like the Pharaonic or Sunna circumcision. Later on we shall observe the moderate ritual that is performed in Israel. Although we do not justify its existence we nevertheless do not find sufficient reasons to ask the state to interfere and prohibit this practice.

11 For a discussion of how this assumption came to dominate post-World War II discussions of human rights, in opposition to the earlier belief in the need for minority rights, see Claude (1955). Claude notes: '[T]he general tendency of the postwar movements for the promotion of human rights has been to subsume the problem of national minorities under the broader problem of ensuring basic individual rights to all human beings, without reference to membership in ethnic groups. The leading assumption has been that members of national minorities do not need, are not entitled to, or cannot be granted rights of a special character. The doctrine of human rights has been put forward as a substitute for the concept of minority rights, with the strong implication that minorities whose members enjoy individual equality of treatment cannot legitimately demand facilities for the maintenance of their ethnic particularism' (1955: 211).

12 For a discussion of the liberal tradition's hostility to minority rights, see Kymlicka (1995: chapter 4).

13 If female members marry outside the tribe, their children are denied membership. But if men marry outside the tribe, the children are members. This discrimina-

tory rule was upheld in *Santa Clara Pueblo* v. *Martinez* 436 US 49 (1978). For further discussion see Resnik (1989: 671–759).

14 For a discussion of conflicts between some East Asian immigrant groups and the British government over girls' education and arranged marriages, see Poulter (1987: 589–615).

15 For examples of liberals who subordinate considerations of autonomy to tolerance, see Galston (1995: 516–35) and Kukathas (1997).

16 The autonomy-based view is often described as the 'Enlightenment', 'comprehensive' or 'Kantian' conception of liberalism, in contrast to the 'Reformation', 'political', or 'modus vivendi' conception which is grounded on the value of tolerance. For these contrasts, see Galston (1995); Rawls (1993) and Larmore (1987).

17 For a detailed discussion of the millet system as an illiberal form of group-based religious tolerance, see Kymlicka (1996b: 81–105).

18 In Israel, the autonomous education system that is run by ultra-religious Jews prevents children from learning certain secular teachings and practices and Israel condones this.

19 For a detailed discussion of the Court's (divided) reasoning on this case, see Arneson and Shapiro (1996: 365–411) and the reply by Burtt (1996: 412–37).

20 Things are more complicated if an immigrant group was exempted from liberal requirements when it arrived, and so has been able to maintain certain illiberal institutions for many years or generations (e.g. the Amish in the United States). These groups were given certain assurances about their right to maintain separate institutions, and so have built and maintained self-contained enclaves that depend on certain internal restrictions. Had those assurances not been given, these groups might have emigrated to some other country. It is not clear how much weight, morally speaking, should be given to these sorts of historical arguments, but it seems that these groups do have a stronger claim to maintain internal restrictions than newly-arriving immigrants.

21 It was opposed even by Indian groups which were liberal in their basic outlook. Many Indian leaders argued that Indian governments should be exempt from the Bill of Rights, not in order to impose illiberal internal restrictions within Indian communities, but to defend the external protections of Indians *vis-à-vis* the larger society. They feared that their rights to land, or to guaranteed representation, which help reduce their vulnerability to the economic and political pressure of the larger society, could be struck down as violating the equality rights of the Bill. Also, Indian leaders fear that white judges may interpret certain rights (e.g. democratic rights) in ways that are culturally biased. Hence many liberal Indian groups seek exemption from the Bill of Rights, but affirm their commitment to the basic human rights and freedoms which underlie the American constitution. For a more detailed discussion, see Schneiderman (1997).

22 The basic attitude of the American Supreme Court towards Indian sovereignty was determined by Chief Justice John Marshall's judgement in *Johnson* v. *M'Intosh*, 21 U.S. (8 Wheat.) 543 (1823). In this judgement, Marshall said that 'Conquest gives title which the courts of the conqueror cannot deny', the validity of which 'has never been questioned by our courts' (587–8). Marshall's approach continues to determine the Court's approach to Indian rights, not just in the United States, but also in other settler societies, such as Canada and Australia. On this, see Williams Jr. (1995: 146–202); Wilkins (1994: especially 161–8).

23 It is important to distinguish these cases from ethnocultural groups which have no formal constitutions or courts, and which therefore provide no effective check on the exercise of arbitrary power by powerful individuals or traditional elites.

24 For a survey of the arguments against imposing liberalism on other countries, see Walzer (1977; 1980). Virtually all of Walzer's points also argue against imposing liberalism on national minorities, although Walzer himself doesn't always make this connection.

25 What the Pueblo object to is not external review *per se*, but rather being subject to the constitution of their conquerors, which they had no role in drafting, and being answerable to federal courts, which legitimised the unjust coercion and discrimination against them.

26 The ability of members to leave is a very important proviso. However, unlike some commentators, Svensson (1979: 437); Kukathas (1992: 133), we do not think it is sufficient to justify internal restrictions, any more than racial segregation in the American South was made legitimate by the fact that Blacks could move north (although some defenders of segregation did make this argument). The consideration of physical harm is no less important. See Green (1994); Cohen-Almagor (1995b) and Kymlicka (1995: chapter 8).

27 This paper was presented at the pluralism conference, the Royal Irish Academy, Dublin.

BIBLIOGRAPHY

Appiah, K. A. (1991) *In My Father's House: Africa in the Philosophy of Cultures*, New York: Oxford University Press.

Arendt, H. (1958) *The Human Condition*, Chicago, IL: University of Chicago Press.

Aristotle (1995) *Nicomachean Ethics*, trans J.A.K. Thomson, Harmondsworth, Penguin.

Arneson, R. and Shapiro I. (1996) 'Democratic Autonomy and Religious Freedom: A Critique of *Wisconsin* v. *Yoder*, in I. Shapiro and R. Hardin (eds) *Political Order: Nomos* 38: 365–411.

Arrow, K. (1963) *Social Choice And Individual Values*, 2nd edn, New York: Wiley.

Asali, A., Khamaysi, N., Aburabia Y., Letzner S., Halihal B., Sidovsky M., Maoz B. and Belmaker R.H. (draft paper) 'Ritual Female Genital Surgery among Bedouin in Israel'.

Ayer, A.J. (1968) *The Origins of Pragmatism: Studies in the Philosophy of Charles Sanders Peirce and William James*, London: Macmillan.

Barry, B. (1989) *Theories of Justice*, Hemel Hempstead: Harvester-Wheatsheaf.

Barry, B. (1995) *Justice as Impartiality*, Oxford: Oxford University Press.

Becker, G. (1981) A *Treatise on the Family*, Cambridge, MA: Harvard University Press, (2nd edn 1991).

—— (1995) 'The Economic Way of Looking at Behaviour', the Nobel Address 1992, in R. Febrero, and P. S. Schwartz, (eds) *The Essence of Becker*, Stanford, CT: Hoover Institution Press.

Belmaker, H., letter in *Newsweek*, 31 January 1994, 5C.

Ben-Gurion, D. (1959) *Rebirth and Destiny in Israel*, London: Thomas Yoseloff.

Benhabib, S. (ed.) (1996) *Democracy and Difference*, Princeton, NJ: Princeton University Press.

Benn, S.I. and Gaus, G. (1983) 'The Public and the Private: Concepts and Action' in S.I. Benn and G Gaus (eds) *Public and Private in Social Life*, London: Croom Helm.

Berlin, I. (1969) *Four Essays on Liberty*, Oxford and New York: Oxford University Press.

—— (1981) 'The Originality Of Machiavelli', in H. Hardy (ed.), *Berlin, Against The Current*, Oxford: Oxford University Press.

—— (1990) *The Crooked Timber of Humanity*, London: John Murray.

—— (1991) *The Crooked Timber Of Humanity*, H. Hardy (ed.) New York: Knopf.

251

—— (1999) *The Roots Of Romanticism*, H. Hardy (ed.) Princeton: Princeton University Press.

Berlin, I. and Williams, B. (1994) 'Pluralism and Liberalism: A Reply', *Political Studies* 42: 306–9.

Bird, G. (1986) *William James*, London: Routledge.

Bissoondath, N. (1994) *Selling Illusions: The Cult of Multiculturalism in Canada*, Toronto: Penguin.

Blackburn, S. (1984) *Spreading the Word*, Oxford: Clarendon Press.

—— (1993)*Essays in Quasi-Realism*, Oxford: Oxford University Press.

Boserup, E. (1970) *Women's Role in Economic Development*, New York: St. Martin's Press, (2nd edn Aldershot: Gower Publishing, 1986).

Bradwell v. *Illinois*, (1873), 83 US (16 Wall.) 130.

Brandom, R. (1994) *Making It Explicit: Reasoning, Representing, and Discursive Commitment*, Cambridge, MA: Harvard University Press.

Broome, J. (1997) 'Incommensurable Values', Paper Delivered at the Fifth Conference of the International Society for Utilitarian Studies, New Orleans, March 21–23, 1997.

Burtt, S. (1996) 'In Defense of Yoder: Parental Authority and the Public Schools', in I. Shapiro and R. Hardin (eds) *Political Order: Nomos* 38: 412–37.

Carr v. *Allison Gas Turbine Division, General Motors Corporation*, (1994) 32 F. 3d 1007.

Chalmers, D. (1996) *The Conscious Mind: In Search of a Fundamental Theory*, New York: Oxford University Press.

Chang, R. (ed.) (1998) *Incommensurability, Incomparability and Practical Reason*, Cambridge: Harvard University Press.

Chen, C., Huq, E. and D'Souza, S. (1981) 'Sex Bias in the Family Allocation of Food and Health Care in Rural Bangladesh', *Population and Development Review* 7: 55–70.

Chen, M. (1983) *A Quiet Revolution: Women in Transition in Rural Bangladesh*, Cambridge, MA: Schenkman.

—— (1995) 'A Matter of Survival: Women's Right to Employment in India and Bangladesh', in M. Nussbaum, and J. Glover, (eds) *Women, Culture and Development*, Oxford: Clarendon Press.

—— (forthcoming) *The Lives of Widows in Rural India*.

Child, W. (1994) 'On the Dualism of Scheme and Content', *Proceedings of the Aristotelian Society*, XCIV, Part 1: 53–71.

Chodorow, N. (1978) *The Reproduction of Mothering*, Berkeley, CA: University of California Press.

Chomsky, N. (1966) *Cartesian Linguistics*, New York: Harper and Row.

Cinar, D. (1994) 'From Aliens to Citizens: A Comparative Analysis of Rules of Transition', in R. Baubock (ed.) *From Aliens to Citizens: Redefining the Legal Status of Immigrants*, Aldershot: Avebury.

Claude, I. (1955) *National Minorities: An International Problem*, Cambridge, MA: Harvard University Press.

Cohen, J. (1993) 'Moral Pluralism and Political Consensus', in D. Copp, J. Hampton and J. Roemer (eds) *The Idea of Democracy*, Cambridge: Cambridge University Press.

—— (1996) 'Democracy, Difference and the Right of Privacy' in S. Benhabib (ed.) *Democracy and Difference*, Princeton NJ: Princeton University Press.

Cohen-Almagor, R. (1991) 'The Intifada: Causes, Consequences, and Future Trends', *Small Wars & Insurgencies* 2,1: 12–40.

—— (1994) *The Boundaries of Liberty and Tolerance: The Struggle Against Kahanism in Israel*, Gainesville, FL: The University Press of Florida.

—— (1995a) 'Cultural Pluralism and the Israeli Nation-Building Ideology', *International Journal of Middle East Studies* 27: 461–84.

—— (1995b) 'Liberalism, and the Limits of Pluralism', *Terrorism and Political Violence* 7, 2: 25–48.

—— (1996) 'Female Circumcision and Murder for Family Honour among Minorities in Israel', in K. Schulze, M. Stokes and C. Campbell (eds) *Nationalism, Minorities and Diasporas: Identities and Rights in the Middle East,* London: I.B Tauris.

Cooke M. (1997) 'Are Ethical Conflicts Irreconcilable?', *Philosophy and Social Criticism* 23:1–19.

Crocker, D. (1995) 'Functioning and Capability: the Foundations of Sen's and Nussbaum's Development Ethic', in M. Nussbaum, and J. Glover, (eds) *Women, Culture, and Development,* (WCD) Oxford: Clarendon Press.

Crowder, G. (1994) 'Pluralism and Liberalism', *Political Studies* 42: 293–305.

Dasgupta, P. (1993) *An Inquiry into Well-Being and Destitution,* (Chapter 11) Oxford: Clarendon Press.

Davidson, D. (1978) 'What Metaphors Mean', *Critical Inquiry* 5: 31–47.

—— (1980) *Essays on Actions and Events,* Oxford: Oxford University Press.

—— (1984) 'On the Very Idea of a Conceptual Scheme', in *Inquiries into Truth and Interpretation,* Oxford: Oxford University Press.

—— (1989) 'The Myth of the Subjective', in M. Krausz, (ed.) *Relativism: Interpretation and Confrontation,* Notre Dame, IN: University of Notre Dame Press.

—— (1990) 'A Coherence Theory of Truth and Knowledge', in A. Malachowski (ed.) *Reading Rorty,* Oxford: Basil Blackwell.

—— (1984) 'On the Very Idea of a Conceptual Scheme', in *Inquiries into Truth and Interpretation,* Oxford: Oxford University Press.

Dennett, D. (1979) *Brainstorms,* Brighton: Harvester Press.

Deshen, S. and Shokeid M. (1974) *Predicament of Homecoming: Cultural and Social Life of North African Immigrants of Israel,* Ithaca, NY: Cornell University Press.

Doi, T. (1971) *The Anatomy of Dependence,* Tokyo: Kodansha.

Drèze, J. and Sen, A. (1989) *Hunger and Public Action,* Oxford: Clarendon Press.

—— (1996) *India: Economic Development and Social Opportunity,* Oxford: Clarendon Press.

Dryzek, J. (1990) *Discursive Democracy,* New York: Cambridge University Press.

Dworkin, G. (1974) 'Non-Neutral Principles', *Journal of Philosophy* Vol. 71: 491–506.

Elazar, D. (1987) *Exploring Federalism,* Tuscaloosa, AL: University of Alabama Press.

Elster, J. (1993) *Sour Grapes,* Cambridge: Cambridge University Press.

Erikson, R. (1993) 'Descriptions of Inequality' in M. Nussbaum, and A. Sen (eds) in *The Quality of Life,* Oxford: Clarendon Press.

253

Fausto-Sterling, A. (1992) *Myths of Gender*, 2nd edn, New York: Basic Books.

Fraser, N. (1992) 'Rethinking the Public Sphere: A Contribution to the Critique of Actually Existing Democracy' in C. Calhoun (ed.) *Habermas and the Public Sphere*, Cambridge, MA: MIT Press.

Frazer, E. and Lacey, N. (1993) *The Politics of Community*, Brighton: Harvester Wheatsheaf.

Galipeau, C. (1994) *Isaiah Berlin's Liberalism,* Oxford: Oxford University Press.

Galston, W. (1995) 'Two Concepts of Liberalism', *Ethics* 105, 3: 516–34.

Gans, C. (1992) *Philosophical Anarchism and Political Disobedience*, Cambridge: Cambridge University Press.

Gibbard, A. (1991) 'Constructing Justice', *Philosophy and Public Affairs* 20: 264–79.

Goodman, N. (1978) *Ways of Worldmaking*, Indianapolis, IL: Hackett.

Gopalan, C. (1990) 'Undernutrition: Measurement and Implications', in S. R. Osmani (ed.) *Nutrition and Poverty*, Oxford: Clarendon Press, WIDER series.

Gray, J. (1989) *Liberalisms: Essays in Political Philosophy*, London and New York: Routledge.

—— (1993) *Post-liberalism: Studies in Political Philosophy*, London and New York: Routledge.

—— (1995a) *Berlin*, London and Princeton, NJ: Harper Collins and Princeton University Press.

—— (1995b) *Enlightenment's Wake: Politics and Culture at the Close of the Modern Age*, London and New York: Routledge.

—— (1996) *Mill on Liberty: a Defence*, 2nd edn, London and New York: Routledge.

—— (1997) *Endgames: Questions in Late Modern Political Thought*, Cambridge: Polity Press.

—— (1998) 'Where Pluralists and Liberals Part Company', *International Journal of Philosophical Studies* 6: 17–36.

Green, L. (1994) 'Internal Minority Rights', in Judith Baker (ed.) *Group Rights*, Toronto: University of Toronto Press.

Griffin, J. (1986) *Wellbeing*, Oxford: Oxford University Press.

—— (1998) 'Incommensurability: What's The Problem?' In R. Chang (ed.) *Incommensurability, Incomparability and Practical Reason*, Cambridge, MA: Harvard University Press.

Gutmann, A. and Thompson, D. (1996) *Democracy and Disagreement*, Harvard, MA: Belknap.

Habermas, J. (1994) 'Three Models of Democracy', *Constellations* 1: 1–10.

Hacker, P.M.S. (1987) *Appearance and Reality*, Oxford: Blackwell.

Halliwell, S. (1994) *Plato: Republic V*, Warminster: Aris & Phillips.

Hampshire, S. (1983) *Morality and Conflict*, Oxford: Blackwell.

—— (1989) *Innocence and Experience*, London: Allen Lane/The Penguin Press.

Hart, H.L.A. (1975) 'Rawls on liberty and its priority', in N. Daniels (ed.) *Reading Rawls*, New York: Basic Books.

Hobsbawm, E. and Ranger, T. (eds) (1983) *The Invention of Tradition*, Cambridge: Cambridge University Press.

Hofer et al. v. *Hofer et al.* (1970) 13 DLR (3rd) 1.

Human Development Report (1996) New York: United Nations Development Programme.

Ignatieff, M. (1999) *Isaiah Berlin: A Life*, New York: Henry Holt.

Irwin, T.H. (1995) 'Prudence and Morality in Greek Ethics', *Ethics* 105: 284–95.

Jackson, F. (1982) 'Epiphenomenal Qualia', *Philosophical Quarterly* 32: 127–36.

—— (1986) 'What Mary Didn't Know', *Journal of Philosophy* 83: 291–5.

—— (1998) *From Metaphysics to Ethics: A Defence of Conceptual Analysis*, Oxford: Oxford University Press.

Jackson, F. and Pettit, P. (1995) 'Moral Functionalism and Moral Motivation', *Philosophical Quarterly* 45: 20–40.

—— (2002) 'Response-dependence without Tears', *Philosophical Issues* (supplement to *Nous*) vol.12.

Jahanbegloo, R. (1992) *Conversations with Isaiah Berlin*, London: Peter Halban.

James, W. (1975a) *Pragmatism: A New Name for Some Old Ways of Thinking*, Cambridge, MA: Harvard University Press.

—— (1975b) *The Meaning of Truth: A Sequel to Pragmatism*, Cambridge, MA: Harvard University Press.

—— (1976) *Essays in Radical Empiricism*, Cambridge, MA: Harvard University Press.

—— (1977) *A Pluralistic Universe*, Cambridge, MA: Harvard University Press.

—— (1978) *Essays in Philosophy*, Cambridge, MA: Harvard University Press.

—— (1979) *The Will to Believe*, Cambridge, MA: Harvard University Press.

—— (1983) *The Principles of Psychology*, Cambridge, MA: Harvard University Press.

—— (1996) *Some Problems in Philosophy: A Beginning of an Introduction to Philosophy*, Lincoln and London: University of Nebraska Press; reprint of 1911 edn.

Janzen, W. (1990) *Limits of Liberty: The Experiences of Mennonite, Hutterite, and Doukhobour Communities in Canada*, Toronto: University of Toronto Press.

Kant, I. (1929) *Critique of Pure Reason*, trans. Norman Kemp Smith, London: Macmillan.

Kekes, J. (1993) *The Morality of Pluralism*, Princeton, NJ: Princeton University Press.

—— (1997) *Against Liberalism*, Ithaca and London: Cornell University Press.

Kelly, P.J. (1998) *Impartiality, Neutrality and Justice: re-reading Brian Barry's Justice as Impartiality*, Edinburgh: Edinburgh University Press.

Klosko, G. (1992) *The Principle of Fairness and Political Obligation*, Lanham, MD: Rowman and Littlefield.

Krausz, M. (ed) *Relativism: Interpretation and Confrontation*, Notre Dame, IN: University of Notre Dame Press.

Kraut, R. (1983) 'The Third Dogma' in E. Lepore (ed.) *Truth and Interpretation*, Oxford: Oxford University Press.

Kressel, G. M. (1981) 'Sororicide/Filiacide: Homicide for Family Honour', *Current Anthropology*, XXII, 2: 141–58.

Kripke, S.A. (1982) *Wittgenstein on Rules and Private Language*, Oxford: Blackwell.

Kukathas, C. (1992) 'Are There any Cultural Rights?', *Political Theory 20*, 1: 105–39.

—— (1997) 'Cultural Toleration', in I. Shapiro and W. Kymlicka (eds) *Ethnicity and Group Rights: Nomos* 39: 69–104.

Kymlicka, W. (1995) *Multicultural Citizenship: A Liberal Theory of Minority Rights*, Oxford: Oxford University Press.

—— (1996a) 'Federalismo, Nacionalismo y Multiculturalismo', *Revista Internacional de Filosofia Politica* 7: 20–54.

—— (1996b), 'Two Models of Pluralism and Tolerance', in David Heyd (ed.) *Toleration: An Elusive Virtue*, Princeton, NJ: Princeton University Press.

—— (1998) 'Ethnic Associations and Democratic Citizenship', in Amy Gutmann (ed.) *Freedom of Association*, Princeton, NJ: Princeton University Press.

Lakoff, G. (1987) *Women, Fire, and Dangerous Things*, Chicag, IL: The University of Chicago Press.

Larmore, C. (1987) *Patterns of Moral Complexity*, Cambridge: Cambridge University Press.

—— (1996a) *The Morals of Modernity*, Cambridge: Cambridge University Press.

—— (1996b) *The Romantic Legacy*, New York: Columbia University Press.

Leiter, B. (1994) 'Perspectivism in Nietzsche's Genealogy of Morals', in R. Schacht (ed.) *Nietzsche, Genealogy, Morality*, Berkeley, CA: University of California Press.

Leplin, J. (ed.) (1984) *Scientific Realism*, Berkeley and London: University of California Press.

Levine, J. (1993) 'Putnam, Davidson and the Seventeenth-Century Picture of Mind and World', *International Journal of Philosophical Studies* 1, 2: 193–230.

Lewis, C.I. (1929) *Mind and the World Order*, New York: Dover Publications.

Lewis, D. (1983) *Philosophical Papers* Vol. 1, Oxford: Oxford University Press.

—— (1990) 'What Experience Teaches', in W.G. Lycan (ed.) *Mind and Cognition: A Reader*, Cambridge, MA: Blackwell.

—— (1996) 'Elusive Knowledge', *Australasian Journal of Philosophy* 74: 549–67.

Liebman, C.S., and Don-Yehiya, E. (1982) 'Israel's Civil Religion', *The Jerusalem Quarterly* 23: 57–69.

Locke, J. (1988) *Two Treatises of Government*, ed. P. Laslett, Cambridge: Cambridge University Press.

Lovejoy, A.O. (1963) *The Thirteen Pragmatisms and Other Essays*, Baltimore, MD: Johns Hopkins Press.

Lundberg, S. and Pollak, R.A. (1996) 'Bargaining and Distribution in Marriage', *Journal of Economic Perspectives* 10: 139–58.

Lundberg, S., Pollak, R. and Wales, T. J. (forthcoming) 'Do Husbands and Wives Pool Their Resources? Evidence from the U.K. Child Benefit', *Journal of Human Resources*.

MacIntyre, A. (1985) *After Virtue*, 2nd edn, London: Duckworth.

Malia, M. (1999) *Russia Under Western Eyes,* Cambridge, MA: The Belknap Press of Harvard University Press.

Margalit, A. (1997) *The Decent Society*, trans. N. Goldblum, Cambridge, MA: Harvard University Press.

Marglin, F. A. (1990) 'Smallpox in Two Systems of Knowledge', in F.A. Marglin, and S.A. Marglin, *Dominating Knowledge: Development, Culture, and Resistance*, Oxford: Clarendon Press.

Marglin, F. A. and Marglin, S. A. (eds) (1990) *Dominating Knowledge: Development, Culture, and Resistance*, Oxford: Clarendon Press.

Marglin, S. A. (1990a) 'Toward the Decolonization of the Mind', in F.A. Marglin, and S.A. Marglin, *Dominating Knowledge: Development, Culture, and Resistance*, Oxford: Clarendon Press.

—— (1990b) 'Losing Touch: The Cultural Conditions of Worker Accommodation and Resistance', in F.A. Marglin, and S.A. Marglin, *Dominating Knowledge: Development, Culture, and Resistance*, Oxford: Clarendon Press.

Martin, J.R. (1985) *Reclaiming a Conversation*, New Haven, CT: Yale University Press.

Matilal, B.K. (1989) 'Ethical Relativism and the Confrontation of Cultures', in M. Krausz, (ed) *Relativism: Interpretation and Confrontation*, Notre Dame, IN: University of Notre Dame Press.

—— (1995) *Perception*, Oxford: Clarendon Press.

McDowell, J. (1983) 'Aesthetic value, Objectivity and the Fabric of the World', in E. Schaper (ed.) *Pleasure, Preference and Value*, Cambridge, MA: Cambridge University Press.

—— (1994) *Mind and World*, Cambridge, MA: Harvard University Press.

Meyers, R.G. (1971) 'Meaning and Metaphysics in James', *Philosophy and Phenomenological Research* 31: 369–80.

Mill, J. S. (1859) 'On Liberty', in J. Robson (ed.) *Collected Works of J.S. Mill*, vol. 18, London and Toronto: Routledge and University of Toronto Press.

—— (1861) 'Considerations On Representative Government', in J. Robson (ed.) *Collected Works of J.S. Mill*, vol. 18, London and Toronto: Routledge and University Of Toronto Press.

—— (1865) 'An Examination of Hamilton's Philosophy', in J. Robson (ed.) *Collected Works Of J.S. Mill*, vol. 9, London and Toronto: Routledge and University Of Toronto Press.

—— (1869) *The Subjection of Women*, in S.M. Okin, (ed.) *The Subjection of Women* (1988) Indianapolis, IN: Hackett.

Miller, D. (1995) 'Citizenship and Pluralism' *Political Studies* XLII: 432–450.

Moon, D. (1993) *Constructing Community*, Princeton, NJ: Princeton University Press.

Nagel, T. (1986) *The View from Nowhere*, Oxford: Oxford University Press.

—— (1987) 'Moral Conflict and Political Legitimacy', *Philosophy and Public Affairs* 16: 227–37.

Nandy, A. and Visvanathan, S. (1990) 'Modern Medicine and Its Non-Modern Critics', in F.A. Marglin and S.A. Marglin, *Dominating Knowledge: Development, Culture, and Resistance*, Oxford: Clarendon Press.

Nedelsky, J. (1989) 'Reconceiving Autonomy', *Yale Journal of Law and Feminism* 1: 7–36.

Nozick, R. (1974) *Anarchy, State and Utopia*, Oxford: Blackwell.

Nussbaum, M. (1988) 'Nature, Function and Capability: Aristotle on Political Distribution', *Oxford Studies in Ancient Philosophy* Supplementary Volume 1.

—— (1990) 'Aristotelian Social Democracy', in R. B. Douglass *et al.* (eds) *Liberalism and the Good*, New York: Routledge.

—— (1992) 'Human Functioning and Social Justice: In Defense of Aristotelian Essentialism', *Political Theory* 20: 202–46.

—— (1993) 'Non-Relative Virtues: An Aristotelian Approach', in M. Nussbaum and A. Sen (eds) *The Quality of Life*, Oxford: Clarendon Press.

—— (1995a) 'Human Capabilities, Female Human Beings' in Nussbaum, M. and Glover, J. (eds) *Women, Culture, and Development*, Oxford: Clarendon Press.

—— (1995b) 'Aristotle on Human Nature and the Foundations of Ethics', in J.E.J. Altham and R. Harrison (eds) *World, Mind and Ethics: Essays on the Ethical Philosophy of Bernard Williams*, Cambridge: Cambridge University Press.

—— (1997) 'Capabilities and Human Rights', *Fordham Law Review* 66: 273–300.

—— (1998) 'The Good as Discipline, the Good as Freedom' in D. Crocker and T. Linden (eds) *The Ethics of Consumption and Global Stewardship*, Lanham, MD: Rowman and Littlefield, 312–41.

—— (1999) *Sex and Social Justice*, Oxford: Oxford University Press.

Nussbaum, M. and Sen, A. (1989) 'Internal Criticism and Indian Relativist Traditions', in M. Krausz, (ed.) *Relativism: Interpretation and Confrontation*, Notre Dame, IN: University of Notre Dame Press, 299–325.

Nussbaum, M. and Sen, A. (eds) (1993) *The Quality of Life*, Oxford: Clarendon Press.

O'Leary-Hawthorne, J. and Pettit, P. (1995) 'Strategies for Free-Will Compatibilists', *Analysis* 56: 191–201.

Okin, S.M. (1979) *Women in Western Political Thought*, Princeton, NJ: Princeton University Press.

—— (1989) *Justice, Gender, and the Family*, Now York: Basic Books.

Osmani, S. (1990a) 'On Some Controversies in the Measurement of Undernutrition', in S.R. Osmani, (ed.) *Nutrition and Poverty*, Oxford: Clarendon Press, WIDER series.

—— (ed.) (1990b) *Nutrition and Poverty*, Oxford: Clarendon Press, WIDER series.

Papineau, D. (1995) 'The Antipathetic Fallacy and the Boundaries of Consciousness', in T. Metzinger (ed.) *Conacious Experience*, Schoeningh: Imprint Academic.

Pateman, C. (1983) 'Feminist Critiques of the Public-Private Dichotomy' in S.I. Benn and G. Gaus (eds) *Public and Private in Social Life*, London: Croom Helm.

Peacocke, C. (1993) *A Study of Concepts*, Cambridge, MA: MIT Press.

Perry, J. (1979) 'The Essential Indexical', *Nous* 13: 3–21.

Perry, R.B. (1958) *In the Spirit of William James*, Bloomington, IN: Indiana University Press.

Pettit, P. (1990) 'The Reality of Rule-Following', *Mind* 99: 1–21.

—— (1991) 'Realism and Response-dependence' *Mind* 100: 587–626.

—— (1993) 'A Definition of Physicalism', *Analysis* 53: 213–23.

—— (1996) *The Common Mind: An Essay on Psychology, Society and Politics*, New York: Oxford University Press.

—— (1998a) 'Practical Belief and Philosophical Theory', *Australasian Journal of Philosophy* 76: 15–33.

—— (1998b).'A Theory of Normal and Ideal Conditions', *Philosophical Studies* 96: 21–44.

Pettit, P. and Smith, M. (1996) 'Freedom in Belief and Desire', *Journal of Philosophy* 93: 429–49.

Pitkin, H. (1981) 'Justice: On Relating Public and Private', *Political Theory* 9: 327–52.

Plato, (1955) *Republic*, Book V, trans H.P.D Lee, Harmondsworth, Penguin.

Popper, K. (1994) 'The Myth of the Framework' in *The Myth of the Framework*, K. Popper (ed) London: Routledge.

Poulter, S. (1987) 'Ethnic Minority Customs, English Law, and Human Rights', *International and Comparative Law Quarterly* 36, 3: 589–615.

Price, H. (1992) 'Metaphysical Pluralism', *Journal of Philosophy* 89: 387–409.

—— (1997) 'Naturalism and the Fate of the M-worlds', *Proceedings of the Aristotelian Society* Supp.Vol. 68.

Putnam, H. (1981) *Reason, Truth and History*, Cambridge: Cambridge University Press.

—— (1989) 'Truth and Convention: On Davidson's Refutation of Conceptual Relativism', in M. Krausz, (ed.) *Relativism: Interpretation and Confrontation*, Notre Dame, IN: University of Notre Dame Press.

—— (1997) 'James's Theory of Truth', in R. A. Putnam (ed.) (1997).

Putnam, R.A. (ed.) (1997) *The Cambridge Companion to William James*, Cambridge: Cambridge University Press.

Quine, W.V.O. (1960) *Word and Object*, Cambridge, MA: MIT Press.

—— (1969) *Ontological Relativity and Other Essays*, New York: Columbia Press.

—— (1981) 'On the Very Idea of a Third Dogma', in *Theories and Things*, Cambridge, MA: Harvard University Press.

Rawls, J. (1970) *A Theory of Justice*, Cambridge, MA: Harvard University Press.

—— (1971) *A Theory of Justice* , Oxford: Oxford University Press.

—— (1980) 'Kantian Constructivism in Moral Theory', *Journal of Philosophy* 77: 515–72.

—— (1988) 'The Priority of Right and Ideas of the Good', in *Philosophy and Public Affairs* 17: 251–76.

—— (1993) 'The Domain of the Political and Overlapping Consensus' in D. Copp, J. Hampton and J.E. Roemer (eds) *The Idea of Democracy*, Cambridge: Cambridge University Press.

—— (1993) *Political Liberalism*, New York: Columbia University Press.

Ray, S. 'Introduction', *Our Films, Their Films*, (1994) (reprint) New York: Hyperion, 5.

Raz, J. (1986) *The Morality of Freedom*, Oxford: Clarendon Press.

—— (1994) *Ethics in the Public Domain*, Oxford: Clarendon Press.

Resnik, J. (1989) 'Dependent Sovereigns: Indian Tribes, States, and the Federal Courts', *University of Chicago Law Review* 56: 671–759.

Riasanovsky, N.V. (1992) *The Emergence Of Romanticism*, New York: Oxford University Press.

Richardson, H. (1978) 'Self-Determination, International Law and the South African Bantustan Policy', *Columbia Journal of Transnational Law* 17: 204–13.

Riker, W. (1982) *Liberalism Against Populism*, San Francisco, CA: W.H. Freeman.

Riley, J. (1988) *Liberal Utilitarianism*, Cambridge: Cambridge University Press.

—— (1998) *J.S. Mill: On Liberty*, London: Routledge.

—— (2000) *Mill's Radical Liberalism*, London: Routledge.

Rorty, R. (1982) 'The World Well Lost', in *Consequences of Pragmatism*, Minneapolis, MN: University of Minnesota Press.

—— (1989) *Contingency, Irony and Solidarity*, Cambridge: Cambridge University Press.

—— (1997) 'Faith, Responsibility, and Romance', in R.A. Putnam (ed.) (1997).

—— (1998) 'Feminism and Pragmatism', in *Truth and Progress*, Richard Rorty Philosophical Papers vol III, Cambridge: Cambridge University Press.

Rosenberg, J.F. (1980) 'Coupling, Retheoretization, and the Correspondence Principle', *Synthese* 45: 351–85.

—— (1986) *Linguistic Representation*, Dordrecht: Reidel.

—— (1988) 'Comparing the Incommensurable: Another Look at Convergent Realism', *Philosophical Studies* 54: 163–93.

Ross, W. D. (1930) *The Right and the Good*, Oxford: Clarendon Press.

Rousseau, J.J. (1968) *The Social Contract*, Harmondsworth: Penguin.

—— (1979) *Emile: or On Education*, trans. Allan Bloom, New York: Basic Books, Book V.

Russell, B. (1956) *Logic and Knowledge*, ed. R.C. Marsh, London: Macmillan.

Schlesinger, A.(1992), *The Disuniting of America*, New York: Norton.

Schneiderman, D. (1997), 'Human Rights, Fundamental Differences? Multiple Charters in a New Partnership', in G. Laforest and R.Gibbins (eds) *Beyond the Impasse: Toward Reconciliation*, Montreal: Institute for Research in Public Policy.

Searle, J. (1995) *The Construction of Reality*, London: Penguin.

Sellars, W. (1963) 'Some Reflections on Language Games', in *Science, Perception and Reality*, Atascadero, CA: Ridgeview.

—— (1968) *Science and Metaphysics*, London: Routledge.

—— (1969) 'Language as Thought and Communication', *Philosophy and Phenomenological Research* 24: 506–27.

—— (1974) 'Meaning as Functional Classification', *Synthese* 27: 417–37.

—— (1981) 'Mental Events', *Philosophical Studies* 39: 325–45.

—— (1997) *Empiricism and the Philosophy of Mind*, ed. Robert Brandom, Cambridge, MA: Harvard University Press. (Also in Sellars, 1963).

Sen, A. (1970) *Collective Choice and Social Welfare*, San Francisco, CA: Holden-Day.

—— (1982) 'Equality of What?' in *Choice, Welfare, and Measurement*, Oxford: Basil Blackwell.

—— (1987) *On Ethics and Economics*, Oxford: Blackwell.

—— (1990) 'Gender and Co-operative Conflicts', in Tinker, I. (ed.) *Persistent Inequalities*, New York: Oxford University Press.

—— (1993a), 'India and the West', *The New Republic,* June 7.

—— (1993 b) 'Capability and Well-being' in M. Nussbaum, and A. Sen, *The Quality of Life*, Oxford: Clarendon Press.

—— (1994) 'Freedoms and Needs', *New Republic*, January 10–17: 31–8.

—— (1995) 'Gender Inequality and Theories of Justice', in M. Nussbaum, and J. Glover, (eds) *Women, Culture, and Development*, Oxford: Clarendon Press.

—— (1996) *Justice and Assertive Incompleteness*, Draft paper, Harvard University, Department of Philosophy.

—— (1997a) 'and the Act of Choice', *Econometrica* 65: 745–79.

—— (1997b) 'Human Rights and Asian Values' *The New Republic*, July 10–17.

Simmons, A.J. (1979) *Moral Principles and Political Obligations*, Princeton NJ: Princeton University Press.

Skinner, Q. (1990) 'The Republican Idea of Political Liberty' in G. Bock, Q. Skinner and M. Viroli (eds) *Machiavelli and Republicanism,* Cambridge: Cambridge University Press.

Skorupski, J. (1996) 'Value Pluralism', in D. Archard (ed.) *Philosophy and Pluralism*, Cambridge: Cambridge University Press.

Smith, M. (1994) *The Moral Problem*, Oxford: Blackwell.

Sprigge, T.L.S. (1993) *James and Bradley*, Chicago, IL: Open Court.

—— (1997) 'James, Aboutness, and his British Critics', in R. A. Putnam, 1997.

Stalnaker, R.C. (1984), *Inquiry,* Cambridge, MA: MIT Press.

Stocker, M. (1990) *Plural and Conflicting Values*, Oxford: Clarendon Press.

260

Strawson, P.F. (1979) 'Perception and its Objects', in G.F. Macdonald (ed.) *Perception and Identity: Essays presented to A. J. Ayer*, London: Macmillan.

—— (1982) 'Freedom and Resentment', in G. Watson (ed.) *Free Will*, Oxford: Oxford University Press.

—— (1985) *Skepticism and Naturalism: Some Varieties*, London: Methuen.

Sunstein, C. (1993) 'Democracy and Shifting Preferences', in D. Copp, J. Hampton and J.E. Roemer (eds) *The Idea of Democracy*, Cambridge: Cambridge University Press.

Svensson, F. (1979) 'Liberal Democracy and Group Rights: The Legacy of Individualism and Its Impact on American Indian Tribes', *Political Studies* 27, 3: 421–39.

Taylor, C. (1989) *Sources of the Self*, Cambridge: Cambridge University Press.

—— (1992) *Multiculturalism and 'The Politics of Recognition'*, Princeton, NJ: Princeton University Press.

—— (1994) 'Reply and Re-articulation' in J. Tully (ed.) *Philosophy in an Age of Pluralism: the Work of Charles Taylor in Focus,* Cambridge: Cambridge University Press.

Tinker, I. (ed.) (1990) *Persistent Inequalities,* New York: Oxford University Press.

Van Inwagen, P. (1983) *An Essay on Free Will*, Oxford: Oxford University Press.

Verma, R. R. (1995) 'Femininity, Equality, and Personhood', in *Women, Culture, and Development*, in M. Nussbaum, and J. Glover, (eds) Oxford: Clarendon Press.

Walker, G. (1997), 'The Idea of Nonliberal Constitutionalism', in I. Shapiro and W. Kymlicka (eds) *Ethnicity and Group Rights: NOMOS* 39: 154–84.

Walzer, M. (1977) *Just and Unjust Wars*, New York: Basic Books.

—— (1980) 'The Moral Standing of States', *Philosophy and Public Affairs* 9, 2: 209–29.

Whorf, B.L. (1956) *Language, Thought and Reality*, Cambridge, MA: MIT Press.

Wild, J. (1969) *The Radical Empiricism of William James*, New York: Doubleday.

Wilkins, D. E. (1994), 'Johnson v. M'Intosh Revisited: Through the Eyes of *Mitchel* v. *United States*', *American Indian Law Review* 19, 1: 159–181.

Williams Jr., R. (1995) 'Sovereignty, Racism, Human Rights: Indian Self-Determination and the Postmodern World Legal System', *Review of Constitutional Studies* 2: 146–202.

Williams, B. (1978) *Descartes*, Harmondsworth: Penguin.

—— (1980) 'Introduction' to *Isaiah Berlin, Concepts and Categories*, Oxford: Oxford University Press.

Wilshire, B. (1968) *William James and Phenomenology*, Bloomington and London: Indiana University Press.

Wisconsin v. Yoder (1972) 406 US 205, 92 S.Ct 1526.

Wittgenstein, L. (1974) *On Certainty*, Oxford: Blackwell.

Wolff, J. (1990/91) 'What is the Problem of Political Obligation?', *Proceedings of the Aristotelian Society* 91: 153–69.

—— (1991) *Robert Nozick: Property, Justice and the Minimal State*, Cambridge: Polity.

—— (1993) 'Review of Chaim Gans, *Philosophical Anarchism and Political Disobedience* and George Klosko, *Political Obligation and the Theory of Fairness*, *Mind* 102: 500–4.

261

—— (1995a) 'Political Obligation, Fairness and Independence', *Ratio* (New Series) 8: 87–99.

—— (1995b) 'Pluralistic Models of Political Obligation', *Philosophica 56:* 7–27.

—— (1996a) 'Anarchism and Scepticism', in J. Narveson and J.T. Sanders (eds) *For and Against the State*, Lanham, MD: Rowman and Littlefield.

—— (1996b) 'Rational, Fair and Reasonable', *Utilitas* : 263–71. Reprinted in P.J. Kelly (ed.) (1998).

Young, H.P. (1988) 'Condorcet's Theory of Voting', *American Political Science Review* 82: 1231–44.

—— (1995) 'Optimal Voting Rules', *Journal Of Economic Perspectives* 9: 51–64.

Young, I. M. (1990) *Justice and the Politics of Difference,* Princeton NJ: Princeton University Press.

—— (1996) 'Communication and the Other – Beyond Deliberative Democracy', in S. Benhabib (ed.) *Democracy and Difference*, Princeton, NJ: Princeton University Press.

INDEX

Note: Page numbers followed by 'n' refer to notes